THE HUNT FOR
BLACKBEARD

THE HUNT FOR BLACKBEARD

The World's Most Notorious Pirate

CRAIG CABELL, GRAHAM A. THOMAS
& ALLAN RICHARDS

*'I judged it high time to destroy that crew of villains,
and not to suffer them to gather strength in the neighbourhood
of so valuable a trade as that of this Colony.'*
Alexander Spotswood, Lieutenant-Governor of Virginia, December 1718

Pen & Sword
MARITIME

First published in Great Britain in 2012 by
PEN & SWORD MARITIME
an imprint of
Pen & Sword Books Ltd
47 Church Street
Barnsley   South Yorkshire
S70 2AS

ISBN 978 1 84415 959 8

Typeset in Ehrhardt by Chic Media Ltd

Printed and bound in England
by the MPG Books Group

Pen & Sword Books Ltd incorporates the imprints of
Pen & Sword ~~Aviation, Pen & Sword Family History, Pen &~~ Sword Maritime,
Pen & Swor ~~Military, Pen & Sword Discovery, Wharncliffe~~ Local History,
Wharncli ~~Transport, Pen &~~ word Select,
Pen & ~~Classics, Leo Cooper, Remember~~ When,
The Pra ~~orian Press, Seaforth Publishing and Frontline~~ Publishing.

Contents

Acknowledgements

We would like to thank the following people and establishments who made this book possible. First and foremost is David Moore, Curator of Nautical Archaeology for the North Carolina Maritime Museum. He is one of the world's leading experts regarding Blackbeard and assisted us when we were carrying out preliminary research for this book in the United States; he then answered our questions and gave further advice during the writing stages.

Thanks are due to the staff of the Historic Dockyard Portsmouth, the National Maritime Museum and The National Archives, for all the associated research concerning the Royal Navy and their strategies during the eighteenth century.

The authors would also like to thank the various antiquarian book dealers who were involved – you are a great bunch of professionals.

Sincerely, many thanks to all.

CC, GAT & AR

Foreword

The reason why three writers came together to produce this book is that three writers who knew each other happened to be interested in the same subject. We also thought we could write an accessible biography and challenge certain legends that had built up about the infamous pirates of whom we intended to write, and, as this foreword was the last thing written to support this project, I can say that I believe we have.

What makes this book different from others on the same subject is that this one is really, at its heart, about two men: the notorious pirate Blackbeard, and Alexander Spotswood, Governor of Virginia, the man who eventually brought him down. While there are other key players in the Blackbeard saga, these two are at its core. In Spotswood's time Blackbeard was just a footnote in comparison to the various Indian, Spanish and French wars with which he had to contend, along with the almost continual opposition to his political policies throughout his time as governor.

One of the key reasons for writing this book was to confront the myths and legends surrounding Blackbeard and the 'media' image that has built up around him, and it is right that books continue to do this. Society sometimes seems to glorify evil, sadistic people; rarely does it create heroes of victims. This shattering of a 'designer' image is something I have been keen to achieve over the years with regard to the Kray twins, and who is to say that Blackbeard was any better than them? Indeed, was he not the most notorious pirate who ever sailed the high seas? That is what the myths and legends regarding him would tell us, but are they true?

If we look at the popular culture of the last few centuries, the evil people seem to have a better ride than the good, especially those steeped in war and violence. Are we being pessimistic here? Perhaps, but why the fascination with bad people? So many books about Jack the Ripper; so many books about Adolf Hitler. We seem to need to over-analyse our evil past, to cleanse, to understand, to solve the riddle of 'Why?' or 'Who?' Ultimately we need to understand why the human race has to be cruel to its kin. We need justification. The bravery of the good seems to go out of the window and is only documented concerning individuals from the major wars of the twentieth century, or Lord Nelson of course. Why? Well, perhaps the bad guys are more interesting, more extreme, and that's why we thirst for knowledge concerning them: because they did things we couldn't dream of doing, to read about them is a safe way of taking part in those dark, forbidden things. It's probably the reason why we read horror novels and crime fiction.

However, Spotswood is a different kettle of fish altogether. He walks the tightrope between good and bad. Some might see him as a hero, while others might paint him as being bad because he threw convention out of the window. He paid for and equipped a clandestine expedition into a neighbouring state, where he had no jurisdiction, to get Blackbeard. It was an extraordinary act by a man who, in order to maintain security and prosperity in his state, trod a thin line between light and dark. He is inextricably mixed with the dark pirate. As we journey through the story of Blackbeard we will be asking questions that challenge standard thinking. Was Blackbeard really as bad as his reputation claims or was he really one of the best PR men the world has ever seen? Was Spotswood a tyrant or a man acutely aware of the fragility of prosperity and what was necessary to ensure the state of Virginia continued to enjoy growth and prosperity?

This story is not for the faint-hearted. It is one of violence, greed, bloodshed and death. Here then, is the dark world of Blackbeard. Enjoy the horrors and be enlightened.

Craig Cabell

Introduction

*Indeed, they were a stark and ignorant lot, and if you'd asked them
what day it was, it wouldn't have occurred to them to reply 'February the
second, good neighbour'; they would more probably have responded with
'Candlesmass, ye iggerant booger', because that is how they talked. . .*

The Reavers, George MacDonald Fraser

At dawn, they passed Cape Henry, the southern edge of the Chesapeake
Bay. As they headed out into the Atlantic Ocean, the Lieutenant felt anxious
and excited at the same time. Ahead lay battle and with God's will they
would prevail. His gaze wandered over the deck of the sleek, fast sloop and
at the men, quietly preparing their weapons. He suddenly wished they'd
loaded guns onto the sloop but quickly pushed the thought away. They
needed speed and surprise and the cannon would simply slow them down.

This fight was going to be a different one to the many he'd had
against the French where there were some rules of engagement. Against
pirates there were none. The pirates were not just rabble; they were all
experienced fighters and gave no quarter. Their leader was the most
notorious and ruthless pirate of all. At least, that's what the Lieutenant
had heard but he didn't put much stock in stories.

He looked out across the sea watching the *Ranger*, the smaller of the
two sloops, heading away from them to take up a line abreast station
eight miles away. Standard procedure but with the wind getting up and
the sea frothing and rolling he had to make sure the other vessel
remained in sight. High above the deck the lookout would ensure the
Ranger was always in visual range.

The deck heaved under his feet and he quickly looked around at the
men for any sign of weakness but if they felt the motion of the sea none
of them showed it.

Were they ready? The crew were handpicked from the two Royal
Navy warships that were anchored in the James River. They had been
sent to Virginia to protect the colony from pirates and keep the trade
routes open. The Lieutenant was second in command of HMS *Pearl* a
forty gun fifth rate ship of the line, the larger of the two warships. He
wished they could have used the warships. The pirates would have had

no chance against such naval power. But the ships were too big to navigate the inlets and sand bars around Ocracoke Island, so faster, smaller ships were needed.

He glanced round at the men. They were experienced, capable and ready. But the old familiar cocktail of anxiety, apprehension, adrenalin and excitement that came before every battle coursed through him. He wondered if the rest of the men were feeling it as he was.

Clouds were gathering, blocking the sun as the wind rose. The rough sea might slow them down but that meant they would arrive under the cover of darkness. True to his reckoning night had fallen by the time they reached the seaward side of the Ocracoke Island. The tide was ebbing. He scanned the shore for any sign of movement. All was still, save for the trees swaying in high November winds.

Quietly he called for sails to be lowered, the anchor dropped. Over the sand dunes on the southern tip of the island the tall masts of the pirates' ships could just be made out. He ordered lookouts to keep watch for any sign that pirates might have discovered their presence.

Now all he had to do was wait until dawn to launch his attack.

The above is an interpretation of the events leading up to the battle that would result in Blackbeard's death. The full account of the action we will look at in a later chapter. In the meantime, there are questions that need to be asked about Blackbeard and to some degree about Spotswood as well.

Was Blackbeard really as vicious as the myths and legends say he was? His legend has lived on over the centuries and he is probably one of the most well-known pirates ever. While these myths and legends tell of a vicious ruthless man, there are contradicting stories about him. Who was he really and what were the actions he committed that forced Spotswood to finance and organise an expedition against him?

That brings us to another key question: why did Spotswood organise the expedition into the neighbouring state of North Carolina where he had no jurisdiction or legal right to do so? What was it that made him spend his own money to fit out two sloops to carry Lieutenant Robert Maynard and his crew to the inevitable battle that would see the end of Blackbeard?

Most stories or accounts of Blackbeard, or Edward Teach (Thatch, or Thach, depending on which source you use) tell of a man who was a vicious, ruthless, calculating criminal who built a reputation as the most feared pirate on the open seas that has lasted to this day. He was a tough criminal who met a spectacular and unsavoury end.

Because so little is known about the man behind the legend, to find the truth about him we need to examine the key players who influenced him, pursued him and eventually caused his downfall. This book is about the hunt for the truth about him; in particular the truth about why his legend above all has endured. Was he a consummate PR man and spin doctor? Did he understand the need to create reputation above all else? Did he know how to manipulate people in such a way that they were forever telling stories about him? Or was he just a vicious, cold criminal?

Let's first of all look at the players in the Blackbeard story.

Chapter 1

The Players

In our hunt for the truth we will look at the basic things that helped to shape the legend of Blackbeard: the key players who influenced him, chased him and killed him; the actions of the man himself; stories told about him from a wide variety of sources such as those members of his crew who were captured and put on trial; along with personal letters, reports and logs taken from some of the people involved.

The main source of information on Blackbeard comes from Captain Charles Johnson whose book, *A General History of the Robberies and Murders of the Most Notorious Pirates* has a detailed account of the life of Blackbeard. What makes this book special is that it appeared on the bookshelves in 1724, six years after Blackbeard was killed. It is the closest thing we have to 'the truth'. 'Captain Johnson's book took the lid off a shocking world of crime on the high seas and had all the ingredients for a bestseller.'[1]

Another thing that makes Johnson's source important is its accuracy. Indeed, pirate historian David Cordingly wrote in his preface for the 1998 edition of Johnson's work that most of the facts in his account of Blackbeard have proven to be broadly accurate, which is true of most of the other accounts in his *History*. However, Cordingly tells us that Johnson did take a large degree of licence in the biographies when he brings conversation into the mix. For example, his account of the pirate kingdom of Libertalia and his account of Captain Mission are 'certainly fictitious although it was inspired by the pirate communities on Madagascar'.[2] That said, what we do know is that his accounts of Blackbeard, Major Stede Bonnet, Jack Rackham and Bartholomew Roberts are accurate. Documents, letters and logbooks found in the Public Records Office the Colonial Office papers have, over the years, corroborated Johnson's accounts of these men.

Cordingly tells us that Johnson wrote in his introduction to the first edition that where he himself had not been an eyewitness to events, he had interviewed or spoken with the people responsible for capturing the pirates. Adding to that, Johnson says that some of the information also comes from 'the mouths of the pirates themselves after they were taken'.

So it is from this basis that we start our hunt for the truth, and we will be returning to Johnson on many occasions because it is he who provides us with the basis of the legend of Blackbeard: 'He provided a sweeping account of what came to be called the "Golden Age of Piracy".'[3]

At this point it is necessary to list the key players in the story of Edward Teach. We will go into detail in later chapters but for now, we will set the scene to enable the drama to unfold.

The first key player is Teach himself, better known as Blackbeard. No-one really knows exactly who this pirate was. Even his real name is shrouded in mystery. Despite his fame he was not the most prolific, nor the most powerful, nor were his activities the most widespread. For example, Bartholomew Roberts was active on both sides of the Atlantic and took over 400 prizes, while Cheng I Sao controlled 1,800 vessels and 80,000 pirates.[4] Yet, what has been his enduring appeal is the persona that surrounded him, the efforts put in place to find and dispose of him and the spectacular way in which he was taken down.

Criminals have come and gone over the centuries but Blackbeard's legend and fame have managed to live on. Some popular historians say that Captain Kidd is legendary because of his buried treasure, but why is Blackbeard a legend? Was it because of the way in which he was killed, and that his head was cut off and displayed for all to see? We know that by the time of his death he was already of legendary status.

Indeed, the name of Blackbeard continues to thrill to this day and we will try to show that he was a calculating man bent on making a name for himself at the cost of everything the civilised world held dear at the time. Perhaps he was a psychotic, or perhaps deep inside him there was a hole that could never be filled, no matter what outrageous action he performed. Perhaps he was a desperately lonely man inside, and was driven by his desire to be admired and noticed. Perhaps he craved attention and so created his reputation to ensure he always had that attention.

Second to Blackbeard was Alexander Spotswood. This man was the Lieutenant-Governor of Virginia. Although he did not take an active role in the fighting that eventually brought Blackbeard down, he was a key player in the pirate's life. Some of the legend that we know about Blackbeard today was created by the multitude of letters written by him.[5] Although the two men never met, Spotswood was the man who set the wheels in motion to capture and kill the pirate. So he is a crucial player and his information is one of our main sources.

So who was he? He was born in the English garrison at Tangier around 1676, the son of an army surgeon who died when he was 4 years old. He came back to England with his mother in 1683 when King Charles II ordered the troops home. When William III plunged England into a nine-year war with France and

Spain, Spotswood joined the Earl of Bath's Regiment in 1693 and distinguished himself as a soldier in Flanders, becoming an infantry captain in 1698. By 1703 Spotswood was a lieutenant-colonel and was appointed to the Duke of Marlborough's staff where once again he distinguished himself as the quartermaster-general. In 1710 he was selected as lieutenant-governor of the colony of Virginia by the 1st Earl of Orkney, George Hamilton, who was the governor but who never actually set foot in the colony.

In late 1710 Spotswood arrived in Williamsburg to take up his post, and almost from the beginning he faced strong opposition from a radical element within the colony. Indeed, for most of his twelve years in office he faced one crisis after another. Blackbeard was one such crisis and it was one that he could do something about.[6]

Next is Lieutenant Robert Maynard, a Royal Navy officer who led the assault against Blackbeard.[7] Though he distinguished himself in the battle against Blackbeard and became a captain in the Royal Navy, he seems to have faded into obscurity. By anyone's standards he was a hero but perhaps his star has fallen for the reasons we mentioned in the foreword – that most people prefer to read about villains rather than heroes? We will go into greater detail on Maynard later when we discuss Blackbeard's death.

Then we have Charles Eden, Governor of North Carolina and a man whom many scholars have speculated colluded with Blackbeard. The evidence to support this is sketchy. Eden issued a Royal Pardon to the pirate and they knew each other, but the nature of their relationship is crucial in helping us find the truth about the man we call Blackbeard.

In his book, *Blackbeard: America's Most Notorious Pirate*, Angus Konstam states the case that Eden was not corrupt but was a little 'foolhardy' in his dealings with the pirate. However, there may be evidence against Eden depending on the way in which the facts are interpreted. Blackbeard was supposed to have given up piracy in Eden's colony, where he was also eventually killed. Items were found in Eden's possession that were taken from a ship that was possibly stolen by Blackbeard and given to Eden as gifts. We shall look into this in further detail later in the book.

Alongside Eden is Tobias Knight, the Secretary of the Colony for North Carolina. Many historians believe his involvement and collusion with Blackbeard went far deeper than Eden's, but his guilt could never be proved despite the famous letter he wrote to the pirate just before the final battle. This guarded letter to Blackbeard is open to interpretation. For example, he ends it by saying 'I have not the time to add save my hearty respects to you, and am your real friend.'[8] Konstam suggests the letter was a warning to Blackbeard of the coming battle:

If this finds you yet in harbour I would have you make the best of your way up as soon as possible your affairs will let you. I have something more to say to you than at present I can write: the bearer will tell you the end of our Indian Warr, and Ganet can tell you in part what I have to say to you, so refer you in some measure to him.[9]

Whether Knight was complicit or not we will never know, as he died shortly after Blackbeard was killed and nothing was ever proved against him.

Early in Blackbeard's career we find Benjamin Hornigold, a privateer who turned pirate and is thought to have been Blackbeard's mentor. Both Hornigold and Blackbeard served together as privateers and it was Hornigold that first turned pirate. They served together as fellow pirates before Hornigold abandoned the pirate's way of life and accepted the King's Pardon. Indeed, when the new governor arrived on the island of New Providence, a pirate haven at the time and the place which both Blackbeard and Hornigold used as a base, Hornigold turned away from piracy, accepted the pardon and became pirate-hunter under the command of the newly-arrived Governor, Captain Woodes Rogers.[10]

Rogers, like so many other men of this time, was an ex-privateer who had been given a commission as Colonial Governor of New Providence. The difference between him and men like Hornigold and Blackbeard is that he never turned pirate. Although his role may at first appear to be superficial, it is in fact very prominent. It is more than likely that his arrival in the previously lawless New Providence may have been the trigger that encouraged Blackbeard to move northwards in search of a new base of operations; a move that eventually brought him into the path of Alexander Spotswood.[11]

Of course, we must also look at Johnson as a key player in the story because he documented Blackbeard's life with considerable detail and accuracy. We don't just use Johnson's *History* as a major source; we also need to look at him as a player in the overall scheme of things. In his 1724 edition, Johnson thanks the many persons who had been taken by the pirates as well as those people who were involved in the taking for giving him detailed facts. He also drew on accounts of pirates written in the London newspapers and other journals, with the *Boston News Letter* being a rich source of pirate stories from America.

As with Blackbeard, no-one really knows who Johnson was. For decades historians believed that he was Daniel Defoe, the famous author of *Robinson Crusoe*, but that theory has recently been exploded. Cordingly states that it is likely that Johnson was an ex-privateer or even a pirate himself because of his extensive knowledge of the sea.[12]

So while we don't really look into the man we know as Captain Charles Johnson, his presence permeates this book and just about every other book on

Blackbeard because we know the facts in his account are largely accurate. That means Johnson's story of Blackbeard is the closest we have to an eye-witness account and so should be believed.

The story that culminated in Blackbeard's death was a story that only lasted a couple of years. It encompassed the east coast of North America, from the Caribbean to Delaware. As we hunt for the truth about the man and his legend these key players will help us paint a picture of the pirate and his nemesis – Spotswood.

Each lonely scene shall thee restore;
For thee the tear be duly shed:
Belov'd, till life could charm no more;
And mourn'd, till pity's self be dead.

Cymbeline, William Shakespeare

Chapter 2

The Man and the Myth

*It was his custom to invite five or six of his
brutal companions to come ashore, and
he would force her to prostitute herself
to them all, one after another, before his face.*[13]

Captain Charles Johnson, 1724

The early life of Blackbeard is a mystery. Like many of his
contemporaries, the years before he became a pirate are shrouded in
the swirling mists of time.

Most historians believe he was born in Bristol, although the date of his birth
is uncertain. The best guess we can make comes from pictures, drawn at the
time of his death, alluding to a man in his mid-30s. This places his birth in the
1680s. Indeed, Johnson states that 'Edward Teach was a Bristol man born but
had sailed some time out of Jamaica in privateers.'[14]

Let's start with the basics – the name he was born with – but that too is
uncertain. While there are many different variations of it the most commonly-
held version today is Edward Teach, although Edward Thatch, Edward Tach,
Edward Thack and Edward Thache are also likely candidates. For example,
Captain Mathew Musson – perhaps the first to encounter the pirate – wrote to
the Council of Trade and Plantations, and used the spelling Thatch.[15] Even
Edouard Titche has appeared in a document of the era as a possible spelling.[16]

The principal nemesis of Blackbeard – Alexander Spotswood, who we shall
look at in more detail later – clouds the issue of the correct surname. He refers
to the pirate by the name of Tach, as in 'Tach's crew' and in the very next
sentence uses the spelling Tache, as in 'Tache's Quarter Master'.[17]

To complicate the issue even further, the first person to make a detailed chart
of the Ocracoke area, where Blackbeard met his demise, may have known the
pirate. Edward Moseley was the Surveyor General of North Carolina and made
his chart of the region in 1733, some years after the battle of Ocracoke. The
site of the battle, or the most likely site, is known locally as Teach's Hole.
Moseley referred to this as Thatch's Hole.[18]

When Blackbeard's former quartermaster – William Howard – was captured and brought to trial, prior to the battle that claimed the life of the pirate captain, another spelling was used: 'That the said William Howard ... did some time in the Year of our Lord 1717 Join and Associate himself with one Edward Tach and other Wicked and desolate Persons...' Ordinarily, we would assume that any legal documents used in a trial would use, wherever possible, the correct names of individuals mentioned during the proceedings unless, of course, the only source of information at that time was Howard himself and he did not know for sure.[19]

Until there is any evidence to the contrary it seems reasonable to refer to Blackbeard as Edward Teach. It is the most accepted version of his name and it appears in many of the texts available for studying Blackbeard; it is also the spelling that Johnson uses in his narrative.

Studying the early life of Teach means that we have to make some assumptions. One of the main ones is that he came from a wealthy family or a family of merchants because he had an education; that is, he could read and write. Robert E. Lee in his book *Blackbeard the Pirate* says this about his early life:

> Apparently he was an educated man, for there is no doubt he could read and write. He corresponded with merchants, and, at the time of his death, he had a letter in his possession addressed to him by the Chief Justice and Secretary of the Province of North Carolina, Tobias Knight.

We looked at the body of his letter in the previous chapter, and whether it was meant as a warning to Teach or not, the fact is that Knight would have assumed the pirate could at least read what he had written and indeed understand it, as it was a letter that had some instructions to it. It told Teach to look to the bearer of the letter for more information. Knight began this letter with the salutation 'My friend', so it is reasonable to assume that Knight and Teach had met before on a few occasions and Knight would know that Teach was educated. He'd had dealings with Teach so he would know his 'friend' was an intelligent man who could read and write.[20]

Lee sites several references including the entry in the Encyclopaedia Britannica stating that Teach was born in Bristol.[21]

Indeed, Konstam states that Blackbeard was by all accounts a 'literate, somewhat educated' man who would have received enough formal education to allow him to read and write.[22]

So we can make the assumption that he came from a family affluent enough to be able to give their son an education. Another assumption that we can make about his origins is of his ability to be fully at ease in the company of his fellow pirates as well as with the higher end of society where politicians, wealthy landowners, merchants and planters mingled. If he did have more than a basic education and came from a family used to socialising with important people, this easiness with such extremes of society makes sense. In order for him to create the myth and the legend he would need to have been intelligent and highly perceptive of people's feelings and fears to play them as well as he did.

It is also quite likely that his family earned their living from the seafaring trade in Bristol. At the time it was a thriving port town and the second-largest town in England and much of the wealth of Bristol came from trade with the American colonies. Sugar, cocoa, and other luxury items that entered England came in through Bristol. Bristol was also heavily involved in the slave trade from which many wealthy merchants gained their fortune. So for a small boy growing up in daily view of the ships coming and going from Bristol, the temptation to look westwards towards the Atlantic Ocean and the colonies of North America must have been great indeed.[23]

However, there is no real evidence to suggest that Blackbeard was from Bristol. It is an assumption made by many historians because Johnson states that is where Blackbeard came from. Konstam cites the survey conducted in 1698 by the authorities in Bristol as a place where some proof could be found but no-one by the name of Thatch or Teach is mentioned or even anyone with a variation of the two names such as Tach or Tache. Yet, Konstam does put forward a convincing theory that might shed some light on whether Blackbeard may have come from Bristol.

In our previous chapter we mentioned Captain Woodes Rogers as being one of the key players in Blackbeard's life. Indeed, the two men were roughly the same age. In 1708 Rogers embarked on a round-the-world voyage to plunder Spanish ships, leading a squadron of two small frigates. He was a privateer with money from Bristol backers behind him and Letters of Marque that gave him the authority to attack enemy vessels, primarily Spanish.

He sailed round Cape Horn into the Pacific Ocean. One of the best-known incidents of this voyage is when Rogers put into the remote archipelago of Juan de Fernández Islands to take on wood and water and discovered the marooned Scots mariner Alexander Selkirk. This discovery and Selkirk's description of his years of solitude on the islands formed the basis of Daniel Defoe's *Robinson Crusoe*. By the time Rogers returned in 1711 after having circumnavigated the globe, he had won wide acclaim for his exploits to which he added by publishing an exciting account of his voyage a year later.

Konstam states that Bristol was a city of just under 20,000 at that time and if both Blackbeard and Rogers came from Bristol then the possibility exists that the two men could have known each other by sight. Local legend has Blackbeard being brought up in Redcliff which is a riverfront suburb, while Rogers was brought up in the heart of the city. 'If Blackbeard went to one of Bristol's half dozen schools during the last decade of the seventeenth century, the two would surely have met at some stage.'[24]

If both men growing up in Bristol had access to the books published about round-the-world voyages by mariners of the mid- to late-seventeenth century, it is quite likely that both were lured by the adventures on the high seas. Both men were privateers, although Rogers was considerably more successful. There is a strong likelihood that the two men had heard of each other and that their paths may even have crossed at some point during their careers, prior to Blackbeard turning pirate.

Rogers arrived in New Providence as the new governor in 1718 with an objective of ridding the island of pirates once and for all. It was the main base for pirates attacking shipping in the waters of the West Indies and the southern American Atlantic coast.[25]

One of the key things that Rogers brought with him was an official pardon from the King to pirates who denounced their piratical ways and turned to legal trade. At the time Blackbeard was using New Providence as his headquarters. His mentor and friend Benjamin Hornigold, along with several other pirates, took up the pardon while Blackbeard didn't, and he set sail from the Bahamas to North Carolina. Why didn't he stay, like so many of his shipmates and friends? Could the reason be that he did not want to be seen by Rogers? If Edward Teach was not his real name and he knew Rogers, it is likely the new governor would have recognised him and also known his real name.[26]

Why would Blackbeard be worried about Rogers knowing him? If Blackbeard was interested in returning to England and living off the fortune he made as a pirate and Rogers knew who he really was he would be forever a hunted man, unable to return to his family and his home and live the life of a wealthy man. Ironically, Blackbeard's decision to move up the Atlantic coast would be his undoing, all because he might not have wanted to be recognised by Rogers. Of course, this is speculation but the theory does make sense and seems logical.

However, this is not just about Blackbeard being a literate man coming from Bristol and possibly knowing Rogers. That sets the stage for what follows – his actions. If, as we suggest, he was intent on building his reputation, creating his own legend, then his actions would have to be different and outrageous in order for him to be seen as the most notorious pirate who ever sailed. On the surface, many of his actions seem to be just whims or turn of fancy, but if we look closely at them then we believe they are calculated actions designed to create an extreme effect that would continue to build his reputation, such as maiming one of his crewmates, Israel Hands, when he pulled out his pistols under the table and fired.

An action like this would rip through the crew very quickly and instil fear and awe in all of them. Their ship would have sailed into many ports, the crew would hit the taverns and inns in those ports and the stories of Blackbeard would be told, embellished with each pint. Blackbeard would have relied on the fact that his crew would start telling stories about him and their exploits once they were ashore, along with the crews of the ships he captured and sent on their way after robbing them, which in turn would have created the legend and myth of Blackbeard as the worst and most feared pirate who ever lived.

Another myth that is part of the Blackbeard legend is that he had fourteen wives. Though there are no records of these, it is Captain Johnson who provides us with that number: 'As it is the custom to marry here by priest, so it is there by a magistrate, and this I have been informed, made Teach's fourteenth wife, whereof about a dozen might be still living.'[27]

The so-called fourteenth wife was Mary Ormond, and although Johnson doesn't name her, other historians such as Lee have done. She was the daughter of a Bath County plantation-owner in North Carolina and was 16 when Blackbeard married her. Johnson states that the marriage ceremony was performed by the Governor of North Carolina, Charles Eden, so if this was the case, we know that Blackbeard knew Charles Eden.

According to Lee there is a letter written by a Mrs Ada S. Bragg to Mrs E.P. White stating that Mrs White's great-great-aunt was Mary Ormond who became Blackbeard's last wife.[28] If we take this letter at face value then it provides us with some connection to Blackbeard and reinforces the claims from historians that Mary Ormond was Blackbeard's wife. However, we must look at this with some scepticism. In Johnson's account the poor girl was badly treated on her wedding night by Blackbeard who forced her to have sex with some of his brutal shipmates:

> While his sloop lay in Ocracoke Inlet, and he ashore at a plantation where his wife lived, with whom after he had lain all night, was the custom to invite five or six of his brutal companions to come ashore, and he would force her to prostitute herself to them all, one after another, before his face.[29]

Now as we don't have any records that reinforce Johnson's statement we can look at it in the following two ways.

It may be that Johnson was adding the lurid detail to his narrative to spice it up or he had heard this from other pirates, from sitting in on trials of pirates, from shipmates of Blackbeard, or from hearsay. One source that Johnson used would have been Blackbeard's first mate Israel Hands who was maimed by Blackbeard when the pirate shot him and survived his career of piracy. Around the same time as Johnson was writing his accounts of the various pirates in his book, Hands was back in London. Indeed, it is Konstam who states we 'can be fairly certain that the writer met the pirate during this period and that the latter was the source of many accounts of Blackbeard's career'.[30] If this is right then it means that Hands was one of Johnson's principal sources on Blackbeard. The account, where after Blackbeard had finished with his wife and then forced her to make herself available to his friends with her protests falling on deaf ears, could have some basis of truth to it, albeit tenuous.[31]

Alternatively, what if it was Blackbeard who concocted this story and he was the one who related it to the rest of his men? Johnson doesn't name the other pirates who had their way with Mary. So if Blackbeard himself created the story in collusion with a few of his closest shipmates, men who were probably too scared to go against the pirate, they would certainly agree to have taken part in such actions, even if they didn't. After all, it is highly unlikely that the whole ship's company were there. The impression we get from Johnson is that there were only a few other 'brutes' who abused Blackbeard's young wife. So with their collusion the whole story could have been a fabrication told to Israel Hands by Blackbeard and the other men. Hands could have told it to Johnson, but if it's true then we can see the ruthless pirate at work. It may have been something he did on the spur of the moment or something he'd planned beforehand.

However, there is no official record of Blackbeard, Edward Teach, ever having been married and there is no official record of a wedding that took place where he was the groom. Then if he did take up with a woman, she would have been a mistress and not his wife. If she was his mistress then having her available for some of his men makes a little more sense.

As a contrast to this crude treatment of his own wife/mistress, others have suggested that he treated women with great respect. He had no power of resistance when confronted with an attractive woman and would find himself twisted around their fingers.[32] This may account for the rumours and gossip that he had thirteen wives before he met and took up with Mary Ormond.

Much has been written about Blackbeard's physical image by a variety of writers. Many people talk about his imposing height, the multitude of weapons he carried into battle with him, the lighted fuse wire under his hat and of course, the flowing black beard that gave him the name that became more famous than his own. 'An evil reputation was a great aid in persuading prospective victims of surrender quickly with a minimum of resistance. With this in mind he deliberately attempted to emphasise the evil side of his character.'[33]

It is indeed possible that some of Blackbeard's characteristics have been invented and re-invented by storytellers over the years. Again, it's Johnson's narrative that is the starting point for many of the descriptions that depict the pirate: 'Captain Teach, assumed the cognomen of Blackbeard from that large quantity of hair which, like a frightful meteor, covered his whole face and frightened America more than any comet that has appeared there a long time.'[34]

There was one man who had actually met him and left us with a brief description of the pirate in his deposition.

Captain Henry Bostock, master of the sloop *Margaret* must have been shaking in his boots when he was run down by the large pirate ship. There was nowhere for him to run and his much smaller vessel simply rode the swell; the much larger ship only a few hundred yards from him had her gun ports open. Smoke drifted in the air from the guns on the mighty ship that signalled the gunners were ready to fire. On the top deck of the ship men jeered and taunted him and his small crew. Ordering his sloop's tender to be lowered into the water, he clambered into it and was rowed across to the pirate vessel where he was roughly hauled aboard. On the deck of this pirate ship, Bostock came face to face with the most frightening man he'd ever seen – Blackbeard. However, later in his deposition he simply described him as a 'tall spare man with a black beard which he wore very long'. It was Johnson who took the sparse description and expanded upon it to provide us with the image we have today of the famous pirate and since then, other writers and storytellers have expanded it further and embellished it even more:[35]

> This beard was black which he suffered to grow of an extravagant length: as to breadth it came up to his eyes. He was accustomed to twist it with ribbons, in small tails, after the manner of our ramilies wigs, and turn them about his ears. In time of action, he wore a sling over his shoulders with three brace of pistols hanging in holsters like bandoliers, and stuck lighted matches under his hat, which, appearing on each side of his face his eyes naturally looking fierce and wild, made him altogether such a figure that imagination cannot form an idea of a fury, from hell, to look more frightening.[36]

These 'lighted matches' stuffed under Blackbeard's hat would have been impressive and frightening to his shipmates and certainly to his victims. They were the same fuses that were used for lighting the fuses to fire the cannon. What we don't know is if he had them in his hat all the time or just put them on for boarding captured ships.

However, there is one thing of note about this encounter between Bostock and Blackbeard. He and his crew were prisoners of the pirates for eight hours after they'd ransacked the *Margaret* and taken his cargo consisting mostly of cattle and pigs. Once he'd taken everything from the *Margaret*, Blackbeard let Bostock and his crew sail away in their own vessel, free and unhurt.

If Blackbeard was trying to cultivate an image of the most ruthless and brutal pirate who ever sailed, why did he let Bostock and his crew go? If, however, the image he was trying to create was the antithesis of the real Edward Teach then this makes sense. If the truth was that Teach was a benign and lenient man, then this act of leniency does make sense, but it may just be that he was feeling particularly magnanimous that day.

As we shall see later, Teach was prone to sudden violent actions but if he was projecting an image, then these violent outbursts had to be part of it. Few would even consider raising a hand against him and that was his genius. He played on his fearsome image to build this reputation. However, to maintain this kind of image, Blackbeard would have to work hard especially in front of his crew to prove to them he was more ruthless, unpredictable, ferocious and violent than any of them. Johnson reinforces this by relating an action that he believed helped his crew to think he was the devil:

> For being one Day at Sea, and a little flushed with drink: – Come, says he, let us make a Hell of our own, and try how long we can bear it; accordingly he, with two or three others, went down into the Hold, and closing up all the Hatches, filled several Pots full of Brimstone, and other combustible Matter, and set it on Fire, and so continued till they were almost suffocated, when some of the Men cry'd out for Air; at length he opened the Hatches, not a little pleased that he held out the longest.

Of course it may be that the above incident didn't happen, but if something similar did and Johnson heard it from Israel Hands or other pirates, then we can see Blackbeard hard at work building his reputation. Being magnanimous and letting a ship go only adds to his unpredictability, certainly in the face of actions like this one.

Although Blackbeard was a violent man, there is no actual record of him killing anyone. However, killing and maiming are not too far apart from each other and we know that Blackbeard had no qualms about maiming people, even his own crew.

Chapter 3

Nemesis – Alexander Spotswood

Governor Spotswood was irritated. The hammering and sawing that had been going on in his mansion for months was still not finished. The house was half-built and the endeavour he was about to embark upon needed concentration. It was a bleak November Wednesday when the two Royal Navy captains arrived at his mansion at his request. They sat across from him now, sipping their port. Although the big oak door to his large drawing room was closed the incessant banging and sawing could still be heard coming from the bowels of the mansion.

Spotswood's two guests were Captain Ellis Brand, commanding HMS *Pearl* and Captain George Gordon, commanding HMS *Lyme*. They were there because he had a plan and he needed them to carry it out. The problem he had was one of protocol. Even though he had a title of Admiral of Virginia, his authority over the Royal Navy in Virginian waters was extremely limited. He knew the two captains reported directly to the Admiralty in London and that his own chain of command back to the King was through their Lordships at the Council for Trade and Plantations. Even trickier was that this expedition was to be undertaken in the neighbouring colony of North Carolina where he had no jurisdiction whatsoever.

The two naval officers could easily say no to his plan and that would be that. After a few pleasantries, Spotswood poured the men another glass of port each and said, 'Gentlemen. I have decided to expurgate that nest of vipers at Bath Town once and for all.' He was, of course, referring to Blackbeard and his crew who were anchored at Ocracoke Island near Bath Town in North Carolina. The two naval officers listened as Spotswood outlined his decision to attack the pirates and both men agreed to the proposal.[37]

It was that meeting between the three men that ultimately sealed Blackbeard's fate. To all intents and purposes, Spotswood was Blackbeard's nemesis. For this reason a chapter devoted to Spotswood is crucial for us to understand the kind of man he was and his importance to Teach.

Even if Blackbeard had accepted the King's Pardon, there is no telling if he would have turned back to piracy and so without Spotswood, Blackbeard would have been free to roam the American coast for many more years, plundering ships and towns at will until he was stopped or until he chose to give up piracy and live as a wealthy man. So to understand the Blackbeard story it is necessary to understand Spotswood, bearing in mind he overstepped his authority, funded and planned the expedition himself that would see the death of the pirate. From his letters and other sources we know much more about Spotswood than we do about Blackbeard – Edward Teach. Spotswood's duration as Lieutenant-Governor of Virginia lasted twelve years, from 1710 to 1722. He ruled in the place of Governor George Hamilton who selected him while he was a lieutenant-colonel in the Army.

Taking up the post in 1710, Spotswood's initial objectives were to increase the power of the governor's office, end piracy, and improve relations with the American Indians through regulated trade. Not a man to mince words and a very moral man, he often and openly expressed his utter contempt of the members of his Council and those of the House of Burgesses who were at odds with his actions and polices.[38] Indeed, his main objective was to impose the will of England on the colony of Virginia but by the end of his term in office, he had become a Virginian himself by investing heavily in the colony. For example, he built his own ironworks in Spotsylvania County which became the largest producer of iron throughout the colonies. Also Spotswood designed and built the Governor's Palace, the powder magazine in Williamsburg and the Bruton Parish Church building. He was given the position of deputy postmaster-general for North America in 1730 and died in 1740 of a short illness while he was in Maryland raising troops for a military campaign by the British against the Spanish in South America.

He was born in Tangier, an English colony, in 1676 to Catherine and Robert Spotswood; the latter was a surgeon for the garrison. When Spotswood was only 4 years old his father died and his mother decided to stay in Tangier where she married the schoolteacher for the garrison, the Rev. George Mercer. There they stayed until the troops were ordered home in 1683. As a young boy growing up in Tangier he would have been exposed to military action; the regular skirmishes with the Moors just outside the walls of the colony. It was an exciting and exotic place to grow up. However, back in England life became more conventional. Warfare was a constant thing in his life. 'His elder half-brother Roger Elliot (the product of Catherine's first marriage) helped to secure Alexander an appointment as an ensign in the Earl of Bath's Regiment in 1693.'[39] Eventually he rose to the rank of lieutenant.

Some historians suggest that he was wounded, quite seriously, during the War of Spanish Succession (1701–14) at the Battle of Blenheim (1704), at which time he was the quartermaster-general for the English Army. However, our sources make no reference to his being wounded or to the legend that says

Spotswood was hit by a 4lb cannonball which he managed to keep and show off to his guests whenever he had any.[40]

Also there is some consensus indicating that he was taken prisoner during the Battle of Oudenarde and was released through the negotiating skills of the Duke of Marlborough, John Churchill, but not every historian agrees with this. Disillusioned with his lack of progress in terms of promotion within the military he began looking elsewhere and on 18 February 1710 he was commissioned by Queen Anne to be the Lieutenant-Governor (Deputy to the Governor) of Virginia. Some scholars say he obtained this post through his friendship with George Hamilton, 1st Earl of Orkney and Governor of Virginia (1704–37), or through the good offices of Marlborough himself.

Hamilton was Marlborough's trusted deputy and a fellow Scotsman like Spotswood. While Hamilton had been given the title of Governor of Virginia he certainly wouldn't be the man to run it. He gave that privilege to Spotswood and he would stay in England and receive half the revenues from the colony for doing nothing.

Spotswood arrived in Virginia in late 1710 and set about tackling the major issues of the colony: Indian relations, economic depression and security. He found the colony was poorly defended:

> I cannot but be of the opinion that a small fort built upon Point Comfort would be of good use, the very name of it would strike an awe in the Enemy, it would afford a Retreat for Ships when pursued by Privateers in time of War or by Pirates as must be expected in time of Peace.[41]

Also of concern was the economy as he states in his letter to the Council of Trade: 'The price of tobacco is fallen so low that it has brought many of the Owners in Debt at London, and lessened the Supplys of goods for their familys.'[42]

However, he soon found himself unable to effect real change because his responsibility to the colony exceeded his resources and his power. Committed to efficient and effective leadership, he faced a radical element in the colony and soon found that he had little support from the General Assembly. The twelve men of the Governor's Council resented his arrival because they had ruled the colony for four years without a governor. Indeed, the power struggle in Virginia reflected the old battles between King and Parliament in Britain but this time fought out on a different stage. 'Spotswood frequently tried to use prerogatives that were no longer available to King George I back in Britain, and his colonial assemblies knew that,' writes Angus Konstam in his book on Blackbeard. In Britain Parliament held power over the King and the Council and the House of Burgesses believed the same should be true of Virginia. Their view was that they represented the rights of the American people rather than serving the governor who, essentially, acted for the King.

In 1711 Spotswood shows his willingness to step outside of his own borders and interfere in other colonial states. In this case it was North Carolina, where an insurrection was taking place. In a letter to the Lords Proprietors of Carolina dated 28 July 1711, Spotswood blames the Quakers for the uprising, saying that they had poisoned 'the minds of all those who had any remains of a peaceable disposition'.

The prime antagonist in this affair was one Colonel Thomas Cary who had been the former deputy governor of North Carolina but had 'afterwards been removed by an order of the Lords Proprietors'. Cary, however, did not hang around but

> being joined by certain Quakers entrusted by the proprietors in some part of the Administration, gathered together a Rabble of the looser sort of people and by force of arms turned out the President and most of the Council, and by his own Authority assumed the administration of the Government.[43]

Some historians claim that the Tuscarora Indians were involved in this insurrection but as Spotswood states, they were divided in their feelings:

> There are now further discoverys made of the ill designs of Colonel Cary and his party, there being several Affidavits sent in hither to prove that Mr. Porter, one of Mr Cary's pretended Council was with the Tuscaruro [*sic*] Indians endeavouring by promises of great Rewards to engage them to cut off all the Inhabitants of that part of Carolina that adhered to Mr Hyde. The Indians own the proposal as accepted by their young men, but that their old men who have the greatest Sway in their Councils being of their own Nature suspicious that there was some trick intended them, or else directed by a Superior providence, refused to be concerned in that barbarous design.[44]

Spotswood consulted his Council and the decision was taken to act, despite the fact that they were meddling in the internal affairs of another colony:

> I had the unanimous opinion of Her Majesty's Council here to send an armed Force for the protection of that government against this Insurrection, there being now no other way but Force left to restore the peace of Your Lordships' Country.[45]

Spotswood sent a party 'of Marines from our Guardships, in hope that will fright the people from joining in the mad designs of Cary and his party, when they see their Governor will be supported from hence'.[46]

Fortunately for Spotswood this action worked as he stated in a letter to the Lords Proprietors of Carolina, dated 31 July 1711:

> The Marines are returned after having frighted the Rebellious party so
> as to lay down their arms and disperse, and I with joy tell your Lordships
> that there is now some prospect of tranquillity in Your Government, and
> that I have brought this about without effusion of blood, or disorders
> committed.[47]

However, it was not all wine and roses. Indeed, Spotswood exacerbated the issue
by not bothering to conceal his contempt of the House of Burgesses throughout
his tenure as governor. For ten years he was at odds with his Council and the
House of Burgesses, which constant strain would have laid many other men low
but not so for Spotswood.

Yet, he did try to quell some of the discontent by bringing in the Tobacco
Inspection Act in 1713. This put into law the requirement for the tobacco from
Virginia to be inspected before entering the European market which would
ensure that only highest-quality leaf would get through, increasing demand and
increasing prices, rather than the poor quality of leaf that was, at the time, being
exported to England:

> It may be reasonably suspected if what they carry home rather diminishes
> y'n increases the duties at the Custom House and serves for no other Use
> than Vile practices, whereby the Staple Commodity of this Country has
> been brought into Disteem and the markets thereof entirely ruined in
> Europe.[48]

The new Act was designed to increase the prices and improve the lot of the
growers and planters:

> This Law, therefore, by obliging all Planters to have their Tobacco viewed
> by a Sworn Officer in ye manner your Lordships may see more fully from
> ye several parts of the Act, has made provision against the exportation
> of all such Trash as is said to be allowed by the Custom House officers in
> the Out Ports as damaged Tobacco and thereafter frequently re-exported
> without the benefit of the Draw-back, and thus it is hoped the reputation
> of Virginia Tobacco may be retrieved when none but such as is found to
> be worth paying the duty at home shall be sent to foreign markets.[49]

The Assembly was made up of the elite of Virginia tobacco planters and
Spotswood decided to create forty patronage positions, of which twenty-nine
sitting burgesses were awarded these positions – some additional £250 per year.
However, Spotswood's scheme backfired as tobacco prices did not quickly go
up and the Act was highly unpopular with the farmer elite in Virginia. In the
following election after the Act was introduced, all but one of the burgesses who
had been awarded these inspectorships lost their seats.

A year later, he brought in the Indian Trade Act that helped to make his relationship with the Councils and the Virginia planters even worse. The idea for the Act was to grant the 'Virginia Indian Company, a joint-stock company, a twenty-year monopoly over American Indian trade, and charge the company with maintaining Fort Christanna, a settlement in southern Virginia for smaller Indian tribes':[50]

> I formed a settlement on the Frontiers for the Tributary Indians, pursuant to their Treaties, and by the Temptation of a fine tract of Land of Six Miles Square, the building a Fort thereon and placing a Guard of Twelve men and an Officer to be assisting to them.

Spotswood named this new settlement Christanna. As for the Indian Trade Act he mentions this in a letter dated 27 January 1714 claiming

> By the means of a late Act which I have obtained to be passed in the Assembly here, confining all Trade with ye Indians on the South side of James River (which are the most considerable of all our Tributaries), to Christ-Anna alone.[51]

Spotswood goes on to say that he formed a company to take on the responsibility of monitoring the Indian trade:

> It became the more easier for me to draw 'em to the passing the above mentioned Act for the better regulation of the Indian Trade, by which that Trade is not only confined to ye Settlement at Christ-Anna, as is above related, but a Company is established for carrying it on, who has as they have, the Sole benefit thereof for 20 years, are under an Obligation to contribute towards the Education of the Indian Children, namely by erecting forthwith, at their own Charge, a School-house at Christ-Anna.[52]

Spotswood hoped that by creating the company he would head off any political opposition by passing the responsibility for defence against Indian attack to private enterprise, taking it away from the colonial government along with the associated costs of defending the colony. However, like the Tobacco Act this also angered many Virginians, especially those who had heavy investments in private trade.

In the autumn of 1715, Spotswood dissolved the House of Burgesses in frustration:

> I am obliged to give an Account of the Transactions of this Government, wherein the several unwarrantable Schemes they had formed, and their whole proceedings thereupon are faithfully Sum'd up, and told them in so public a manner as will leave no room to doubt of the truth of ye matters of fact; and after such a Behaviour of the House of Burgesses as

is there truly represented, I hope the Expressions will not appear so Severe nor their dissolution too unadvised.[53]

The wrangling continued, and to get away from it he led an expedition in 1716 to expand Virginia's western frontier. His expedition crossed the Blue Ridge Mountains and took the Shenandoah Valley which Spotswood claimed for the King and by doing so, expanded the colony of Virginia. This area was later settled in the 1730s to act as protection against French and Indian aggression. He also created a frontier fortified outpost at Germanna on the Rapidan River. None of these actions were really contested by the two assemblies of the colonial Virginian government.

Looking beyond his political policies, Spotswood also left a mark on Virginian architecture. He is responsible for much of the design of Williamsburg and he helped to restore the College of William and Mary that was damaged after a fire in 1705. He designed the structure for a new church in Bruton Parish in 1710 shortly after his arrival. This church served as a model for the design and style of many other churches and buildings throughout the colony. In 1715 he had a new powder magazine built in Williamsburg. Perhaps the most memorable and outstanding project is the magnificent Governor's Palace which he oversaw from 1710 to 1722:

> Spotswood was criticized for the project's high cost, but plantation owners began to emulate the building's Georgian architecture in their own homes as early as the 1720s, and by the mid-eighteenth century, the style was an indicator of wealth and power.[54]

Yet, despite these achievements Spotswood could not get away from the political wrangling and he discovered too late that he had many more masters than he initially realised, including English merchants, the Virginia planter elite and imperial bureaucrats, in addition to the Earl of Orkney and their Lordships at the Council of Trade and Plantations.

The Virginia planter elite were the biggest thorn in his side because they were very well-connected to the Privy Council in Britain and could bring a lot of influence and power to bear on policies that they opposed. For example, they brought so much pressure to bear on the Tobacco Inspection Act and the Indian Trade Act that the government in Britain disallowed those acts in 1717:

> Immediately upon the Receipt of his Majesty's Order in Council, I issued a proclamation for repealing both ye Indian and Tobacco Laws, but as the Country are almost Generally sensible of the loss of the Tobacco Law, so the Government found it Self no less embarrassed by the repeal of the Indian Law.[55]

Part of the problem was Spotswood's desire to increase his power without realising that it was actually diminishing. He appointed judges, called for new elections, and appointed new parish ministers without consulting the local politicians. He tried to remove members of the Council that opposed him. All of this added up to a weakening of his power as the influence of the Virginia planters continued to grow, the latter being manifest in the House of Burgesses and in the Colonial Council.

However, Spotswood reached an accord with his council on 29 April 1722 when both sides agreed to act in friendship in the running of the colonial government. This was largely achieved by Spotswood agreeing to become a permanent Virginian resident: 'Later that year, as part of a series of land grants awarded to settlers to create a buffer against the French, the Council granted Spotswood 86,000 acres in the newly created Spotsylvania County.' In a letter dated 11 June 1722, Spotswood wrote to the Board of Trade that the 'angry proceedings of the Assembly in 1718' were 'balanced by their good agreement in 1722'.[56]

That same year Spotswood was replaced, despite the new detente between him and the Council. The new Lieutenant-Governor, Hugh Drysdale arrived on 25 September 1722 to take up his post. Historians believe that there were several factors that may have contributed to Spotswood's removal. One is the ten years of constant wrangling that took place prior to the new detente. The government in London would have had a string of letters and complaints against Spotswood and it could be that after ten years they'd had enough. Another reason could be the massive land grant that he accepted which went against the stated policy that no person or persons could claim more than 1,000 acres of Virginian land. Perhaps the most plausible theory of all is that two of Spotswood's most antagonistic opponents, the Reverend James Blair and William Byrd, had not reconciled with him when the rest of the Council had and both men, powerful and influential in Virginia as well as having potent friends in the English government, were in London when the decision to replace Spotswood was taken. If this is the case he would be the third governor in a row that Blair had had a hand in unseating. If Spotswood had cooperated with the Virginia planter elite he may have been able to hang on much longer as governor. It was a lesson taken to heart by future governors.

True to his agreement, Spotswood settled in Virginia, in the frontier town of Germanna in Spotsylvania County. Here he built a mansion that was even larger than the Governor's Palace and far more ornate and impressive than that building. Sadly by 1750 it had been destroyed. He also built the largest ironworks in the colonies and relied on slave labour to run it. The biggest market for his iron was England.

Spotswood married Anne Butler Brayne of St Margaret's Parish,

Westminster in 1724 when he returned to England to work out the taxes on his vast land holdings in Virginia as well as secure his title to those lands. The couple had two sons and returned to Virginia in 1729. A year later the government appointed him as deputy postmaster for all of North America and he distinguished himself in this role as well, extending the postal service much further south from Philadelphia, where it was before he took up the post, to Williamsburg. It was Spotswood who selected Benjamin Franklin as the postmaster for Philadelphia in 1737.

Two years later Britain went to war with Spain. Spotswood had always dreamed of military advancement and this he finally achieved when he was brought back into the Army as brigadier general. This position saw him as second-in-command to Major-General Charles Cathcart, but Spotswood didn't see any action. He was travelling to Maryland to consult with colonial governors on how to raise and organise new troops for the war against the Spaniards; on arriving at Annapolis he fell ill suddenly and died shortly afterwards on 7 June 1740.

That is his life story. From the letters and actions in this chapter we can get an idea of what kind of man Alexander Spotswood was. He had no qualms about extending his authority beyond the borders of Virginia into neighbouring colonies, specifically North Carolina; he set up settlements on the borders and expanded the lands which were later settled. We see a man of action, a decisive man who was driven to get things done and would use unorthodox methods to achieve his aims. He was a builder, a man of some vision who left a lasting legacy on Virginia. By contrast, Blackbeard was the opposite; a man who left nothing behind but a terrible reputation.

If Spotswood had not been governor at the time and if there had been another man who was softer, more pliable than and not as single-minded as Spotswood, would Blackbeard's reign of terror have continued virtually unchecked? We will never know but what we have provided here is a little of Spotswood's character; at heart a military man and therefore accustomed to action, to people doing what he told them to do and being single-minded and dedicated to his purpose. The two men were on a collision course that would see Blackbeard's end and, in some ways, the end of the 'Golden Age of Piracy'.

Chapter 4

Contemporaries and the Times

Now that we've looked at Spotswood's life and had a glimpse at Teach's early life it is worth looking at the times and some of the people within them that influenced these two men. Turning to the criminal fraternity, one man whose life was broadly similar to Teach's was Dick Turpin, a famed highwayman who was alive during the same period as Edward Teach, although Turpin was much younger when Teach died and wasn't hung until several years later.

Why look at Turpin? Simply because his legend, like that of Blackbeard, has become much larger over the centuries than the actual exploits of the man. His image is of a dashing and daring highwayman who rode from London to York in less than twenty-four hours on his mount 'Black Bess'. In reality this ride was undertaken by another highwayman, John 'Swift Nick' Nevison who, having robbed a sailor near Gad's Hill in Kent, set off on this momentous journey in order to give himself an alibi. This took place before Turpin was even born.

Turpin's criminal ventures had been unremarkable and certainly nothing of legend up until the time when he was captured and waiting to be hung at York racecourse. Only then did he exhibit the daring traits of a dashing highwayman usually attributed to him.[57]

The legend of Turpin is one of a lone highwayman, but during most of his criminal career he was part of the Essex Gang. This gang operated not by holding up people on the highway but by robbing isolated farmhouses and torturing the occupants into giving up their valuables and money. Turpin did not get involved in highway robbery until towards the end of his criminal career and his brashness at the end of his life was recorded in an account of his execution in the *York Courant* where he finally showed some courage and 'threw himself off the ladder', dying five minutes later.

By the time of Turpin's death, Teach was already dead but his legend would have become common knowledge due to the account of his exploits being published in Captain Johnson's *History* as well as accounts appearing in newspapers. So by the time Turpin was gaining notoriety it is quite likely that he must have known of the accounts of Blackbeard. We could speculate that these accounts may have contributed in some small way to Turpin wanting to gain as much infamy, kudos and fortune as he could. He acquired these through his acts of lawlessness, torture and murder and was no hero, but Teach could have been. The latter fought in 'Queen Anne's War', also known as the War of Spanish Succession, as a privateer. When it was over he could have continued with this line of work but instead, he chose to let go of all the shackles of civilisation and turn to piracy.

The times would also have had a heavy influence on Teach. Most of the major battles that England was fighting at the time took place at sea and the news of these maritime victories by the Royal Navy would, of course, be brought back to England and published. Between 1689 and 1697 England was at war with France. In 1702 the War of Spanish Succession broke out. Hostilities continued until 1713 when the signing of the Utrecht Treaty ended the war.

Last of the Stuart monarchs, Queen Anne's reign spanned twelve years. These were dominated by the War of Spanish Succession and, by the uniting of the English and Scottish parliaments, resulted in the creation of the Parliament of Great Britain on 1 May 1707 which was known as the Act of Union. The years were also marked by Marlborough's famous victories at Blenheim, Ramilies, Oudenarde and Malplaquet.[58]

Anne was born to the Catholic King James II but was raised as a Protestant under her uncle King Charles II. She married the Prince of Denmark and experienced seventeen pregnancies but only produced five children and only one, her son, managed to outlive infancy but died before he could inherit the throne.

The greatest influence on Queen Anne was her relationship with Sarah Jennings Churchill, her childhood companion and lady of the bedchamber. According to the BBC *Online History* account of Queen Anne, in 1688 Sarah persuaded her friend, then monarch-to-be, to support her brother-in-law the Protestant William of Orange of the Netherlands when he took the English throne from James II:

> It was after William's death in 1702 that Anne became monarch, but prior to her succession she agreed to the Act of Settlement in 1701, signed by William, which promised the throne to the Electress of Hanover (and her heirs) as heir of James I (VI of Scotland). Anne had by this point abandoned the idea of producing an heir.[59]

Politically, Anne believed in mixed ministries and the two major political parties of the day were the Whigs and the Tories. The Tories came to power in 1710 and when it came to foreign policy she found herself at odds with them, believing, as did the Whigs, that a war on the continent would be more successful than a naval campaign, which the Tories supported.

The Duke of Marlborough was Sarah Churchill's husband and also a Whig sympathiser. He won several battles as the commander of the British and allied forces on the continent during the War of Spanish Succession. As the Queen's lady of the bedchamber, Sarah was always trying to pressure Anne to promote more Whigs and by the same process, her husband. However, the Queen resisted these attempts and finally, having had enough, dismissed Sarah and her husband from her service.

Sarah's successor, Abigail Masham, was a confidante who had been planted by the Tories into Anne's closest circle. She was a cousin to the Tory, Robert Harley who later became the Earl of Oxford; and in 1708, Harley also lost favour with the Queen. She then admitted the Whigs into her administration while leading Tories tried to plot the succession of Anne's exiled Catholic brother James, the Old Pretender to the throne. Anne was having none of it and ensured that Protestant succession would take place through the Lord Treasurer, Charles Talbot, and the Duke of Shrewsbury who presided over the accession of the Prince of Hanover, George Louis, crowned George I, who reigned from 1714 to 1727.

During these years, Blackbeard rose to prominence. As we have seen from earlier chapters the conventional wisdom is that Teach was from Bristol. That said, his early life must have been dominated by the bustling seaport. Located at the joining of the Avon and Frome rivers, Bristol is about 8 miles from the Bristol Channel and the open sea. The city is unique for having the docks right in the heart of the city. At the time when Teach was a young man, the thriving Bristol port owed its prosperity to the sea trade that many explorers, adventurers and privateers had opened up with foreign countries. Indeed, in the fifteenth century the Society of Merchant Adventurers was organised in Bristol and by 1500 the Society collected port dues and regulated all of the city's foreign trade. The discovery of America increased the prosperity of the city dramatically as the slave trade grew. The merchants of Bristol constructed ships to carry African slaves to the West Indies and America in return for a wide variety of items such as sugar.

Bristol merchants had financed several voyages to the newly-discovered America in a bid to find a short route to Asia by sailing westward across the Atlantic. These rich merchants began financing voyages of discovery by adventurers such as John and Sebastian Cabot. Many other voyages from this area of England were launched as people came from all over the country to find their fame and fortune in adventures far across the seas. William Hawkins and his son John, who came from Plymouth, were among this group of intrepid seafarers seeking the New World and all the riches it could offer.

However, it was pirates or privateers like Francis Drake, arguably the original and most famous privateer and pirate, who helped to make England rich.

Drake's exploits and his close friendship with Queen Elizabeth I turned him into a household name, making him one of the most famous of all seafarers. In 1577, Drake had sailed from Plymouth on his round-the-world voyage of plundering. Philip Gosse, in his *History of Piracy*, states that Drake returned with a fortune from his expedition in 1580 and that Queen Elizabeth ordered the royal barge be rowed down the Thames so that she could 'knight the master thief of the known world on the deck of his *Golden Hind*'.[60]

Gosse also states that Queen Elizabeth was severe with pirates operating in English waters but was much more lenient with English pirates operating in foreign seas. She shut her eyes or turned her back on their exploits as the hostility between Spain and England increased. While England was at peace with the world, piracy, principally against Spain, was done in secret with Elizabeth's encouragement. These nefarious activities brought wealth into the country and helped to create a race of very tough and able seafarers who, in England's hour of need, took on the might of the Spanish fleet and defeated it, bringing about that nation's ultimate downfall and making England 'the proud mistress of the seas'.[61]

Drake's exploits could not have been lost on Teach who, as a young boy growing up in Bristol would very likely have had a youth dominated by tall tales of the sea. It is highly likely that he pored over any journals or books about the voyages and adventures of Drake and others like him whenever he could. As we have already seen we know that Teach was an educated man for he could read and write, so for those who were educated there was ample literature from sailors, privateers and others who had embarked on various adventures around the world. For example, in 1582 Richard Hakluyt published his *Divers Voyages Touching the Discovery of America* and seven years later his best work, *Principal Navigations, Voyages and Discoveries of the English Nation* was published. In 1679 *Bucaniers of America* by A.O. Esquemeling was published in Amsterdam and the English translation was published in London in 1684. William Dampier, who had already circumnavigated the globe, published the first volume of his *Voyages* in 1697, with further volumes appearing in 1699 and 1707. Also, in 1709 John Lawson's *A New Voyage to Carolina* was published. So it is clear that there was ample reading matter that probably made the young and impressionable Teach keen to make his mark, to seek adventure, fame and fortune.

Yet, did he go to sea because he had no choice, or because it was the best choice, or because he just drifted into it? There were choices and it seems most likely that he made the choice to follow in the steps of all those other sailors before him, especially if he lived in Bristol and if his family was already involved in the seafaring trade in some way. The influence of adventures on the high seas and lure of the sea would have been very strong indeed.

So what was life on the high seas like during the time of Blackbeard?

The published works by the seafarers and adventurers of the day that were available to Teach would have romanticised life to some degree, but the reality was that life at sea was hard. The film industry paints a far more glorious picture of life on an early eighteenth-century vessel than was actually the case, and there was very little difference in the quality of life between sailors serving their country and those serving themselves. In fact, in some cases, those in the Royal Navy suffered more.

On board pirate ships a captain was never placed in command by a higher authority. Unlike the Royal Navy which had rules, regulations and traditions, pirates were literally their own bosses, hence the often higher living standards. While the Royal Navy had a rank structure which meant that ratings did what lieutenants ordered, lieutenants did what commanders ordered, commanders did what captains ordered, captains did what admirals ordered and ultimately, admirals did what the government and monarch, through the Admiralty, ordered, pirates did none of these things.

Despite the apparent lawless nature of life on a pirate vessel compared to a military vessel, pirates did have codes: a list of ethics that everyone on board had to abide by. These covered the very basic provisions, such as discipline, each individual's share of the 'treasures' taken and compensation when a crew member was injured. Some codes were far more detailed and were not far removed from standard corporation contracts we may see today. The more detailed ones covered discipline, shares and compensation, gambling, drinking, curfews on board, theft between the crew, clothing, rewards for scaling another vessel first and therefore being at higher risk of death, keeping weapons fit for their purpose, women on board (although in exceptional cases women were a part of the crew), voting status on whether to attack a vessel, desertion, in-crew fighting, work of musicians on board and perceived cowardice. Clearly, some pirate captains were keen to run a vessel almost as efficient as their Royal Navy counterparts.

However, as far as Blackbeard is concerned we do not have detailed evidence of what code or ethics were aboard his ships but we must assume that he had instilled some, if not just to prevent total anarchy on board. While much is known about Teach's feared reputation as the pirate Blackbeard, in order to build the reputation within his crew he must have instilled some form of crude and cruel discipline aboard his ship.[62]

Like most other pirates, Blackbeard did not advertise his presence when approaching a prize. The famous black flag with the skull and crossbones was rarely flown. Instead, most pirate captains would use a ruse that many privateers used which was flying the flag of a friendly or neutral country to lure their unsuspecting prey into a false sense of security and make it easier to board the ship and capture it. This was common practice amongst privateers, and to some degree naval vessels hunting for both pirates and enemy ships. If you could draw close to your prey before the trick was realised, it simplified the chase.[63]

Quite often though, pirate activities did involve a great deal of chasing. These chases could last for hours, depending on how determined the prey was to escape. The chase would begin with the pirate lookout, perched high up in the crow's nest, sighting the sails of a ship on the horizon and the pirate captain then deciding to give chase. The target then had a massive head start. Several miles of open sea separated the ships and it was up to the skills of the pirate crew and the speed of their vessel to catch up with the intended target. To gain the advantage of speed, pirates often stripped down their ships, ripping out anything that would add weight and slow them down. In this respect, Blackbeard was no exception.

Chapter 5

The New Pirate Captain

Though he had often distinguished himself for
his uncommon boldness and personal courage, he was
never raised to any command till he went a-pirating ...
when Captain Benjamin Hornigold put him into
a sloop that he had made a prize of. [64]

Captain Charles Johnson, 1724

The ship most associated with Blackbeard is the *Queen Anne's Revenge*. This did not mark the start of his career in piracy, nor did it mark the end, but some of his major exploits were conducted while he commanded this ship. Its eventual demise has created one of the lasting mysteries of his career.

Before he took command of that ship, he served under the guidance of the man who was his mentor – Benjamin Hornigold. 'Blackbeard the onetime privateer had become Blackbeard the notorious pirate and the transformation was largely due to the leading pirate captain of the time.'[65] Benjamin Hornigold may not have been the first person that Blackbeard served under but, according to most sources he was certainly the most influential. He was the one who gave Blackbeard his first command, so he must have recognised the talent and ability of his protégé.

Little is known about Hornigold except that he was an Englishman and was a privateer fighting in the War of Spanish Succession ('Queen Anne's War'). Konstam suggests that Hornigold may have come from Norfolk as Hornigold was and still is a common surname in that county. Norfolk has two main ports, King's Lynn and Great Yarmouth which were both important fishing ports and centres of coastal trade between Britain and the rest of Europe. He maintains that it is likely that Hornigold started his seafaring career in one of these ports, even though they faced Europe instead of the Atlantic which limited their importance as long-range international trading ports.

So it is likely that Hornigold made his way to London to start his ocean-going career. Though the War of Spanish Succession was fought between

European nations, much of the fighting took place off the coast of North America.[66]

There is no record as to how Hornigold got to the Bahamas but by the time Blackbeard arrived he was already a pirate having been a privateer in the war and refusing to give up the fight against the French and Spanish when the war ended in 1713. Johnson gives us the date of 1716 when Blackbeard was sailing with Hornigold so the latter must have arrived around the end of the war.

Now Konstam suggests that in the first account of pirates operating from the Bahamas they were using small boats and not the large ships such as the ones that Blackbeard later captured. Through Captain Johnson we know that Hornigold was commanding a 30-gun vessel by 1717 probably known as the *Ranger*. It is highly likely that Hornigold's ship was probably the largest in the harbour at Nassau on New Providence Island.[67]

In reality privateering is the legalised version of piracy. The difference is that piracy is theft for personal gain when the victim is anyone, while privateering is theft for the gain of whichever government or monarch issued the warrant, or Letters of Marque, to steal from its enemies at the time. Privateering was far more prevalent in wartime than during periods of peace since the warrants often specified ships of certain nationalities that were fair game. However, like piracy, the crews were not paid by anything other than a share of the spoils.[68]

By March 1717, Blackbeard and Hornigold were sailing in tandem. Captain Johnson writes that

> in the spring of the year 1717 Teach and Hornigold sailed from Providence, for the Main of America, and took in their way a billop from Havana, with one hundred and twenty barrels of flour, as also a sloop from Bermuda, Thurber, master, from whom they took only some gallons of wine and then let him go.

Also around this time, they captured a sloop and Hornigold put Teach in command of it.[69]

At the time, Hornigold would have been the top pirate in the Bahamas; a pirate king highly involved in the running of the community in Nassau. One of the earliest official records of Blackbeard being mentioned comes from Captain Mathew Musson (Munthe according to some historians). By this time, Blackbeard was one of several operating from New Providence and had clearly taken command of a vessel:

> ... five pirates made ye harbour of Providence their place of rendezvous
> ... Hornigold, a sloop with 10 guns and about 80 men; Jennings, a sloop

with 10 guns and 100 men; Burgiss, a sloop with 8 guns and about 80 men; White, in a small vessell [*sic*] with 30 men and small armes [*sic*]; Thatch, a sloop 6 gunns [*sic*] and about 70 men.[70]

The above report tells us that Blackbeard was in command of his own ship, albeit still in the company of Hornigold. We can't be sure what this ship was. Some accounts believe it to be the *Revenge*. We go with this because it is known from other later documents that Blackbeard was in command of this vessel fairly early on. This ship, a sloop, was formerly under the command of the pirate Stede Bonnet.[71]

However, there is some discrepancy around the dates when Hornigold and Blackbeard parted. Johnson states that it was sometime in late November 1717 that they separated. However, we have some documentation that might suggest their parting was earlier. One of the documents we can look at is the charge brought against Blackbeard's former quartermaster, William Howard, by none other than Governor Spotswood of Virginia.

> Howard did together with his Associates and Confederates on or about the 29th day of September in the year Aforesaid (1717), in an Hostile manner with force and Arms on the high seas near Cape Charles in this Colony (Virginia) within the Jurisdiction of the Admiralty of this Court attack & force a Sloop Called the *Betty* of Virginia belonging to the Subjects of our said Lord the King, and the said Sloop did then and there Rob and plunder of Certain Pipes of Madera Wine and other Goods and Merchandizes and thereafter the said William Howard did Sink and destroy the said Sloop with the remaining Part of the Cargo.

In this charge against Howard, Blackbeard is named specifically stating that he did 'in the year of our Lord 1717 Join and Associate himself with one Edward Tach and other Wicked and dissolute persons'. In the same charge, the sloop is also named 'and with them did combine to fit out in Hostile manner a Certain Sloop or Vessel Called the *Revenge* to commit Piracies and depredations upon the High Seas'.[72]

From this document it would seem that Blackbeard was operating alone when he met the *Betty* which would have been sometime in September 1717. Hornigold isn't mentioned anywhere in the charges against Howard and if the two pirates had still been operating together he would most likely have been mentioned at some point as he was, to all intents and purposes, still a highly influential pirate. It may be that he is included as one of those 'dissolute persons'.

Perhaps the key document here is a report that was in the November edition of the *Boston News Letter* filed in Philadelphia on 24 October 1717 that stated a certain Captain Codd had been taken '12 days since off our Cape by a Pirate Sloop called *Revenge*, of 12 Guns, 150 Men, Commanded by one Teach, who Formerly Sailed Mate out of this Port'.[73]

This report confirms that by October 1717 Blackbeard was sailing alone. However, as with any historical trail there are discrepancies and the key one here is the time and date that Blackbeard met Stede Bonnet.

Major Stede Bonnet was something of an oddity in the circle of piracy. He had been a gentleman and a landowner, having at one time been in possession of some property in Barbados. As a land-lover, he knew very little about sailing a ship or commanding a crew, features that made him susceptible to a takeover bid by the more capable and determined Blackbeard.[74]

He was known as the gentleman pirate, but this seems to be more in keeping with his habit of walking the deck of the ship in his morning suit, and then returning to his onboard library, than to his exploits at sea.[75]

Bonnet had been a wealthy landowner in Barbados. Born in St Michael's Parish in 1688, he inherited the family estates (sugar plantations), was made a major in the militia and married a neighbour's daughter. All of this he gave up at the age of 29 and turned to piracy, something he knew nothing about. Johnson tries to come up with a reason as to why Bonnet did this in his account of the man:

> He was afterwards rather pitied than condemned, by those that were acquainted with him, believing that this humour of going a-pirating, proceeded from a disorder of his mind, which had been too visible to him, some time before this wicked undertaking, and which is said to have been occasioned by some discomforts he found in a married state.

Bonnet also broke with pirate tradition and bought his vessel. While other pirates used ships they had stolen to rob other ships, Bonnet chose to part with money for his vessel. Some historians even believe that he paid his crew a regular wage rather than rely on the standard form of remuneration, that being shares of the spoils of plunders. At a time when many national navies were too bankrupt to pay their sailors a regular wage, this, if true, not only made him unique in piracy, but also made him almost unique in the maritime world.

The November edition of the *Boston News Letter* stated that Captain Codd had been taken by Blackbeard commanding the 12-gun sloop *Revenge* – Bonnet's ship that he'd paid for – but it doesn't stop there. The same edition had another three reports of piratical acts carried out in the month of October.

Codd's ship had little of interest for Blackbeard as they were carrying indentured servants and so was allowed to continue her voyage into Philadelphia. Further attacks took place according to the *Boston News Letter* reports: 'Two Snows, outward bound, *Spofford* leaden with stave for Ireland and

Budger of Bristol and the *Sea Nymph* leaden with Wheat for Oporto.' At the time Blackbeard was cruising near the mouth of the Delaware River when these vessels were taken as they headed out to sea. The reports also stated that a sloop from Madeira was attacked, one Peter Peters commanding, while another sloop, 'One Grigg Master, bound hither for London', another from Madeira heading for Virginia was attacked and then 'they took a sloop from Antigua, belonging to New York'.[76]

All of these attacks took place in the Delaware Bay according to the reports in the *Boston News Letter*, which also stated that Blackbeard kept the *Sea Nymph* and turned it into a pirate ship. Blackbeard then took three more ships, one of which was commanded by Captain Goelet, a fast sloop from Curacao whose holds were half-full with cocoa. According to the newspaper report the pirates threw the cargo overboard and kept this sloop for themselves, putting all the crew, passengers and other prisoners into the *Sea Nymph* which was much slower.

So what of Bonnet? Our information on him comes from the same source published in the *Boston News Letter* where there is a paragraph in which Bonnet is mentioned:

> On board the Pirate Sloop is Major Bennet, but has no Command, he walks about in his Morning Gown, and then to his Books, of which he has a good Library on Board, he was not well of his wounds that he received by attacking a Spanish Man of War, which kill'd and wounded thirty to forty men. After which putting into Providence the place of Rendezvous for the Pirates, they put the afore said Captain Teach onboard for this cruise.

So if we replace Bennet with Bonnet we have a report that puts Bonnet on board with Blackbeard.

If we take the information from the article at face value then the story of the Spanish man-of-war was true, but there are problems with dates as Konstam explains in his book. Captain Johnson suggests that Blackbeard and Bonnet met around December 1717, while Lee suggests they met in March 1717. However, the article in the *Boston News Letter* was filed on 24 October and it stated that Codd had been taken some twelve days earlier. This would mean that it is likely that Bonnet's story about encountering the Spanish man-of-war is a fabrication and that it sounded better than him just meekly surrendering to Blackbeard: 'Faced with someone as intimidating as Blackbeard, it is little wonder that he allowed himself to become a passenger on his own sloop.'[77]

So what is the significance of Bonnet to Teach? Why would the notorious and ruthless pirate allow another pirate to walk about his deck in his morning coat and have his own library and have nothing whatever to do with the running of his own ship? Lee states that these two men went into the captain's cabin and got on very well, 'the two men apparently proved congenial, since great laughter was soon heard'.[78]

Konstam states that Bonnet was to all intents and purposes a prisoner on his own ship. So why didn't Blackbeard just dump him; if he was of no value why not just lock him up? If we look at Blackbeard as the supreme spin-doctor, a man steadily building his reputation, then having Bonnet around and apparently free to walk the deck and read his books shows that Blackbeard was in complete control – in essence complete control of Bonnet's fate.

Most historians agree that within weeks of being captured Bonnet was mumbling to anyone who would listen that he would give up piracy and go and live a simple life because he was becoming increasingly worried about Blackbeard's actions. So we could say that Bonnet was the perfect eye-witness for Blackbeard – a literate man who could accurately describe the actions of the pirate to whomever would listen. Perhaps Blackbeard might have been thinking that Bonnet could be a useful spokesman for him at some point?

Chapter 6

Flagship

On the far side of the Atlantic a ship was leaving port. The date was 24 March 1717 and *La Concorde* commanded by Captain Pierre Dosset was sailing from Nantes for the last time. It had made two previous transatlantic voyages, one in 1713 and one in 1715. The first voyage carried around 500 slaves from the West Coast of Africa to Martinique and 456 of them were sold, while the fate of the remainder is not known. On the second voyage, the cargo of slaves was sold to owners in and around Leogane, a French colony in what is now Haiti.[79]

There are two versions surrounding the origins of *La Concorde*. The first states that the ship was built around 1710, that it was used to protect British interests during the War of Spanish Succession and was captured by French privateers a year later and was refitted as an armed escort that was part of a squadron that attacked the town of Rio de Janeiro. At the end of hostilities the ship became an armed merchant vessel.[80]

The second version, and the one most historians go with, is that the ship, already named *La Concorde*, was built in the river port of Nantes as a French naval frigate. It served as an escort for a convoy bound for the naval port of Brest. The ship sailed for the West African coast, then across the Atlantic to Martinique, Tobago and Hispaniola. After a couple of captures, she returned to Nantes, and at the end of the war, she was abandoned.[81]

The ship eventually ended up in the possession of the Montaudoin family. This influential family conducted its business in and around Nantes, the centre of the French slave trade.[82] They had made their fortune in the profitable selling of slaves and not only owned the ship but also all of its cargo, and that included the men, women and children being transported.

Captain Dosset filed a report on the capture of his ship to the French authorities in Martinique. There the manager of public affairs, Charles Mesnier, compiled his own detailed report which he sent back to his superiors in France. Dosset's report states that *La Concorde* was 200 to 300 tons, making it a large ship for its time. Ships during the early part of the eighteenth century were weighed by the amount of cargo they could carry rather than the amount of water they displaced in the sea as they are today. Measuring the tonnage of a ship by the cargo it could carry was based on two principal trades of medieval times, that of grain and wine, and was of primary importance when it came to taxes and port duties.

La Concorde was refitted by the Montaudoin family with two vital criteria in mind, neither of which was comfort for either the crew or the slaves, but would have been of great interest to a pirate. 'She began life as a privateer,' Konstam states in his book. 'A clean, fast hull, ample cargo capacity, and three masts, providing a maximum press of sail for a vessel of her size.'

Storage space was crucial. The more slaves that could be crammed into the hold, the higher the profits would be at the markets on the other side of the ocean. Conditions on board these ships for the slaves would have been appalling and the conditions for the crew not much better. Modern rush-hour trains by comparison would seem positively spacious. For pirates, a large storage space like that of *La Concorde* would be ideal for holding large amounts of plunder between ports that were open to dealing with them. Also the massive size of the ship as a whole could threaten crews of smaller vessels into surrendering their cargoes without much of a struggle.

That brings us to the second criteria – speed. It was expected that a few of the slaves would die on the long voyage and the more the number of deaths could be reduced by a swifter voyage, the more the potential for profits. Also, for a pirate, speed was essential when chasing other vessels.

The final voyage of *La Concorde* saw Dosset in command of this impressive ship with his second-in-command Lieutenant François Ernaut.

On 8 July 1717 the ship, armed with sixteen cannon and manned by a crew of seventy-five, arrived at the port of Whydah. This was a thriving coastal port of West Africa known today as Benin, and in 1717 it was one of the hubs of the African slave trade which it had supported for 300 years. In this flat country human sacrifice was normal, and holidays were celebrated with public beheadings of slaves and captured warriors. Despite this, there were still plenty of slaves available to maintain this area's reputation as the Slave Coast. Around this region, the Royal African Company had once enjoyed a monopoly but that control had vanished in 1698 when it became just one of several.[83]

From Whydah the ship collected around 500 captured Africans: a mixture of men, women and even children. Their futures, assuming they survived the transatlantic voyage, would be serving whichever owner chose to purchase them in the New World.[84]

The voyage across the Atlantic was arduous. Even without the dangers of attack there were many other hazards, chief of which was disease. Because conditions on board were so poor and there was no hygiene to speak of, diseases like scurvy and dysentery were rampant. Survival was hindered by people's lack of understanding on how to prevent disease and how to cure it. Once disease prevention became more and more widespread, people understood how to prevent scurvy, for example, and the death rates on long voyages declined. Proper nutrition was far from understood and in those days, the preservation of meat was maintained by dousing it in salt.[85]

Biscuit was another form of food, as were beans. Biscuits were hard and brittle, could last a long time in the hold of a ship and could be eaten either whole or crushed into powder to mix with other rotting foods. These were difficult to eat when your teeth were decaying from lack of care or from scurvy.[86]

We know from the reports of Dosset and his lieutenant that during the crossing of this stretch of the Atlantic Ocean sixteen crewmen and sixty-one slaves died, mostly from scurvy or dysentery. Judging by the appalling conditions the slaves would have endured, their higher death toll in numbers is not surprising. What is interesting is that, in percentage terms, a higher percentage of the crew perished than the slaves – 21 per cent against 12 per cent in favour of the slaves. Out of the remaining crew, another thirty-six were suffering from scurvy and dysentery. That left twenty-three able-bodied crew members. Considering more than one person would be needed to man each cannon for the rapid fire needed in a direct attack (pumping the powder, loading the ball, lighting the shot, controlling the recoil), they were not enough and there was no chance that *La Concorde* would have been able to resist an attack by a pirate.

Crews were always terrified of not only losing their cargo, but also their ship. The fear of being tossed overboard, abandoned on some desert island or being taken hostage and tortured was always prevalent in their minds, but for slavers it was even worse. The crews of those ships were afraid of the slaves rising up against them and overwhelming them, which is the reason why, in many cases, slave ships had barriers constructed between the waist of the ship and the quarterdeck, turning the ship's stern into a mini fortress should the slaves revolt. Common practice was to have guards posted on the quarterdeck with small-arms when the slaves were brought up from the hold to be washed or exercised. Also common practice was mounting swivel cannon on the quarterdeck, loaded with grapeshot so that their range of fire would be inwards and facing the middle of the ship, should the slaves revolt.[87]

La Concorde, with her reduced crew and much-reduced defensive capability, was heading for the Caribbean island of Martinique. Apart from the early inhabitants being tribes of Arawak and Carib Indians, the island had spent the majority of its inhabited history under the control of France. The plan was to unload and sell the human cargo and perhaps some of the other cargo, reload with sugar and return to France. This triangular-shaped voyage of Europe to

Africa to the Caribbean to Europe was common. Most of the slaves that could be sold would then be put to work on the sugar cane fields of Martinique, Guadeloupe or Saint Dominique.

The date when Blackbeard sighted *La Concorde* was 28 November 1717. This is given to us in the French documents and so uses the calendar applicable to France. If we compare this to the calendar being used in Britain at the time, that same date would be 17 November 1717.[88]

In the account left by Charles Mesnier, the Administrator of Martinique, regarding the capture of *La Concorde*, he tells us that the ship was just 60 miles from its destination, at 14° 27 north latitude when it was intercepted by two sloops:

> Two boats of English pirates, one of 12 and the other of 8 guns armed with 250 men controlled by Edouard Titche, English, was removed by these pirates with 455 negroes who remained with him – the aforementioned Dosset with his crew to the Grenadines onto the island of Becoya [Bequia], near Grenade [Grenada].[89]

By the time Blackbeard captured *La Concorde*, he was in command of a small fleet of vessels which explains the report of the two pirate sloops attacking Dosset's vessel.

Some historians suggest that both sloops came up on either side of the large slaver and opened fire. Lee, in his book *Blackbeard the Pirate*, states that the two sloops 'came with such speed upon the merchantman that her captain was unable to manoeuvre her into battle position'. He claims that before Dosset could do anything both sloops fired broadsides into his ship, killing half his crew and terrifying the remainder into surrender.[90]

However, there could be another reason why Dosset did not put up much of a fight: he had the two swivel guns that were mounted on either side of the ship covering the waist of the ship pointing inwards. They were only 60 miles away from Fort de France, the harbour at Martinique. For slave vessels the landfall was a vulnerable time as it provided opportunities for slaves to escape, so covering this offloading with guns was always a prudent idea. This means that these swivel guns were not part of the main armament for firing broadsides outwards to enemy vessels but were for firing inwards into the waist of their own ship to put down any rebellion.[91]

Whether or not Dosset knew about Blackbeard before his ship was captured is something about which we can only speculate. However, we can safely assume that he knew about pirates operating in the waters he was heading into, and while they would have been a big concern to him, his greatest was a revolt by slaves during the unloading process. He also must have been very anxious about the depleted number of his crew and was likely trying to get to port as quickly as possible.

After this capture and with Dosset's report to Mesnier who then sent a detailed report back to Paris, Blackbeard's reputation had increased by leaps and bounds. With two pirate ships coming in on either side of him firing their guns, it's highly doubtful that any of Dosset's remaining crew would have stood their ground and fought back, even if he'd ordered them to. The cargo didn't belong to Dosset, so losing it would have cost him nothing and with his depleted crew and inability to resist he had no other choice but to surrender.

It wouldn't have taken Blackbeard long to realise that his new prize was a fine catch indeed. It was the perfect ship for his growing status and reputation. It seems he had more interest in the ship than in the cargo, though certainly some of the cargo he may have kept for himself. Items like the gold dust the ship was known to be carrying would have found their way into his possession. As for the human cargo, we can only presume that Blackbeard retained some of the more capable as part of his own crew. He now had a larger ship and so needed a larger crew.[92] The remainder of the slaves would very soon find themselves back in captivity and on the auction block.[93]

In most slave ships the hold was subdivided to stop slaves from mixing together, but they did not suit a pirate ship and it is likely that Blackbeard had the dividers completely removed in order to make a large open hold. This meant that all the crew could see that none of their comrades were receiving any larger shares of captured booty. Even pirates had a code, and while they would happily steal from anyone, they would not steal from each other.

We don't know exactly what Blackbeard did to reconfigure the ship from being a slaver into a fast pirate ship, though in his account of Captain Bartholomew Roberts Johnson describes what Roberts and his crew did to turn a large slave ship, the *Onslow*, owned by the Royal African Company into the *Royal Fortune*:

> They fell to making such alterations as might fit her for a sea rover, pulling down her bulkheads, and making her flush, so that she became, in all respects, as complete a ship for their purpose as any they could have found.

It's highly likely that Blackbeard did the same. This much larger storage area in the open hold meant that Blackbeard and his crew could continue plundering with impunity until the hold was overflowing and they put into a friendly port to sell their ill-gotten gains. However, the conversion from slaver to fast pirate warship was a big job and would take several days.

There were standard things that could be done relatively quickly, such as knocking down most of the internal bulkheads to create large open spaces in the forecastle, behind the quarterdeck and on any lower decks. The idea behind this was to reduce the risk of flying splinters during a fight, as well as preventing the captain or the quartermaster from placing themselves above their crew which was in keeping with the egalitarian way in which pirate crews operated. Nevertheless, Stede Bonnet was different and Blackbeard had him transferred from the *Revenge* over to his new flagship, complete with his morning coat and his library.

Usually, the quarterdeck and poop deck were used for cabin space and as a gun deck but opening these up provided a much larger space for the crew as well as for stores. Bartholomew Roberts tore down the entire superstructure on the upper deck of the *Onslow* so that he had a flush deck from bow to stern without any kind of impediment getting in the way in order to accommodate larger pirate crews than those of the merchantmen. This also needed more space so the pirates could easily board their captured prizes as they came alongside. The unimpeded upper deck also meant that the pirates could cram as much firepower onto the vessel as possible.[94]

In order to squeeze out every ounce of speed from their captured ships, pirates would also redesign the sails so they would have as much of an edge on their prey as possible. Blackbeard increased the amount of cannon on the new ship up to approximately forty guns, though there is some debate about this number. The more accepted amount, supported by officials in colonial offices, puts the figures at either twenty-six or thirty-six.

Most of the people making these claims were making little more than guesses. None of them had of course stepped aboard and made a count of the amount of weapons the refitted ship was carrying. They based their calculations solely on what they saw of the ship from a distance, or on second-hand information from the crews of ships Blackbeard would go on to plunder in his new vessel.

Archaeologists excavating at the wreckage site of what is thought to be the remains of the ship have not found anything like this number. What guns have been discovered vary greatly in weight, size and origin. These include mostly French and British guns with one that appears to be from Sweden. This mix of nationalities would fit well with the concept of a pirate ship, where the crew would use whatever they plundered from other vessels, but at the time of writing the surveys had only revealed less than thirty cannon.[95] For the purposes of this book we will stick to the accepted norm of up to forty cannon.[96]

The main deck of *La Concorde* did not have the space for so much firepower, so Blackbeard had gun-ports cut into the side of the hull below the main deck, giving it greater firepower for blasting other vessels with broadsides. There were no turret cannon in those days so each side of the ship would hold the largest number of cannon; however, by this time most ships were also placing cannon in the bow and stern of their ships so they could have full coverage and keep up a steady rate of fire when either chasing another vessel or trying to get away from one.[97] Most pirates modifying captured ships would have very quickly increased the firepower in order to intimidate their prey as much as possible without having to fight, while also ensuring they had enough firepower if they did have to fight. We can assume Blackbeard did the same.

In order for Blackbeard to modify this new prize he headed for a sheltered anchorage at Bequia

> an island small enough to lack a British or a French garrison, and a long-established watering place for buccaneers, privateers and pirates. There Blackbeard and his men set to work, building a slave-holding pen, landing *La Concorde*'s human cargo and crew, then converting *La Concorde* for their own use.[98]

Now we have Blackbeard busy at converting the slaver into a fast pirate ship but we are left with one problem. What happened to Benjamin Hornigold?

During the capture of *La Concorde*, two sloops approached the larger vessel one on either side of her, moving fast and firing as they gained. If Hornigold was commanding the other sloop then where did he go after the capture of such a large prize? Captain Johnson says this about what happened to Hornigold:

> By Hornigold's consent, Teach went aboard of her as captain and took a cruise in her. Hornigold returned with his sloop to Providence, where, at the arrival of Captain Rogers, the governor, he surrendered to mercy, pursuant to the King's proclamation.

Historian Robert E. Lee states that Teach asked Hornigold if he could claim *La Concorde* as his prize and be placed in command. Hornigold agreed to this request. He then states that both men shook hands and departed. However, Konstam suggests that Blackbeard and Hornigold had already parted company by this time and the other sloop would have been commanded by one of Blackbeard's most trusted men. The other sloop was a prize that he and Hornigold took earlier in the year.

What we do know is that Hornigold returned to the Bahamas where he approached the new governor, Woodes Rogers, and accepted the King's Pardon. Indeed, Hornigold became invaluable to Rogers, who fitted him out as a pirate-hunter to hunt down and bring back for trial as many pirates as he could.

As a pirate, Hornigold was at one point king of the pirates based out of Providence, so any men joining his crew would have had the highest standing in the pirate community. He had the biggest ship with the biggest guns, but the crews would have been disappointed with the haul under Hornigold because he would only plunder certain ships.

He had always refused to acknowledge the treaty that ended the War of Spanish Succession that had taken away his source of income as a privateer operating in that conflict. Some historians believe that he still considered himself a privateer rather than a pirate, similar to the way in which Captain Kidd claimed right up to the end of his life just before his execution that he was a legally-sanctioned privateer and not a pirate.

Hornigold allowed ships belonging to Britain to pass unhindered, while only attacking those ships that sailed under the flag of her enemies. Pirates, on the other hand, attacked any ship that seemed a good prize regardless of nationality. The crew serving Hornigold, considering themselves pirates and being greedy for whatever they could get – much like Captain Kidd's crew – would have become more and more restless about the lack of activity. Hornigold's crew held a council on board the ship and voted to attack any ship of any nationality as they were fed up with their captain's fussiness about which ships he would or would not attack. This action deposed Hornigold as captain, essentially making him a bystander on his own ship which must have infuriated him as he watched his crew turn their guns on British ships.[99] Perhaps it may have been this that persuaded him to accept the King's Pardon and turn pirate-hunter. Did Blackbeard play a part in this mutiny? There is no evidence to suggest he did but if he was turning his guns on all ships including British his already growing reputation could have helped Hornigold's crew make up their minds – a move of which Blackbeard would have approved.

Back on Bequia we know that Blackbeard landed the crew and human cargo of *La Concorde* onto the island and even built a pen for the slaves and crew. Bequia is in the Grenadines and its name comes from the Arawak Indian language meaning 'island of the clouds'. It is the second-largest island in the chain. In Blackbeard's day the island was home to mostly Carib and Arawak Indian tribes, though pirates used the island as a base for repair and replenishment of their ships due to its safe anchorage. From the reports filed by Dosset and his lieutenant we know the crew of *La Concorde* and those slaves rejected by Blackbeard were left on the island with few supplies and limited weapons.

Imagine Dosset, forced to stand with his crew and the slaves in the pen built by the pirates on the beach, watching his ship being torn apart and refitted by the pirates. With each passing day the ship would look less and less like the one he had commanded. The most notable changes would have been the extra firepower, with cannon barrels aimed in all directions. He had crossed the Atlantic with sixteen, and that number had been more than doubled. The other feature of which he would have been painfully aware was that it was now bustling with crew, some of which were formerly his own. Not only had he lost his ship but he had also lost a proportion of his crew to the pirates, including some of the slaves. One can only imagine his frustration and humiliation.

Of the crew we know of that transferred to Blackbeard, four went willingly and a further ten went under some form of duress. However, as this information comes from the report filed by Dosset's Lieutenant Ernaud sometime later, it is likely that there was some bias involved so we must assume that it is open to interpretation. The crew who were apparently forced to transfer included a pilot (or navigator), three surgeons, two carpenters, two sailors and the cook.[100]

One of the crew who voluntarily defected to Blackbeard was the cabin boy, Louis Arot. According to the reports it was he who told the pirates where to find the gold dust that was on board *La Concorde*. Perhaps he wanted a change of scene, or perhaps he did not like the captain and the officers. We shall never know his motivation.

Yet, while the alterations were taking place Blackbeard carried out a strange act for so ruthless a pirate. He gave the smaller of his two sloops to Dosset and the remainder of his crew so they could leave the island.

There was absolutely no requirement, legal or otherwise, for him to hand over any vessel to those he had attacked. He could quite easily have left them stranded on the island to find some way of making their own way off. However, from his efforts to equip the larger vessel with more guns, ammunition and stores, Blackbeard would have had them stripped from the smaller sloop which he then handed over to the prisoners.[101]

So while Blackbeard had given the French a lifeline with the smaller sloop it was completely unarmed, its guns being used to increase the firepower on *La Concorde*, Blackbeard's new flagship. He very likely would have winched up any extra guns from the hold of the *Revenge* after stripping the smaller sloop of all its ordnance.[102]

All Dosset had were his crew and a quantity of slaves and they were on an island some distance from their original destination. Dosset and his crew renamed their new vessel the *Mauvaise Rencontre*, which in French means *Bad Encounter*. Considering their newfound circumstances, the name seemed painfully appropriate. In a couple of trips, they transported the remaining contingent of slaves from Bequia to Martinique to at least fulfil that part of their voyage.[103]

The French were not on Bequia for the same length of time as Blackbeard and his crew. Indeed, they were there for only a few days before sailing away in the unarmed sloop given to them by Blackbeard.

We could look at this action by Blackbeard in two ways: one is that it was very generous of Blackbeard to give Dosset and his crew a ship; the other that it was extremely cruel to give them one that was unarmed and would be at the mercy of any pirate they encountered. Perhaps that's what Blackbeard felt – let them take their chances on the high seas.

Angus Konstam states it would have taken Blackbeard at least two weeks to transfer the slaves and crew to the island and then make the alterations to the ship. Once the alterations were completed and Blackbeard had his floating fortress, he renamed his new flagship with a name that could have harked back to his days as a privateer in the War of Spanish Succession.

However, this new name could also have been because Blackbeard was, in his own way, doffing his hat to Queen Anne herself and to the era of piracy that she had reigned over as monarch. When she died she left no heirs and her successor was her second cousin George, who became George I and started the rule by the House of Hanover. Perhaps this was Blackbeard's way of showing some loyalty to the House of Stuart and Queen Anne for whom he had fought, and naming his ship after her was him displaying his disapproval of the new monarch. It could have been Blackbeard simply recognising that an era was coming to a close and this was his way of paying homage to it.

Whatever the reason for naming his ship as he did, the vessel that sailed into the anchorage on the island of Bequia as *La Concorde* sailed out, fully refitted as a pirate fortress, ready to take on any victim or naval vessel, as the *Queen Anne's Revenge*.

Chapter 7

Blackbeard's Victims

*Nor had we much time left to us for thought. Suddenly, with
a loud huzza, a little cloud of pirates leaped from the woods
on the north side and ran straight on the stockade.
At the same moment, the fire was once more opened from the
doorway, and knocked the doctor's musket into bits.*

Treasure Island, Robert Louis Stevenson

Before we continue let's look at Blackbeard's actions so far. He took the *Revenge* from Major Stede Bonnet who he let walk freely about the ship in his morning coat as well as letting the major spend vast amounts of time in his library below decks. Bonnet had bought the ship outright and had his library brought aboard so it was there when Blackbeard took the ship from him. We know, too, that when Blackbeard transferred his command from the *Revenge* to the *Queen Anne's Revenge* he had transferred Bonnet as well. If what Lee says is true that they got along well together, then perhaps Blackbeard wanted Bonnet as a friend because he missed Hornigold? However, we also know that Bonnet was unhappy about the arrangement and certainly wouldn't have been glad to transfer to the *Queen Anne's Revenge*. So what's going on here?

Then we have Blackbeard who, after capturing *La Concorde* and sending the crew and slaves ashore and starting his alterations on the ship, gave them one of the sloops under his command but which was stripped of guns. He gave Dosset the means to get off the island on which they were stranded, but in an unarmed ship in an area infested with pirates.

What does this tell us about Blackbeard?

If he was building his reputation as the most feared and ruthless pirate on the high seas, then these actions reinforce that. They show Blackbeard in complete control over Bonnet and in control over Dosset, his crew and the slaves. By giving them the ship he was being generous but by giving them one that was unarmed he was playing God – leaving them to their fate if they faced pirates on the way back to Martinique. Blackbeard was no fool; he knew that Dosset and his lieutenant would report the events to the authorities when they arrived. The rest of Dosset's crew would tell the tales in the dosshouses, taverns and bars in Martinique and the story would spread.

We can see the story of Blackbeard building through the reports filed by his victims.

On 29 September 1717 Blackbeard attacked the *Betty*, a sloop registered in Virginia. Being a Virginia-based vessel this capture would likely have come to the attention of the Lieutenant-Governor of Virginia, Alexander Spotswood, who later instigated the search for and final destruction of Blackbeard.

Blackbeard's crew took the cargo of Madeira wine from the *Betty*. Madeira was known for its quality but it is unlikely that they cared much about the quality preferring quantity, and if we compare other pirate crews to this one then the wine didn't last long. Once they had taken what they wanted they sank the vessel with her hold still bearing a quantity of cargo that the pirates didn't require or couldn't carry. Indeed, in the charges that Spotswood brought against Blackbeard's quartermaster, William Howard, they explicitly state that it was William Howard who sank and destroyed the *Betty* and the cargo remaining aboard. The fate of the crew of the *Betty* is uncertain.[104]

We know from the report filed in Philadelphia from which the reporter for the *Boston News Letter* published his stories of the activities of Blackbeard that the pirate was operating in the Delaware Bay area. The entire area was covered in salt marshes and mudflats fed by numerous rivers. Two capes form the entrance to the Bay – Cape May and Cape Henlopen – where it joins the Atlantic Ocean and it is around these capes and the bay itself that Blackbeard was to go on to claim several of his early victims.

In previous chapters we've seen that Blackbeard took Captain Codd's vessel and it was Codd who filed his report on 24 October 1717 that formed the basis of the reports on the pirate's activities published in the November edition of the *Boston News Letter*. What is interesting about the Codd affair is that there is no mention of cargo being taken from his ship. Codd was carrying 150 indentured servants and presumably other cargo as well. Why would Blackbeard go to all the trouble of chasing the sloop, stopping her, boarding her and then come away with nothing? We believe, like some historians, that the reason why Blackbeard didn't take any cargo and let the ship go was because once the pirates discovered the passengers were largely servants they felt a common bond with these underdogs; knowing the servants had little wealth, they identified with them and so allowed the ship under Captain Codd's command to continue to sail into Philadelphia.[105] However, people do carry their own personal possessions so we can only wonder as to whether the pirates relieved the passengers of some of these.[106]

During this period, September/October 1717 we know from the report that Blackbeard took the *Spofford* which was headed for Ireland with a load of staves, the *Sea Nymph* which was filled with wheat and heading for Oporto, a sloop from Madeira commanded by Peter Peters, another sloop commanded by Griggs, another sloop from Madeira and another from Antigua. Most of the vessels they let go after plundering them of cargo and guns and stores but the *Sea Nymph* they kept, effectively doubling the number of vessels within Blackbeard's fighting force.[107]

There is no indication of what cargo was on the sloop commanded by Captain Peters but on the basis that it had sailed from Madeira and the chief export of that island at the time was wine, it is fairly safe to assume this would comprise part of the cargo.

Another of Blackbeard's victims was Captain Farmer whose sloop had already been looted by pirates before Blackbeard got to him. Sailing from Jamaica, Captain Farmer had very little left to be plundered by the time he reached Delaware Bay, so Blackbeard stripped the vessel of its mast, anchors, cables and any extra money that the preceding plundering had left behind. With no cargo and missing all these items, Farmer was then permitted to complete his journey in what was basically little more than a stripped floating shell.[108]

At much the same time another captain was sailing his sloop through the region. This was Captain Sipkins (in a New York-registered sloop) in command of a 12-gun vessel that was taken by the pirates, though he doesn't name Blackbeard or Teach specifically. We can make the educated guess that it was Blackbeard who took the vessel as it happened in his hunting ground of Delaware Bay and we know that the pirate was adding to his little fleet. Being more useful for their needs they set about converting it to a pirate ship. What isn't clear is what happened to the crew of this sloop or where Blackbeard got the crew to man his new prize, presumably from the former crew? Farmer managed to reach dry land and reported the incident.[109]

By this reckoning, Blackbeard now controlled three vessels – the *Revenge*, the *Sea Nymph* and this latest acquisition.

On 30 October 1717, Captain Goelet sailing from Curaçao to New York became the next known victim of Blackbeard: 'This sloop was half loaded with cocoa which the Pirates threw overboard.'[110] However, the pirates realised the new sloop could be useful and decided to keep it, giving Captain Goelet and his crew the much slower *Sea Nymph*. They made a swift escape while the pirates were still in a generous mood. After Goelet was released, another ship and a brigantine were taken but there is no indication of what happened to the vessels or their crews.[111]

The next report from the *Boston News Letter* tells us that Blackbeard was moving south towards warmer climes. On 18 October 1717 he captured a sloop on the border between North Carolina and Virginia at latitude 36 under the command of Captain Pritchard. Pritchard had left St Lucia and was sailing northwards: 'Pritchard from St Lucia, who on 18th October in Lat 36 and 45 was taken by Captain Teach, in Company with Captain Hornigold.'

As we have seen in earlier chapters there are discrepancies around the issue of Hornigold sailing with Blackbeard in October 1717. However, the report in the November edition of the *Boston News Letter* suggests that Hornigold was still sailing in company with Blackbeard. Nevertheless, as we have seen, by this time Hornigold may have been in command in name only of his own vessel due to his penchant for not attacking British ships. What we do know is that by the middle of October 1717 Blackbeard was no longer the protégé of Hornigold but an experienced pirate captain commanding a small fleet in his own right. Remember, this is prior to the encounter with *La Concorde*. The pirates took from Pritchard's vessel about eight casks of sugar and most of the clothes.

According to the report two more vessels were taken by the pirates; the sloop *Robert* and a ship called the *Good Intent*, both on 22 October 1717.[112] The article ends by saying that a ship from London sailing for Virginia had been 'taken off the Capes of Virginia by Teach and Hornigold'. After being plundered the ship limped into a Maryland port where the report about their experiences was filed, but this ship got off lightly as all the pirates took was a suit of sails and rigging that had been brought across the ocean for a ship being built for Colonel Lloyd in Maryland.[113]

For most of these accounts we have been turning to the *Boston News Letter* for information. This is largely because the information in Johnson's account is so sketchy. We will turn to the same publication again for the account of the taking of the *Great Allen*. The report of this action was filed on 24 February 1718 and claims that the ship was taken in November 1717. It appeared in the March edition of the *Boston News Letter*. This ship, under the command of Captain Christopher Taylor, was cruising near St Lucia and St Vincent in Caribbean waters. Both islands are part of the Lesser Antilles and also part of the British Windward Islands. The *Great Allen* was registered in Boston and was on its way to Jamaica, having come out of Barbados.

What we know is that Blackbeard had two sloops and with those he took *La Concorde* to which he transferred his command and converted her to a pirate ship and launched her as the *Queen Anne's Revenge*. We also know that he gave the French crew he had stranded on the island one of his own sloops, which was unarmed because he'd taken the guns from it and put them onto the flagship. That left Blackbeard with the *Queen Anne's Revenge* and the *Revenge* – a large flagship and a sloop.

The account of Taylor's capture by Blackbeard in the *Boston News Letter* stated that 'a great ship from Boston was taken at or near St Lucia or St Vincent by Captain Teach the Pirate in a French Ship of 32 Guns, a Brigantine of 10 guns and Sloop of 12 guns.' So Taylor mentions Teach by name and he also mentions a brigantine. Being a ship's captain himself he is hardly likely to mistake a sloop for a brigantine. This means we have to assume that Blackbeard took this brigantine before capturing the *Great Allen* and after he had captured and refitted *La Concorde* and relaunched her as the *Queen Anne's Revenge*.[114] Captain Taylor reported sighting a large French vessel armed with thirty-two guns. The assumption is that Blackbeard's new flagship had around forty guns but as most sources have discrepancies in dates, numbers of ships and numbers of guns it is hard to pinpoint an exact total so, again, we make some assumptions and one of those is that this 32-gun ship was the *Queen Anne's Revenge*.

Ordering his men to put on more sail, Blackbeard brought the *Queen Anne's Revenge* closer to the *Great Allen* and soon he was alongside her. Shouting and yelling, waving their cutlasses and pistols, Blackbeard's crew poured onto the deck of the captured ship, rampaging through their new prize stealing anything they could get their hands on. From a deposition filed by Governor Hamilton of the Leeward Islands in January 1718 we know that the ship was carrying a great deal of plate 'and one fine cup they told the despondent they had taken out of Captain Taylor', but there is no record of anything else it was carrying. Blackbeard and especially his crew were convinced that the ship was carrying more and that it had been hidden.

However, Captain Taylor was adamant that there was no currency on board. Frustrated, Blackbeard ordered him to be bound in irons for a full twenty-four hours. During this time, Blackbeard's crew subjected him to a whipping to extract the information from him about any hidden money.[115]

Having taken everything they could from the ship, the pirates stranded the crew on the nearby island of St Vincent. However, once the crew were on the island, instead of handing them another ship to help them get back to civilisation Blackbeard took a different action. Standing on the beach, stranded, the crew and officers of the *Great Allen* watched in desperation as the pirates set fire to their ship, ending any chance they had of getting off the island quickly. As the flames spread, their hearts sank as the ship slowly burnt to nothing.[116]

Why didn't Blackbeard just let them go as he had done with the crew of *La Concorde*? Some months before, captured pirates had been executed in Boston and this ship was from Boston so it just could have been an act of revenge or retribution on Blackbeard's part. He also would have known that as soon as Taylor got to civilisation he would file a report with the local authorities which would eventually appear in something like the *Boston News Letter*. By being lenient with one crew and harsh with another it showed Blackbeard to be unpredictable and violent.

On 29 November Captain Benjamin Hobhouse, commanding officer of the *Montserrat Merchant*, came face to face with the pirates:

> Seeing two ships and a sloop, and thinking one did belong to Bristol, and the other two to Guinea, he went in the long-boat to enquire for letters. They desired us to come on board, but seeing Death Head in the stern we refused it. They compelled us to go on board and asked about the guns and ships at Kingslale and Plymouth. They report the Captain of the pirates name is Kentish and Captain Edwards belonging to the sloop, and they report the ship has 150 men on board and 22 guns mounted, the sloop about 50 white men, and eight guns, and that they burnt part of Guadalupe, when they cut out the French ship.[117]

In the past, Bonnet had used the alias of Captain Edwards and it is likely that he was still aboard the *Queen Anne's Revenge* at the time but we don't know who Captain Kentish is, or do we?[118] Konstam suggests that Kentish was another alias that Blackbeard used, providing us with a clear indication that Blackbeard was not above using several aliases himself. This account was made through Governor Hamilton by Thomas Knight, one of the crew of the *Montserrat Merchant*.

The next morning Captain Richard Joy commanding the *New Division* ran into the pirates. He was lucky. The pirates didn't plunder his ship or attack the crew. They just wanted information on shipping in the area. Perhaps his vessel was so meagre and the cargo of no importance to the pirates that he was spared. We'll never know nor will we ever know what he told them but we do know that, while his ship may not have been plundered, his crew was shrunk by one. Whether that person went voluntarily or by force is also not clear.[119]

The next entry comes from Henry Bostock, the captain of the sloop *Margaret*. According to his deposition published in a letter from Governor Hamilton to the Council of Trade and Plantations, Bostock encountered Blackbeard on 5 December off Crab Island where he met a large ship and a sloop:

> He was ordered on board and Capt. Tach took his cargo of cattle and hogs, his arms books and instruments. The ship, Dutch built, was a French Guinea man, 36 guns mounted and 300 men. They did not abuse him or his men, but forced 2 to stay and one Robert Bibby voluntarily took on with them. They had a great deal of plate on board, and one very fine cup they told the deponent they had taken out of Capt. Taylor, bound from Barbados to Jamaica, whom they very much abused and burnt his ship. They said they had burnt several vessels, among them two or three belonging to these Islands, particularly the day before a sloop belonging to Antego, one (Robert) McGill owner.[120]

In the same letter Governor Hamilton recounted more of Blackbeard's activities. We learn that the pirate continued to plunder vessels through the early part of

December 1717; in one instance capturing a ship loaded with white sugar which he sunk. Hamilton then goes on to give different accounts of the description of the number of guns on the larger vessel from twenty-two up to as many as forty. This letter is one of the first to mention that Blackbeard was married: 'He is believed to have a wife and children in London.'[121]

Some people joined Blackbeard voluntarily, others were forced to join. Captain Bostock's account states that Robert Bibby had jumped ship and joined Blackbeard voluntarily but two other crew members were pressed into the pirate's service. Though Bostock didn't identify them we can assume that they had skills needed by Blackbeard.

Now we come to an event which can only be described as fiction. According to Johnson's account of Blackbeard he stated that the *Queen Anne's Revenge* encountered the Royal Navy warship HMS *Scarborough* 'who engaged him for some hours; but she finding the pirate well manned and having tried her strength gave over the engagement and returned to Barbados, the place of her station, and Teach sailed towards Spanish America.'

If this story was true it would certainly have gone a long way to increasing Blackbeard's notoriety – a pirate ship coming away from an encounter with a Royal Navy warship unscathed? The story would spread like wildfire throughout the ports. There is no official documentation to support this story, so was it true or a complete fabrication?

On the one hand the Royal Navy, having engaged the *Queen Anne's Revenge* and failed to stop the pirate captain known by then to be on board, may not want anyone to know of the failure. If the perceived might of the Royal Navy was insufficient to stop him, what chance did anyone else have? This would, by association, increase his reputation and the fear surrounding him. Conversely, the Royal Navy, having by then heard of the exploits of Blackbeard, would have needed to be seen to be doing something to stop him before he became too powerful and too dangerous.

HMS *Scarborough* was certainly capable of standing up to the *Queen Anne's Revenge*. It could certainly face Blackbeard's vessel on a cannon-for-cannon basis. Also, since pirates on the whole rely on fear in their victims and so have very little opportunity to fight, they would not be as skilled and battle-hardened as the crew of the warship. It is far more probable, if this story were true, that the warship would have had more accurate fire and have been able to keep up a higher rate of fire than the pirate ship. There are many other documented cases where Royal Navy ships have encountered pirate ships and virtually blasted them out of the water. For proof we can look at the rather one-sided fight Bartholomew Roberts found himself in against HMS *Swallow*. He lost the fight and his life.

Johnson claims that the ships engaged each other for several hours. This could mean that it was a running fight with both ships firing off shots from their bow guns or stern guns and never getting into a position to fire full broadsides. However, if it was a full-scale battle and the ships engaged each other for hours, then both would suffer significant damage to their hulls and masts. Yet, no-one giving subsequent reports of seeing the *Queen Anne's Revenge* makes any claim that they saw damage to either the structure or any of the masts. In addition, there was no damage reported on HMS *Scarborough* from any of the ports she subsequently entered, nor was there any mention of it requisitioning replenishments of cannonballs and gunpowder. Interestingly, the logbook from HMS *Scarborough* is still held on file, along with Captain Hume's personal letters and reports and nowhere within them is there a mention of such a battle.[122]

Surely this would be an urgent requirement for a warship that had just emerged from a prolonged battle? While it may have been useful for the Royal Navy to be doing something to stop Blackbeard, it is inconceivable that these vessels, locked in combat for several hours, would both emerge without a single scratch.[123]

Historian Robert E. Lee has a different version of events. He states that Blackbeard waited for the *Scarborough* to get closer to his ship and then when she was in range opened fire with a broadside 'that tore great holes in her sails'. He suggests that the *Scarborough* broke off the engagement and limped back to Barbados. This version goes against Johnson's who doesn't mention the damage done to the *Scarborough*. It also goes against what Angus Konstam says in his book, that 'the closest HMS *Scarborough* and the *Queen Anne's Revenge* ever got to trading blows with each other was when the pirate ship sailed past Nevis on her way north.'[124]

It is likely then that Lee is using sources that propagate the myth of this encounter, for if there is no record of the event taking place in the ships' logs and there is no reference to the encounter in Governor Hamilton's letter, perhaps we can assume that the encounter between these two vessels either didn't take place or was built upon another encounter between two lesser vessels and either used by Governor Hamilton to deliberately show how bad the piracy problem was, or the event was simply confused.

Even if it did happen, the account mentions only the *Queen Anne's Revenge* and HMS *Scarborough*. Where were the sloops that were escorting Blackbeard's flagship? We know from earlier and later reports of sightings that at least one sloop was a constant companion of the *Queen Anne's Revenge*, which was most likely the *Revenge*. Yet, had it conveniently vanished just before the 'battle' and would then reappear as escort to its totally undamaged flagship immediately after the last cannon blast had been fired?

If this event took place then it really would have cemented Blackbeard's reputation as the most feared pirate on the high seas, but suppose it was a fabrication, not by Johnson but by Blackbeard and his crew? Thomas Knight's deposition as reported by Governor Hamilton said that they had spotted a man-of-war when they made Nevis: 'Spying some vessels in Nevis, and among the rest took one for the man of war, they said they would cut her out, but the Captain being ill prevented it.'

Thomas Knight was taken prisoner by Blackbeard when they encountered the *Montserrat Merchant*. Once he was free from the pirates Knight reported to Hamilton and gave his deposition. Henry Bostock in his deposition to Governor Hamilton said 'They owned they had met the man of war on this station, but said they had no business with her, but if she had chased them they would have kept their way.'

So Lee thinks the encounter is true, Johnson thinks it's true and many historians base their facts on Johnson's account. However, as we have the depositions from people who were there that they didn't engage with the *Scarborough*, where does the tale come from? If, when Blackbeard and his crew entered port they bragged about engaging a warship and winning the battle against it then we have the makings of a great story, a great myth that Johnson could have picked up on when he was putting his history of Blackbeard together, especially if he was using Israel Hands as one of his primary sources. Even if Blackbeard and his crew didn't boast about it but the story was around as rumour, then Blackbeard could have picked up on it to enhance his reputation.

Of course we have no evidence either way, but this is certainly food for thought.

Both Johnson and Captain Bostock state that the *Queen Anne's Revenge* sailed towards the coast of Spanish America for cleaning. The implication for cleaning a vessel is to do minor repairs to beams and scrape off the hull to ensure the ship remains as fast as possible; it did not imply that the vessel was limping into port to make massive repairs to its overall structure. In order for Blackbeard to clean the vessel, he put into Samana Bay on the island of Hispaniola to keep away from prying eyes while his ship and men were vulnerable.[125]

For the next few months there were no sightings of the pirate. Some pirates were nicknamed 'snowbirds' because they plagued the northern ports such as Boston and New York during the summer and drifted southwards to the warmer Caribbean when winter arrived. We hear very little from Blackbeard until March 1718 except for a sighting that took place in February in the vicinity of the Leeward Islands.

This sighting comes from a report filed by Captain Hume of HMS *Scarborough*. He states that he had information of a pirate ship of thirty-six guns and 250 men in company with a sloop of ten guns and 100 men operating in the Leeward Islands' vicinity. He sailed on 18 February for Antigua to join with HMS *Seaford* and it was while they were at Antigua that they had information that the pirate ship had moved to the Leeward Islands: 'The 23 December we proceeded for Nevis, and St. Christopher's, from which islands I had an Officer and 20 Soldiers put on board me for the Cruize.'[126]

While this account does not accurately identify the vessel as being the *Queen Anne's Revenge*, we can be fairly sure that there weren't too many pirate vessels of that size operating in those waters and even fewer that were in consort with a 10-gun sloop. Governor Hamilton ordered HMS *Seaford* supported by HMS *Scarborough* to hunt for the pirate ship. They were unsuccessful.

On 28 March 1718 another victim fell into Blackbeard's clutches and this was the *Protestant Caesar*, on the final few days of its long voyage from Boston. It was within a couple of days of Honduras.

Captain William Wyer commanding the *Protestant Caesar* stood on the deck of his ship, watching a small sloop heading directly for him. As his own ship rolled up and down with the motion of the sea he estimated that the sloop had about ten guns and possibly fifty or so men. Were they pirates? Just in case, he ordered more sail, but his ship couldn't go any faster and Wyer watched the much smaller vessel getting closer and closer. Much of the action that followed was later reported in the *Boston News Letter*.

As the sloop came closer he saw the black flag. So they were pirates after all. At this time most pirates relied on creating fear rather than actually fighting in order to induce their victims into surrender, but Wyer was not a man to be easily swayed and his ship outgunned the little sloop. Wyer ordered the cannons to be loaded and made ready to engage the approaching vessel.

It was around nine o'clock that evening when the sloop moved in under the stern of the *Protestant Caesar* 'and fired Several Cannon in upon the said Ship and a Volley of small Shot, unto which he returned two of his Stern Chase Guns, and a like Volley of small Shot'.

A verbal warning, in English, came from the sloop. If the *Protestant Caesar* dared fire another shot, the pirates would not even consider the option of their surrender once the ship had been boarded. This sloop is most likely the *Revenge*, which was now under the command of a man with the rather obscure name of Captain Richard Richards. Nothing much is known about Richards at all, so it is likely that this was an alias.

The warning fell on deaf ears: 'Captain Wyer continued Fighting them till twelve a clock at Night when she left the Ship, and so he continued his Course to the Bay of Honduras.' Clearly, both vessels were close enough for shouts from one to be heard by those aboard the other, so how no damage ensued from this engagement is not known, but if there was any damage it wasn't reported in the *Boston News Letter*.

Some might say that this was a brave act on the part of Wyer and his crew, but if we take the report seriously then the sloop was completely outgunned and would very likely have been completely destroyed had the fight continued. The reason we say this is because of a line in the report and a line that Johnson uses later, 'which said Sloop came under Captain Wyer's Stern'. This implies that the sloop was small compared with the *Protestant Caesar*. The sloop had ten guns, the *Protestant Caesar* had twenty-six, and her crew was trained to use them so the sloop had no chance.

However, if Wyer had known he was being attacked by one of Blackbeard's fleet he might have thought twice about resisting, but as we have seen the battle raged for three hours, then the sloop withdrew and sailed away. The most likely reason for this withdrawal is that it had exhausted its ammunition supply or Richards simply realised they were outgunned and outclassed so withdrew to call in the big guns – the *Queen Anne's Revenge*.

The withdrawal of the *Revenge* from the battle showed that a pirate could be beaten, even one operating together with the most notorious and feared pirate on the high seas. The *Protestant Caesar* had scored a victory that few could match and had resumed its journey to the Bay of Honduras. Having been attacked on 28 March 1718, Captain Wyer made good time and arrived at his destination on 1 April 1718. He planned on remaining in port for around a week, loading logwood into the hold. Wyer must have felt on top of the world.

However, that would soon change.

Chapter 8

The *Adventure* Continues

Meanwhile, beyond the horizon but still in the vicinity, a sloop was making its way around the Turneffe Islands. This little cluster, just off the coast of what is now Belize, is made up of around 200 tiny islands surrounded by coral reefs.

The Turneffe Islands lay in the Bay of Honduras, home to part of the second-largest coral reef in the world. The sloop that was heading into these waters had managed the crossing all the way from Jamaica. It had traversed some of the most pirate-ridden waters in the world and was within just a few miles of its destination when disaster struck. The captain, one David Herriot, was sailing his 80-ton sloop, the *Adventure*, along the coastal waters, searching for a way into the cluster of logwood areas known to be thereabouts.

The *Revenge* appeared from around the islands and headed straight for the *Adventure*:

> At Turniff [*sic*], ten leagues short of the Bay of Honduras, the pirates took in fresh water. While they were at anchor there they saw a sloop coming in, whereupon Richards in the sloop *Revenge*, slipped his cable, and ran out to meet her, who upon seeing the black flag hoisted, struck sail and came to under the stern of Teach the commodore. She was called the *Adventure*, from Jamaica, with David Herriot master.[127]

Blackbeard took a liking to this 80-ton sloop. There was something special about it that fitted his requirements and he claimed the vessel as his own. Captain Herriot and his crew became prisoners and Herriot was forced into joining Blackbeard, a claim borne out by subsequent sighting and events, and by claims that Herriot would subsequently make.

Quite how this enforced recruitment was achieved has never really been established. Perhaps Herriot saw this as the only opportunity he would ever have of some day reclaiming his vessel, and when he later found himself accused of being a pirate by association, the enforced nature of his conspiracy was his only defence.

To all intents and purposes, Herriot was now like Bonnet, a prisoner on his own ship, under the command of Israel Hands, the former ship's master of the

Queen Anne's Revenge and second-in-command, who had been sent over to take command of the *Adventure* by Blackbeard. This gave Blackbeard a flotilla including his flagship and a couple of sloops under his command, along with roughly 300 pirates.

What happened to the crew of the *Adventure* isn't known but it is likely that Blackbeard continued in his tradition of selecting the best men from among them who had specific skills he needed to man the new ship alongside his own comrades, thus ensuring that the conquered crew remained loyal and obedient.

Remember how Richards had failed to capture the *Protestant Caesar*? While there are no records of what actually took place between Blackbeard and Richards when the latter reported his failure in taking the vessel, his action to slip his cable and go out to take the *Adventure* was probably his way of making amends for it. We'll never know. Based on Blackbeard's reputation and his treatment of people who defied him or failed him it is unlikely that Blackbeard took Richards' failure with grace and a polite wish that Richards experience better luck next time. More than likely the pirate threatened Richards with his life; he may even have hit him or pointed a pistol at him giving him one more chance before he killed him. We can never know. At some point, Richards might have wondered whether he was going to walk out of Blackbeard's cabin with all his limbs, and his head, still attached to the rest of his body.

The *Boston News Letter* provides an example of Blackbeard's reaction to Richards' failure to take the *Protestant Caesar*, through the deposition of the master of the *Land of Promise*, Thomas Newton. Newton's ship had been taken by Blackbeard and he stated in his report that the tall, intimidating and powerful English pirate with his black flowing beard had decided on a course of action. There was no way he was going to allow anyone to reach any port with news that he could be beaten. He had a reputation to uphold. He had worked tirelessly to build it up; and he was not going to let some worthless ship's captain destroy it by claiming that they had beaten a ship under his command. Other captains may start to believe the same and the fear factor he relied upon so heavily would diminish even more rapidly than it had grown. That ship, he decided, had to be destroyed and he would divert all his resources to this very important task: 'Captain Teach told Captain Newton after he had taken him, that he was bound to the Bay of Honduras to Burn the Ship *Protestant Caesar*.'[128]

The *Queen Anne's Revenge* set sail, escorted by its flotilla of sloops. The mission was simple, to destroy the *Protestant Caesar*. If plunder could be added into that, all well and good, but it was a low priority. The *Protestant Caesar* had defied him. The *Protestant Caesar* was doomed.

Captain Newton reported seeing only two ships, the *Queen Anne's Revenge* commanded by Blackbeard and alongside it a sloop, tiny by comparison, of ten guns and most likely the *Revenge*. Where then was the *Adventure*? It was either tucked away on the far side of the *Queen Anne's Revenge* or hidden from Captain Newton's sight at that time or it was elsewhere. We know already that Blackbeard told Captain Newton of his intentions, so this must mean that he must have gone aboard the *Queen Anne's Revenge*. Based on Blackbeard's behaviour so far it is likely that Newton was summoned to appear before the pirate captain.

Back in the Bay of Honduras Captain Wyer in command of the *Protestant Caesar* was overseeing the loading of logwood into the hold. The ship had so far taken onboard about 50 tons of logwood with the remainder still to be loaded. Suddenly, there was a shout. On the horizon a sail was spotted, then a few minutes later another, then another and then another. The first sail was from a large ex-slaver bristling with guns and around this formidable ship were four small sloops. Wyer stared at the horizon. As the ships came closer he thought one of the sloops looked familiar.

Earlier we established that there were three ships in Blackbeard's flotilla, his own flagship and two sloops; now we have five ships. He had the *Revenge*, the *Adventure* and the *Land of Promise* with him. Where did the others come from? We believe that Blackbeard had attacked some more shipping but it is not clear what he kept and what he sent away. Perhaps there was a discrepancy in the stories from the two captains – Wyer and Newton – or perhaps there was a discrepancy in the reporting? More than likely the other ship joined Blackbeard at some point between the pirate taking the *Land of Promise* and this meeting with the *Protestant Caesar*.

Wyer's heart must have sunk when he saw the black flags boasting the death-heads. He knew they were pirates. He had battled pirates before and won; perhaps he could do it again? Calling his officers and crew together on the deck of the *Protestant Caesar* he asked them if they would stand by him and defend the ship: 'They answered if they were Spaniards they would stand by him as long as they had Life, but if they were Pirates they would not Fight.'[129]

So what was the problem with fighting? They'd resisted before and won. However, that had been a small sloop that they outgunned, and this was entirely different. The largest ship alone outgunned the *Protestant Caesar*, but with four other sloops also firing at them and then the musket shot from hundreds of pirates they wouldn't stand a chance.

However, if they were Spanish then they had a possibility of survival if they were taken prisoner. The reputation of many pirates was that resistance by those captured meant almost certain death in battle, or torture then death later.

Captain Wyer decided a parlay was in order so he ordered his second mate to row across in the pinnace and find out who they were. Wyer already knew the ships belonged to pirates, so as he watched the pinnace row across to the flagship he must have been playing for time.

He didn't get the parlay and didn't have to wait long to find out which pirate he was facing. It could only be one man. The second mate discovered the identity of the larger ship and of one of the sloops and hurried back to his captain. Of course the large ship was the *Queen Anne's Revenge* and one of the sloops was indeed the one that had attacked them several days before. The first stage of the battle had been to Wyer, but the second stage was going to be very different indeed.

When the second mate returned and told Wyer and his crew who he was facing, Wyer's crew panicked. They must have been convinced they would be tortured and murdered so with this news they jumped ship and fled to the shore to hide. Wyer had no alternative. His crew wouldn't fight and he couldn't resist as one man, so he was compelled to join his crew in hiding in the jungle that covered most of the area. From their hiding places among the trees they would have watched in safety as the pirates poured over their ship taking whatever they wanted.

This rampage took three days as the report in the *Boston News Letter* tells us: 'And on the 11th of April three days after Captain Wyer's ship *Protestant Caesar* was taken, Captain Teach the Pirate sent word on shore to Captain Wyer, that if he came on Board he would do him no hurt.'

Wyer accepted the invitation likely because he knew he had no choice. He was on a fairly desolate island with his ship, his only means of returning to civilisation, in the hands of pirates who, if they wanted to, could start swarming the area in search of himself and his crew.

He met with the pirate captain, who informed him that he was pleased that Captain Wyer had vacated the *Protestant Caesar* before his arrival. Even Blackbeard himself would not have been able to hold his own men back and deny them their desire for revenge if Captain Wyer and any of his crew had remained on board. Judging by Blackbeard's reputation and actions, it seems doubtful that he would even try to restrain them.

The fact that Captain Wyer even survived this meeting also gives us a little more insight into Blackbeard's character. Again we see him as a man in complete control. The lives of Wyer and his crew are in Blackbeard's hands. Imagine the scene: Blackbeard calmly telling Wyer that if he or his crew tried to resist he wouldn't be able to stop his men from killing them all. Very likely Blackbeard could have snapped his fingers and Wyer would have had his throat slit by one of the crew or by Blackbeard himself. His reputation as a ruthless man had been carefully built up over the years. Yet here he was, allowing someone who had stood up to his crew and humiliated him to leave with his life and all his body parts intact. Perhaps, under the surface, the pirate harboured a certain degree of admiration for his fellow captain?

Much to the surprise of his crew Captain Wyer returned to dry land unharmed. The following day on 12 April 1718, Wyer and his crew witnessed the final chapter in the life of the *Protestant Caesar*. We can only speculate on how Wyer must have felt – completely powerless as the pirates scrambled over his ship setting a series of fires. Within minutes the flames were licking the deck and reaching up into the air and the ship was soon engulfed, the wooden hull and the wood in the hold fuelling the inferno. By the time the flames exhausted themselves, there was nothing left of the ship to see above the water line.

Earlier Blackbeard had taken the *Land of Promise* and held its captain, Thomas Newton and the crew under guard, putting his own people in command. Now Blackbeard must have decided to cut the *Land of Promise* loose and let Newton go because the March edition of the *Boston News Letter* tells us that Wyer arrived in Boston on board the *Land of Promise* under the command of Thomas Newton. So Newton must have rescued Wyer from the island after being freed by Blackbeard. Was this another calculated action by the pirate to ensure his activities were known to as many people as possible to keep building his reputation?

We know Blackbeard was an educated man, so it is unlikely he wouldn't know that Wyer and Newton would report what had happened to the authorities. It is very probable that this is exactly what Blackbeard wanted. The burning of the *Great Allen* and the *Protestant Caesar* would send ripples of fear throughout the region to the authorities who had recently executed pirates, but what of his compassionate treatment of the crews of these ships? Perhaps he was thinking ahead that if he was ever caught he could point to these events as part of a defence? Or, as we have stated before, was this part of the Blackbeard control over the lives of his victims?

With his work in the Caribbean completed, ships taken and plundered, his crew and flotilla established, it was time for Blackbeard to head north. The weather along the North American Atlantic coast was improving and for the next few months, those waters would be his next hunting ground until he headed south again into the Caribbean for the winter, but he was destined to never sail into those waters again.

Chapter 9

Charles Town

The unspeakable calamity this poor Province suffers
from pyrates obliges me to inform your Lordships of it in order
that his Majestie may know it and be induced to afford us the
assistance of a frigate or two to cruse hereabouts upon them for we are
continually alarmed and our ships taken to the utter ruin of our trade ...[130]

Robert Johnson
Governor, South Carolina, June 1718

L
ike many settlements in North America, Charles Town (Charleston) was, in the early eighteenth century, a vibrant, small bustling settlement of around 5,000 inhabitants. Its large accommodating harbour located behind the marshy Cummins Point ran for 3 miles inland to the point on the headland where the Ashley River and the Cooper River joined.

The European influence in the area came in 1663. After the English Civil War had ended with the reign of Oliver Cromwell and the subsequent restoration of the monarchy after his death, King Charles II granted several of his friends and supporters portions of land in the territories that would become South Carolina. However, it was several years before the first settlement, Charles Town (named after the King), would start to appear, some miles from the location of the present city.[131]

The concerns about attack were always foremost in the minds of the early population. There was the possibility of attack from the French, the Spanish, the various tribes of Native Americans and, of course, pirates.

The town was situated on the peninsula between the two rivers. Because of its close proximity to Spanish-held Florida, defences were hugely important so a wall was built on the Cooper River banks running north to south, with another wall on the landward side of the peninsula that connected to the walls along the Cooper River. Along the walls were a series of triangular bastions designed to lay down defensive crossfire on any attacking army at any point along the defensive walls. Although it would suffer a series of attacks and blockades during its history, few were as infamous as the one that occurred in May 1718.

Most of the walls were built of earth and a ditch had been dug in front of them. However, the city planners realised that the most likely place for an enemy to attack would be from the sea, so the wall along the Cooper River was made of brick, with five bastions and one semi-circular battery housing cannon that were aimed out over the harbour, but their range was extremely limited.

By this time the town was the fifth-largest settlement in North America and many of the inhabitants were growing wealthy in the booming economy, based initially on rice. The import of slaves, while it existed, was not as extensive here as it was in some of the more southerly areas like the Caribbean. Other trades that soon became prominent were indigo, a dye used in the textile industry in Britain, and timber.

Blackbeard approached Cummins Point from the south in the afternoon of 22 May 1718; part of a flotilla of four vessels, his flagship being the largest. Because of the bank of sand that formed a natural barrier across much of the harbour's mouth, known as the Charles Town Bar some 3 miles from the town itself, the *Queen Anne's Revenge* would have encountered some difficulty getting close enough to the town to really become a major threat. There were ways in but as events transpired, Blackbeard made no attempt to venture closer to the town. Besides, he was not there to attack. Of all the crimes that pirates had achieved throughout history, few could claim to have blockaded a port and brought its trade to a standstill.

The threat was not so much to the town but to any ship trying to enter or leave the harbour. They would first of all have to pass the large pirate warship, bristling with guns, gun ports open and ready. A terrifying sight indeed.

To make matters worse, Charles Town was undefended in terms of warships. New York had a warship to protect it; Williamsburg had a warship for protection; Charles Town had no such defence. The walls that protected the town were in the process of being shifted to make way for the growing population, and while the cannon mounted on the bastions could just reach the other side of the Cooper River, they were utterly useless against Blackbeard and his fleet 3 miles downstream.

There is no record that the *Queen Anne's Revenge* ever entered the harbour at Charles Town. Blackbeard threatened to enter the town and bombard it if his demands weren't met but this never actually took place. For him to enter the harbour and begin shooting would have been tactically unsound. Once the alarm had been raised the Royal Navy could have blockaded the mouth of the harbour, trapping the pirate and then taken their time blasting him to bits.

The harbour itself was 1.5 miles across and 5 miles long with Charles Town sitting at one end on the peninsula and the mouth of the harbour facing the open Atlantic. The harbour's main anchorage lay at the point where the two rivers converged but getting to this point could be treacherous. Running from the anchorage to the open sea were a series of deep-water channels divided by sandbanks and shoals that from time to time shifted under the force of winter storms or hurricanes that roared in from the Atlantic. Large ships such as the *Queen Anne's Revenge* could enter the harbour and sail along the deep-water channels but they needed to have a local pilot thoroughly familiar with these shifting shoals and channels.

Of the vessels with him that made up the rest of his flotilla, all three were sloops. The first was the *Revenge*, formally Stede Bonnet's ship and more than likely commanded by Captain Richards. The second would have been the newly-acquired *Adventure*, formerly commanded by David Herriot and now commanded by Israel Hands. The identity of the last sloop is not known for certain.[132]

These vessels most probably spread themselves across the mouth of the harbour. They were in prime positions to both escape if a fleet of warships appeared and to block transport into and out of the harbour itself. As events were to transpire, sailing into the harbour became unnecessary. An alternative was about to fall into Blackbeard's lap.

Blockading a small city was a daring move by Blackbeard. Few other pirates had the audacity to carry out this action. By doing this, Blackbeard could hold the town to ransom, capture any ship he liked that was either leaving the harbour or entering and plunder them for riches. Also this blockade would see Blackbeard spreading his complete control from that of his own ship and crew, beyond the little flotilla now to a town of more than 5,000 people, all of whom would be completely at his mercy. Once he began communication with the town he said that all he came for was a chest of medicine. This has been well-documented: 'If I did not immediately send them a chest of medicines.'[133]

Back in Virginia, Spotswood had been hearing the news about Blackbeard's actions. Trade between the colonies was starting to suffer because of the pirate. He had not yet heard of the blockade of Charles Town but he would soon enough.

Robert Johnson, Governor of South Carolina, provides us with a narrative of sorts about what went on during those dark days. Disturbed by the presence of so many pirate ships and by the rising level of panic surging through the local population, he wrote an urgent letter to the Council of Trade and Plantations in London which would have arrived long after the blockade was over but one which conveyed his anxieties.[134]

When the little flotilla arrived off the Charles Town Bar the pilot vessel headed out to meet them as they rode the swell off Sullivan's Island. There was nothing uncommon about this. They would have been used to small fleets of ships arriving ready to take their cargo into the harbour. The pilot vessel was especially needed to guide larger vessels over the Bar, down one of the deep channels into the main anchorage. It was perfectly normal. Of course, as the pilot boat drew near, the realisation of the situation struck, but by then, it was too late. Once the pilot had climbed up onto the deck of the *Queen Anne's Revenge* he would have come face to face with the tall, foreboding heavily-armed English pirate with the black flowing beard. Escape was impossible for the unsuspecting pilot and his crew and they were to become the first victims of the blockade – prisoners in the dark hold of the pirate flagship, but they would not be alone for long. Indeed, Governor Johnson confirmed in his letter that the pilot was Blackbeard's first victim, '...appeared in sight of the Town tooke our pilot boat'.[135]

According to Governor Johnson's letter the next victim was the ship *Crowley*. This, under the command of Captain Clark, was proceeding over the Bar, carrying passengers: 'It is not unreasonable to assume that her commander, Captain Clark, had followed the pilot boat out of the harbour and was captured within minutes of his guide.'[136]

This first important catch of the blockade presented Blackbeard with some interesting opportunities as it had many leading citizens from Charles Town aboard.[137] The first of those opportunities was the possession and baggage of all the passengers which the pirates rifled through in quick order. Another opportunity was the hold of the *Crowley* which was packed with rice. Then, of course, there was the value of keeping the passengers as hostages. Blackbeard read the ship's papers and discovered one of the passengers was Samuel Wragg, a prominent wealthy man in Charles Town and a member of the council. He was travelling with his young son William so this provided Blackbeard with even more opportunity. Despite the fearsome reputation pirates often had, it appears that none of these passengers were physically harmed. This shows the control that Blackbeard had over his crew but also a man at the height of his power, having control over his prisoners, more than 300 pirates spread out in his fleet and of course the poor citizens of Charles Town.

The capture of the *Crowley* must have been towards the end of the day as no alarm had yet been raised by fishermen or anyone on the nearest shore. However, when dawn rose the following day the people of Charles Town would soon discover their city was in deep trouble.

That following day the haul was even better. According to Governor Johnson, '8 or 9 sail with severall [*sic*] of the best inhabitants of this place' were to fall victim to the plundering designs of the pirates. The first victim of the new day was a small outbound ship, commanded by Captain Craigh also, like the *Crowley*, starting its long journey to London. As the pilot was nowhere to be found that morning, we can assume that Captain Craigh's concentration would have been on navigating the Bar by himself while quite possibly cursing the pilot's absence. He would have had no time to wonder about the vessels waiting beyond the Bar and by the time he did turn his attention to them it was too late. He would have sailed straight into the range of their guns.

The next victim was the *William* commanded by Captain Hewes, an incoming ship on the last leg of its journey from Weymouth. Even if word had managed to spread across the harbour by then not to put out to sea, this unsighted incoming ship would have stood no chance of avoiding the inevitable.[138]

This encounter would very likely have been witnessed by fishermen and others in small boats or those working along the shore and someone would have headed back to the town to raise the alarm. Panic would have started to spread as fast as the news and the remaining eight ships, now locked up in the harbour, would have been a clear reminder to the traders that they were under siege. The nearest known warship would probably have been in Williamsburg. It would take several days to get a message by land to its captain and then it would have been several more days for his ship to reach the area. The rest of the Royal Navy, sparsely spread out across the then known world, would have been of no use.

Charles Town was sealed off from the outside world. People undoubtedly began worrying about whether the pirates would come ashore and take whatever, or whoever, they wanted. The general population knew nothing of the strategic dangers Blackbeard faced if he entered the harbour. All they knew was that their town was under siege and anything that moved in the waters beyond the harbour was being taken. If the blockade lasted for any length of time the crops that brought prosperity to the growing town would rot in the holds of the stranded ships. At the time, they had no idea whether they would be blockaded for a day, a week, or a month. A war with the local tribes of Native Americans had just ended and they were living through a difficult fragile peace which could change at any moment. 'What made these misfortunes heavier to them was a long expensive war the colony had had with the natives, what was but just ended, when these robbers infested them.'[139] Captain Charles Johnson writing in his *History* gives us a glimpse of what it was like for the people of the town:

> The whole Province of Carolina, having just before been visited by Vane, another notorious pirate that they abandoned themselves to despair, being in no condition to resist their force. They were eight sail in the harbour ready, for the sea, but none dared to venture out, it being almost impossible to escape their hands. The inward bound vessels were under the same unhappy dilemma, so that the trade of this place was totally interrupted.

However, the blockade did not last long enough for things to really deteriorate in the town. Blackbeard continued to capture vessels and on the same day the *William* was taken, two smaller 'vessels with narrow overhanging sterns' known as 'pinks' were taken and plundered. These were most likely coastal craft as they were roughly the same size as a brigantine or a sloop. It is likely that these coastal craft were carrying goods from South Carolina to Virginia, which would bring Blackbeard's actions to the attention of Spotswood.

After the pinks, Johnson states 'a brigantine with 14 Negroes aboard' was taken. This was a slave ship from Angola out of Bristol and Blackbeard chose fourteen of the fittest to reinforce his crew. Right after this another coastal craft was plundered out from Boston. Blackbeard's haul over two days was eight prizes.

Charles Town was now effectively under siege; with the guns from the *Queen Anne's Revenge* covering the North Channel, nothing was getting in or out.

Yet, Blackbeard's only demand to the town council of Charles Town was for a chest of medicine. Here he had the whole of Charles Town in the palm of his hand, at his mercy and yet all he demanded was medicine. Why not more? With the closest Royal Navy warship several days away he could have demanded a substantial amount of wealth from everyone in the town. He had the hostages. On the face of it he had everything on his side. Or did he?

In Blackbeard's time the single biggest killer of sailors was not battle but disease. It was not understood and could run rampant through a ship claiming hundreds of lives. Blackbeard's fleet had been in the Caribbean over the summer where they would have been exposed to tropical diseases such as malaria, typhoid and yellow fever, all lethal. It was estimated that a captain would expect to replenish 50 per cent of his crew by the end of a voyage or return to a home port with barely enough people to man half the guns and sails. As an example, when Captain Kidd was in the Indian Ocean many years earlier, he lost a third of his crew to disease within a week.

To a pirate captain who relied on overwhelming superiority not only of fear and weapons but of manpower, substantial losses could be disastrous. Some members of the crew are more important to a successful operation or a prolonged voyage than others and perhaps it was these crew members who were suffering. Well-trained replacements for these would have been more difficult to find. Or there is another possibility. Since disease makes no judgement on whom it infects, it cannot be discounted that perhaps Blackbeard himself was suffering. What is the point of massive wealth if you die before you have a chance to enjoy it? His apparent lack of action in avoiding the battle that was eventually to take his life and his ignoring of the warnings that preceded it could imply that he knew he was going to die anyway and that he wanted to go down fighting rather than waste away with disease.

According to Angus Konstam there is another suggestion; that the pirates needed a medicine chest to combat venereal disease. In those days the primary treatment for syphilis was an injection of mercury. Recently, in an investigation of what could be the shipwreck of the *Queen Anne's Revenge* a metal urethral syringe was found by marine archaeologists among the debris of the wreckage. It had the recognisable funnel-shaped curved tip which was designed for injecting mercury into the patient to treat venereal diseases. Supporting this theory was the discovery of a high concentration of mercury inside the syringe.[140] Of course the wreckage in question may not be Blackbeard's flagship, but if it is then the syringe had been used before the ship went down, suggesting that the voyage in the Caribbean had been much livelier than most scholars believe.

Whatever the reason, Blackbeard needed medicine. The theft of possessions from the hostages was probably more to keep his crew satisfied.

We have already seen that Samuel Wragg was a member of the Charles Town Council and a prominent wealthy citizen and Blackbeard knew this. Wragg was initially chosen by the pirate to take the list and medical supplies to the council because of his wealth and his position in the city and also because he was travelling with his infant son William, whom the pirates would use as a hostage to ensure Wragg did as he was told.[141] However, Blackbeard seems to have changed his mind about Wragg. Instead, he chose someone lower down on the social scale in Charles Town, a man known only as Master Marks. He went ashore accompanied by two pirates which some accounts speculate may have included Captain Richards.

Along with the list of medicines, the men carried a warning from Blackbeard himself which Johnson states clearly in his account:

> If they did not send immediately the chest of medicines and let the pirate ambassadors return without offering any violence to their persons, they would murder all their prisoners, send up their heads to the governor and set the ships they had taken on fire.

In addition to burning the ships Blackbeard warned he would flatten the town or 'beat the town about our ears' which was the phrase used in a letter written after the event.[142]

Could the residents of Charles Town put up a fight? It seems unlikely. The militia was more of a defensive nature than an offensive one, as one resident described in a letter written after the event:

> The Town is at present in a very indifferent condition of making much resistance if them or any other enemy should attempt it and that we were very desirous to get them off our coast by fair means, which we could not do otherwise for want of such helps as other government are supply'd with from the Crown.[143]

On board the pirate flagship the hostages were in a tense situation. In the hold where they were being kept, men, women and children mixed and worried, perhaps much the same as the African slaves may have done on *La Concorde* when it was a slave ship before being captured by Blackbeard. Ironically, now the whites were locked up in the same hold that only a few months before would have held several black slaves, not knowing what lay in store for them, not knowing whether they would see home again.

Above decks, the little pinnace was lowered into the water, carrying Master Marks and the two pirates. As Blackbeard watched the little boat row away into the mouth of the harbour and out of sight he would have been ill at ease. A hardened sea captain, he did not have the luxury of letting anyone see his uneasiness. He was not a cold-blooded murderer but he had this fearsome reputation which now must have felt like a chain around his neck. He was taking a massive gamble. While he was not above shooting someone if required, it is doubtful whether he would have been prepared to have pistols aimed at the heads of dozens of men, women and children and blast their brains out. If we continue with the possibility that he may have been ill but could not make such a weakness known to his crew, time may have been running out for him too.

Nor was Blackbeard stupid. He knew that once the alarm had been raised the Council would have sent messengers running in all directions for help, so it was only a matter of time before a warship showed up on the horizon. The Royal Navy was stretched thin along the American coast and depleted after the long War of Spanish Succession but it was still powerful enough to mount an attack against him. The longer he blockaded Charles Town, the more likely this attack would take place. Several warships sailing at him from different directions would not only close off his escape, but also send his crew and ships to a watery grave.

So he waited, hoping his gamble would pay off. Now that he had gone this far and built such a reputation, he could not simply pull out and sail away somewhere to sulk. He could not carry out his threat and move in on the town, since each day that passed could bring warships closer and he could be blockaded in himself and the warships would also be carrying troops which they would put ashore and could then fire at him from the shoreline. Then there were the batteries of guns on the walls which, if he was blockaded in the harbour, would catch him in the crossfire. He would be a sitting duck.

He could not execute the hostages, even if he was that way inclined. Once he had exhausted his supply of people to kill and with no further shipping bringing replacement hostages into his grasp, he would have nothing left to bargain with. If he did start killing the hostages, every warship, militia and army in the Colonies would be after him.

Days passed and there was no news from the men in the boat. From Blackbeard's perspective his anxiety would have been mounting and thoughts turning to the fact that the town was not going to comply with their demands and every day that brought nearer the problem he had of having to carry out his threats. As the time dragged on some of the hostages might have been wondering why their lives were being considered to be so unimportant as to be worth less than a chest full of medical supplies. Blackbeard must have been both surprised and disappointed that his very simple demand was apparently not being met.

While some sources speculate that the little boat carrying the three men capsized with the men managing to get to a small uninhabited island before they were rescued and landed at the town, the evidence to support this is sketchy.[144] This could account for the long delay in getting the medicines, but not all the sources on Blackbeard claim that this is what happened to the boat so this incident is in some doubt.

However, a BBC docudrama simply entitled *Blackbeard* suggests that much of the delay was caused by the two pirates, having set foot on dry land, descending on the nearest tavern and pouring as much alcohol as they could down their throats and it goes on to claim that the crewmen sent ashore used the capsizing incident merely as an excuse to conceal the fact that they had spent the entire time drinking and sleeping off the effects.

The BBC drama shows that the *Queen Anne's Revenge* moved further into the harbour putting it some way along the river. Now this move would have bottled up Blackbeard completely if warships arrived at the mouth of the harbour behind him. The three sloops would have remained in a line across the harbour mouth to continue to capture and plunder ships but even the combined firepower of the sloops would have been no match for a heavily-armed warship. We know that the *Queen Anne's Revenge* did not go any closer than where she remained for the entire duration of the blockade. It would have taken considerable time for the three men to get to the Governor to give him the demands and then time for him to collect the medicines demanded on the list, but that does not make for such interesting television.

This was the early eighteenth century when everything happened, by our modern standards, at a much reduced pace. Collecting a chest full of medicines would not have been as easy as a visit to the chemist with a prescription. If some of the medicines were not immediately available, it could have taken several days to find them. Also, the Governor would have had no idea when the pirates would be coming to present Blackbeard's demands or even know if he had any demands until a messenger arrived or the pirates showed up themselves. Everything was by word of mouth, messengers on foot or horseback or, in this case, pirate ambassadors in a small boat. It would all have taken considerable time.

There is some evidence that suggests the two pirates might have gone into the local taverns as the BBC drama asserts, because Captain Johnson says that:

Whilst Mr Marks was making application to the council, Richards and the rest of the pirates walked the streets publicly in the sight of all people, who were fired with the utmost indignation, looking upon them as robbers and murderers and particularly the authors of their wrongs and oppressions, but durst not so much as think of executing their revenge, for fear of bringing more calamities upon themselves, and so they were forced to let the villains pass with impunity.

From Johnson's account above and from Governor Robert Johnson's letters we know the pirates walked the streets with impunity in a 'bold and upright' manner. While Marks was with the Governor the pirates walked the streets. We speculate here that it is highly likely that the pirates entered the tavern while they waited for Marks. After all, they had the upper hand. Marks would not be able to run away because of the hostages; the pirates wouldn't be molested because of the fear of reprisal and again, the fate of the hostages. So it is likely they did go drinking which would account for the delay.

The situation with the townspeople would have been one of wanting to do something but being utterly paralysed by fear of retaliation on a grand scale. The best they could do was either look away in fear or give the pirates a few hard stares. Since there was no evidence of pillaging or plundering by the pirates, or indeed anything more devastating, we can only assume that the pirates were either better behaved than our general view of pirates, or our general view of pirates is distorted; or perhaps, they felt vastly outnumbered, vulnerable and just as ill at ease among the hostile population of Charles Town.

Captain Johnson states that while the pirates walked the streets at liberty, the Governor and the Council:

> ...were not long in deliberating upon the message though 'twas the greatest affront that could have been put upon them, yet for the saving of so many men's lives (among them Mr. Samuel Wragg, one of the council) they complied with the necessity and sent aboard a chest valued at between 300 and 400 pounds.

Blackbeard did get his medicine and 'the pirates went back safe to their ships'. The hostages were released, but not before they were relieved of not only all their possessions but most of their clothing. In terms of the value of items taken from ships and hostages, Johnson states that Blackbeard and his fellow pirates took 'out of them in gold and silver, about 1,500 pounds sterling, besides provisions and other matters'.[145]

After a week of blockading the town and stopping everything that moved in or out, the flotilla of pirate vessels sailed away, and it seems that not even a single shot had been fired by either side. With the city defences in such a poor condition, raiding the town might have been worthwhile. There were around 300 pirates, all ready for a fight, and around 5,000 civilian inhabitants, all trembling behind closed doors, or so it would have seemed. Why then, did Blackbeard not press home his advantage?

There are a number of reasons, and some have already been discussed. Any student of military strategy knows that making a move to attack that also closes off your escape route is unsound. Also, Blackbeard could only guess at the condition of the defences. He was never close enough to make a full survey. Even though he'd captured several ships and from them would have had a rough idea of the town's defences, sailing into an enclosed harbour would have put him in range of the cannon they did have but, more importantly, small-arms fire. Especially, if his navigation wasn't accurate and the massive flagship went aground on one of the many shoals or sand bars, he could be shot at from the shore with impunity. Once stuck, he would then be at the mercy of the town's defences and the arrival of the Royal Navy.

Of course, an attack on the town may have pleased many of his men and given them the opportunity to get more wealth from plundering the people and the town but what of the cost of such an attack? If his overriding need was to get a chest of medicine, then how many of his men were even fit enough to mount such an attack?

In addition, the BBC drama gives us another reason. It claims that, despite the wishes of many of his crew, Blackbeard ordered the flotilla to sail away without attacking Charles Town because to do so would have been, in their view, too easy. Yet, to leave without attacking the town after being in a position where he could have if he had wanted, displayed far greater power and control than if he simply ravaged the place. The actions of blockading the town and then sailing away, leaving it intact would have earned him some more notoriety. In addition, he had received what he had set out to receive – the medicines – and that was sufficient. As a bonus, his crew had a share of the takings from the ships they had plundered during the blockade. In achieving what it had intended, the whole incident was a resounding success, resounding because its impact and the news of it would reverberate throughout the colonies for some time to come.

Governor Robert Johnson's letter to the Council of Trade and Plantations sent after the event illustrates the effect of the blockade. He starts by describing it as an

> unspeakable calamity this poor province suffers from pyrates obliges me to inform your lordships of it in order that his Majestie may know it and be induced to afford us the assistance of a frigate or two to cruse hereabouts upon them for we are continually alarmed and our ships taken to the utter ruin of our trade.[146]

Also in this letter, the Governor raises a fascinating point. He states that this was the second time in nine months since he entered office that Charles Town had been besieged by pirates. Blackbeard's blockade started fourteen days before Governor Johnson wrote his letter and it continued for about a week to ten days.

Governor Johnson's letter to the Council of Trade and Plantations arrived in London in August 1718. He tells their lordships at the Council that 'twice since my coming here in 9 months time they [pirates] lain off of our barr taking and plundering all ships that come into this port'.

The problem we have with this nine months issue is that this then takes us back to around September 1717. Who was in the area at the time? It could have been any number of pirates, but a letter written around the same time as the governor penned his states that the second blockade in May 1718 was by the same pirates who were responsible for the earlier blockade in September 1717. It states that a merchant ship was taken by a sloop with twelve guns and a much larger French ship of forty guns accompanied by two sloops

> for their tenders, having in all about 300 men all English – the ship is commanded by one Teach and the sloop by one Richards, who have been upon this account in those and other vessels about two years, and is, the same sloops and company that was off our barr the last summer and took two vessels inward bound.[147]

So Blackbeard had already been here and had plundered two vessels. This means that Blackbeard would have been off Charles Town when he was commanding the *Revenge* and before he seized *La Concorde*. While being off Charles Town Bar the previous summer he could have then hatched a plan to return to Charles Town and blockade the harbour with a much larger force, so he would need a larger ship with far greater firepower. Hence he seized *La Concorde* for that very purpose. We can't know for sure that this was what lay behind the taking of the French slaver but it does make some sense.

Perhaps he intended to plunder all the ships going in and out and the town itself and get greater riches on his return to the area?

Yet, when he did arrive again and blockade the town he only asked for medicine. If he and his crew were sick then asking for the medicines made sense. He'd had to change his plans of plundering the town so instead he could just take any booty from incoming and outgoing vessels while waiting for his medicine. Then he could move to better hunting grounds, lie low and start plundering all over again.

Governor Johnson predicted that the King's Pardon would do very little to change these pirates. In terms of Blackbeard, it was a prediction that was destined to come true. The Governor also becomes one of the first people to write in his account 'commanded by one Teach alias Blackbeard'.

Resplendent on the deck of his grand flagship, Blackbeard sailed north. With him were the three sloops. He had achieved everything he had set out to achieve, but there was still more to come. The next part of his plan was to come as a shock to almost all of those around him.

Chapter 10

Death of the *Queen*

*Teach began now to think of breaking up the company,
and securing the money and the best of the effects for
himself and some others of his companions he had
most friendship for, and to cheat the rest.* [148]

Captain Charles Johnson

W hen Captain Kidd arrived in the Caribbean aboard the *Quedagh Merchant*, which he had renamed as *Adventure Prize*, he found himself in a dilemma. His massive ship was perfect as a prize to take back to England but it was also a massive target and just about every navy, privateer and even pirates were hunting him.

Two decades later, Blackbeard was in the same dilemma. The blockade of Charles Town had cemented his reputation as the most feared, powerful and audacious pirate sailing in American waters. His fame was spreading, but the blockade had also set him up as public enemy number one. His ship, the *Queen Anne's Revenge*, had become one of the most famous and most recognisable in the world. While Kidd feared attack from both pirates and any of the navies he had managed to upset along the way, Blackbeard had no reason to fear a pirate attack but attacks from the navies, especially the Royal Navy, were a completely different story. His ship was one of the largest pirate vessels afloat and would act as a massive target for anyone hunting him, and they were hunting him. Everyone knew what his ship looked like. However, Blackbeard had a plan.

When Europeans first began to arrive in North Carolina, they were mainly English settlers coming down from the north in search of more farmland. What they found when they arrived was a diverse selection of North American indigenous tribes that included Cherokee, Tuscarora, Cheraw, Pamlico, Meherrin, Coree, Machapungo, Cape Fear, Waxhaw, Saponi, Tutelo, Waccamaw, Coharie and Catawba, all vying for land that would eventually make up North Carolina.

Sir Walter Raleigh was given land in the colony of Virginia in 1584 by Elizabeth I. Raleigh was the man who famously brought tobacco to Europe. As the decades went by, more and more colonists arrived and in 1663 the colony was firmly established by a charter issued by King Charles II that named the entire territory Carolina. In 1710, the area was split into North and South Carolina and the rough line of the modern border was established. Some of the coastline was known as the Outer Banks. This was where Blackbeard was heading.

It was an ideal hiding-place for pirates. Filled with small inlets and shoals, it provided any small pirate vessel with a perfect place to ambush merchant ships traversing the Outer Banks. The multitude of sandbanks made navigation difficult for large ships. Any vessel forced onto these sandbanks by smaller pirate vessels would find they had little choice but to submit to being plundered or face being run aground. One of the many inlets, and the one that Blackbeard was heading for, was Topsail Inlet right in front of Beaufort, North Carolina. During Blackbeard's time Beaufort was a tiny fishing settlement that had been set up as a whaling station. Konstam describes it as having 'a ragged collection of unpainted shacks surrounded by bleached bones and the stench of rotten fish'.[149]

The place Blackbeard was heading for was Topsail Island within Topsail Inlet, so named because any merchant ship passing by would only be able to see the tops of sails above the rolling sand dunes that formed the beaches of the island. Beyond the island was Beaufort and beyond that, Native American territory.

Indeed, the dominant tribe of the area was the Coree, whose territory stretched from the Outer Banks to Cape Lookout and Cape Fear River. The Coree were engaged in a war with the Machapungos and the Tuscarora tribes that nearly wiped them all out, so they had little fight left in them when the white settlers arrived. In 1718, when Blackbeard arrived, the settlement of Beaufort was five years old though it wouldn't officially be recognised as a town until five years later. With such navigational hazards and so few people known to be in the area, it was isolated enough for the next stage of his plan.

He needed to get rid of his flagship. A ship that size was simply too big to operate out of this area, plus it was too well-known, so it had to go. It would certainly not have been the only large ship to have been wrecked in this area. There is only one really safe way through the Outer Banks into Topsail Harbour, even for smaller vessels. If you miss that, you end up beached on one of the many sand bars. No matter which route he took, Blackbeard would have found navigating his way through the sandbanks and shoals difficult with a ship the size of the *Queen Anne's Revenge*. However, it appears that he didn't care. He sailed straight into the sandy beach on Topsail Island.

Captain Ellis Brand, the commanding officer of HMS *Lyme* wrote to the Admiralty on 12 July 1718 providing a rough date of around 10 June 1718 regarding the grounding of the *Queen Anne's Revenge*. We know that Blackbeard lifted the blockade around the end of May 1718 and six days later he beached his flagship so it would be early June. Brand's date will suffice for our purposes.

He describes the flotilla in detail, telling us that the sloops followed the *Queen Anne's Revenge* over the sand bar in the same way that a flock of ducklings would follow their mother wherever she goes. How could Blackbeard be leading them into danger? In Brand's account he believes that Blackbeard was attempting to enter the harbour at Topsail Inlet but instead crashed into the sand bar.[150]

However, other sources tell a different story. Blackbeard knew that his flagship was now a liability. After the blockade of Charles Town he was a hunted man and everyone would be looking for a giant pirate warship of forty guns. Blackbeard was working to a plan. Captain Johnson tells us in his account about the beaching of the *Queen Anne's Revenge*:

> Teach began now to think of breaking up the company, and securing the money and the best of the effects for himself and some others of his companions he had most friendship for, and to cheat the rest. Accordingly, on pretence of running into Topsail Inlet to clean, he grounded his ship, and then as if it had been done undesignedly and by accident, he ordered Hands' sloop to come to his assistance and get him off again, which he endeavouring to do, ran the sloop on shore near the other, and so were both lost.

As we believe that Hands was one of Captain Johnson's key sources it is very likely that this part of the narrative came directly from him. If we take Johnson's account as relatively accurate then it's clear that few of the 300 or so pirates knew what their commander was up to. Blackbeard would only have confided in those he could most trust to keep the plan a secret, and those he had decided were worthy of keeping on as a part of the reduced crew, but whether even they knew in advance the full details is debatable.

From looking at a maritime chart of the area dated 1738, the closest available to 1718, we can see that the deepest channels ranged from 3 and 5 fathoms (18 and 30 feet). The *Queen Anne's Revenge* and any ship like it with a draught of around 10 to 12 feet should have been able to navigate through these deep channels in the Outer Banks to get into the harbour at Topsail Inlet. If Blackbeard intended to sail into the harbour he should have been able to do this.

To create enough damage to a ship so that it is impossible to use without a great deal of repair work, one would need to run the ship aground at some speed. Blackbeard would probably have been running at full sail as he would have for entering a harbour, waiting for the right moment to lower his sails and start to slow down upon entrance. Even if he had lookouts posted for sandbanks, the crew would probably not have realised what was happening until it was too late. Still, he had to have a selected group of the crew in on the plan; probably very few to make it work.

Imagine the scene. The ship moving at full sail; no order yet forthcoming for sail to be reduced. The lookouts in the bow and the rigging seeing the shadow of the submerged sand bar ahead cry out their warning, expecting the order to come to lower the sails to slow down but no order is forthcoming. The crew are wondering what is going on. Why are they still going at full sail? Little do they know their great voyage is about to come to a grinding halt.

Some might even look back anxiously at Blackbeard wondering if he can see what is happening but the tall, intimidating captain seems unaware. More shouts from the lookouts. Time is running out. Suddenly the ship veers to starboard. Then a grinding, tearing, ripping sound as the ship hits the sand bar. Anything not tied down tumbles, rolls and crashes onto the decks as it comes to a final juddering halt.

While the ship had grounded onto soft sand, it had done so at some speed for Blackbeard to ensure it could not be pulled off again. That would mean the damage to the hull would be enough to ensure her days sailing on the high seas were over. Three centuries of the sea's tides and storms have taken their toll on what is thought to be the wreck of the *Queen Anne's Revenge*, making it impossible to analyse the damage created by the crash. Significant structural damage would have been done to the fore sections, likely splintering the planks of the forward underside hull and bow sections which would already have been weakened from the continual pounding of the waves as she ploughed through them during her voyages. We can only speculate on whether the hull was breached in these forward sections, allowing sea water to come cascading into the ship. Nor can we say with any certainty how much of the hull was in water or how high she was riding because of the sandbank. If the hull was breached and water started gushing in, any barrels used for storing water, food and other stores would have been ripped from their moorings from the power of the water blasting in. The more water that came in, the more the ship would sink into the sand, ensuring it stayed fast.

Probably some of the fastened-down parts of the ship may have broken or moved. It seems likely that the main mast could have collapsed on impact. Indeed, Konstam tells us that it shattered on impact.[151] The mast itself was heavy, made of solid wood and the sails fully rigged would have added significantly to the weight, and the jarring impact of the ship hitting the sand bar could well have split the mast, either bringing it down altogether or making it difficult to repair.

We can't know if the ship could have been saved once it had been pulled off the sand bar. Dragging her off and trying to repair her was not part of the plan. The key for Blackbeard was to ensure the ship was firmly and completely beached. Even if the damage could be repaired he needed to be sure the ship was stuck fast and that it would sink further into the sand, unable to be towed off and left at the mercy of the tides and the waves.

From Johnson's account above we can see that Blackbeard made a show of trying to get the *Queen Anne's Revenge* off the sand bar and so summoned the sloop *Adventure*, formerly commanded by the captured David Herriot and now under the command of Israel Hands.

The sand bar was on the starboard side of Blackbeard's ship so Hands brought the *Adventure* up the port side, sending a cable from his sloop to the larger flagship and the *Adventure* made a valiant attempt to haul the *Queen Anne's Revenge* off the sand. However, instead of pulling the *Queen Anne's Revenge* off the sandbank, Hands ended up hauling her further across the bank, driving the *Adventure* onto the shore, springing several of her hull planks so that she too ended up beyond repair. It seems almost certain that Israel Hands was one of those lucky few to know about the plan in advance and so he played his part in the betrayal.[152]

Because both vessels were in shallow water, their hulls completely fixed in the sandbank, they would not have sunk straight away. Indeed, it could have taken hours, days, weeks or months for the ships to completely sink, depending on the tides and the shifting sand. Because of this the pirate crews had enough time to shift what they needed from the ships onto the shore. It's unlikely there would have been a mad dash to drag out as much as they could before the ships descended into a watery grave. The actions by Israel Hands had breached both hulls so both vessels were now wrecks, firmly stuck in the sand and taking on water.

Salvage work in removing everything of value from the two ships would have begun as soon as the crews recovered from the shock. All the light weapons, powder and shot would certainly have been removed, possibly even some of the lighter cannon. Whether or not the locals had a hand in stripping the ships after the pirates had removed everything they could is debatable, but it is a tantalising thought that some of the locals could have plundered both ships. The plunderers of vessels had now become the plundered.[153]

To get a better idea of this event we turn to a deposition written by David Herriot, the former captain of the *Adventure* and who joined Blackbeard, though he later said he had been forced to throw in his lot with the pirate. His account became public information in 1719. It is reproduced in part below:

> That about six days after they left the Bar of Charles-Town, they arrived at Topsail-Inlet in North Carolina, having then under their Command the said ship *Queen Anne's Revenge*, the sloop commanded by Richards, this Deponent's Sloop, commanded by one Capt. Hands, one

of the said Pirate Crew, and a small empty Sloop which they found near the Havana. That the next Morning after they had all got safe into Topsail-inlet, except Thatch, the said Thatch's ship *Queen Anne's Revenge* run a-ground off of the Bar of Topsail-Inlet, and the said Thatch sent his Quarter-Master to command this Deponent's Sloop to come to his Assistance, but she run a-ground likewise about gun-shot from the said Thatch, before his said Sloop could come to their Assistance, and both the said Thatch's Ship and this Deponent's Sloop were wreck'd, and the said Thatch and all the other Sloop's Companies went on board the *Revenge*, afterwards called the *Royal James*, and on board the other Sloop they found empty off the Havana.

Twas generally believed the said Thatch run his Vessel a-ground on purpose to break up the Companies, and to secure what Moneys and Effects he had got for himself and such other of them as he had most Value for. That after the said ship and this Deponent's sloop were so cast away, the Deponent requested the said Thatch to let him have a Boat, and a few Hands, to go some inhabited Place in North Carolina, or to Virginia, there being very few and poor inhabitants in Topsail-Inlet, where they were, and desired the said Thatch to make this Deponent some Satisfaction for his said Sloop; Both which said Thatch promised to do. But instead thereof, ordered this Deponent, with about sixteen more, to be put on shore on a small Sandy Hill or Bank, a league distant from the Main, on which Place there was no Inhabitant, nor Provisions. Where this Deponent and the rest remained two Nights and one Day, and expected to perish, for that said Thatch took away their Boat. That said Thatch having taken what Number of Men he thought fit along with him, he set sail from Topsail-Inlet in the small Spanish Sloop, about eight Guns mounted, forty White Men, and sixty Negroes, and left the *Revenge* belonging to Bonnet there.[154]

In this account, Herriot refers to Blackbeard as Thatch, one of the many versions of his real name, which adds to the mystery of who Blackbeard really was. In England, many surnames we are familiar with today are derived from the professions that people worked in and during this time period many houses were made with thatched roofs, so Thatch could have been a family name.

In Herriot's deposition he refers to the pirates using the words 'their' and 'they' and so on, which gives us a clear indication that when he wrote this he didn't consider himself a pirate. However, if this was written in his defence then it would make sense for him to distance himself from the pirates as much as possible to show that he was forced into their piratical ways.

Also he refers to three sloops: one commanded by Richards, the *Revenge* formerly Stede Bonnet's sloop; another commanded by Hands, the *Adventure* his former ship; and a third, the sloop from Havana which he states was empty. The implication here is that this vessel was empty of both cargo and crew. Had they been stranded somewhere or tossed over the side?

He also tells us that after Blackbeard had stranded them on the sandbank he took their only means of transportation which was the unknown sloop from Havana, but then at the end of his deposition he claims the *Revenge* was left behind. So where then, was the *Revenge* and why couldn't they get to it so they could reach civilisation? We do know from a wide variety of sources, including Johnson, that the *Revenge* was left behind and given back to Bonnet, who two days later came and rescued the stranded pirates.

The chart from 1738, referred to earlier, shows that there are sandbanks throughout the area, some below the water and some above. The larger ones above sea level would have been ideal for stranding someone, especially either of the two that form the outer rim of the inlet. However, Captain Johnson states in his account of Blackbeard that where the men were stranded 'there was neither bird, beast nor herb for their subsistence'. He states they were stranded about a league from the mainland. That's about 3 nautical miles away from Beaufort on the mainland. While there may not have been any animals or plant life on the sand bars there were bound to have been birds. Interestingly, Herriot does corroborate Johnson's account by saying that there was 'no Inhabitant, nor Provisions'.

Johnson tells us that the stranded pirates were taken off the island two days after Blackbeard had sailed away and when Bonnet was back in command of the *Revenge* which at some point had been renamed the *Royal James* (Herriot's claim). By this time Blackbeard and the most trusted and closest men of his crew would have been long gone in the remaining Spanish sloop.[155] This vessel Blackbeard renamed the *Adventure*, perhaps in an attempt to confuse the authorities.

Remember, during the blockade of Charles Town Blackbeard had his flagship and three other sloops and upwards of 300 men under his command. Johnson tells us that he stranded seventeen men on a 'Sandy Island', one of whom was David Herriot, and he took forty men into the Spanish sloop now renamed the *Adventure* (to avoid confusion we will call it *New Adventure*).

This incident marks a turning point in Blackbeard's life and career, which is why we are devoting so many pages to it. However, it is difficult to provide an exact analysis of what happened during the beaching, how much damage was done to the ships and what happened afterwards. We don't know how long it took for both wrecks to slide beneath the waves. Storms and tides could have shifted the wrecks over time. Woodworm attacking the wooden hulls would have had an effect, as well as weakening the structures to such an extent that chunks would have started to come away. If the wrecks had remained above the water for any length of time they would have been subject to heavy storms that could have shifted the vessels sufficiently to drag them below the surface.

The area is also not immune to hurricanes, so we can imagine what a 150 mph wind can do to a wreck over many years and decades, with torrential rain lashing through broken beams. Once the ships started to sink into the sea, with water flooding in through the holes and gaps between the smashed beams, both wrecks would have slowly submerged as they were pounded to pieces by rain, waves and wind. The tides too would have taken their toll over the years, clawing and dragging the wrecks and shifting the sand beneath them until they were claimed by the sea.

In addition to the punishment of nature there is also the effect of man on the area. The US Army Corps of Engineers have been making changes in the area which would have required some dredging, adding to the problem of identifying the wrecks.

It's for these reasons that archaeologists are hesitant to claim with 100 per cent certainty that the site of the wreckage found in the area is that of the *Queen Anne's Revenge* and one other sloop – presumably Herriot's original *Adventure*.

This is also the point where Blackbeard and Bonnet part company. It seems that Blackbeard betrayed Bonnet here by leaving him just the *Revenge* and nothing else of value. Most of the booty the pirates had taken while sailing with Blackbeard was now in the hold of the Spanish sloop in which Blackbeard and his trusted men had sailed away.

The betrayal of Bonnet began with Blackbeard convincing him that the best course of action for all of them was for Bonnet to head straight for Bath Town in North Carolina as quickly as he could, where he would gain an audience with Governor Eden and apply for a pardon. It seems that Blackbeard also convinced Bonnet that he needed the *Revenge* to continue the salvage work from the two wrecks, and so Bonnet took another ship which could either have been a small fishing vessel from the local community at Beaufort or the single-masted longboat from the *Queen Anne's Revenge*. Bonnet sailed away as quickly as he could in search of Eden and a pardon which he got for himself and for the rest of the pirates. He also managed to get permission to take his ship down to St Thomas, a Danish settlement in the West Indies where he planned to obtain a commission to become a privateer. This voyage from Topsail Inlet to Bath Town and back again probably took about a week. Added to that time was an additional week before Bonnet set sail for the salvaging operation from the two wrecks, the fitting out of the small vessel for Bonnet to take on his journey and it appears as if Blackbeard had almost two weeks in the area which would give him enough time to strip the *Revenge* of anything useful.[156]

Indeed, when Bonnet returned he discovered to his horror that Blackbeard had gone, taken all the booty they'd accumulated over the voyage and stripped the *Revenge* of virtually everything – charts, powder, guns and stores – everything Bonnet would need.

Blackbeard would have had upwards of 300 men under his command when the two ships were wrecked. They set up a makeshift camp near Beaufort while the salvaging operations took place. Blackbeard stayed in the camp along with his men, so how was it possible for him to transfer all the loot to the Spanish sloop without the rest of the pirates becoming suspicious? If the men were drinking their way through all the liquor salvaged from the two wrecks, then they would have been drunk most of the time and sleeping it off. Also Blackbeard had a select group of men who were in on the plan and they would be transferring the loot under the auspices of the salvage operations.[157]

Blackbeard selected forty or so men to crew the Spanish sloop; however, some of these would not be sailing with the pirate captain. It is highly likely that David Herriot was one of these men.

Imagine the scene. The hundreds of pirates on shore, slowly coming out of a drunken haze looked out to sea and found that their beloved captain had raised the anchor and was now unfurling the sails of the sloop, catching the wind as the ship moved deftly around the sand bars towards open sea. They ran towards the water, shouting, screaming, bellowing. Nearby on the *Revenge*, the men who had been getting her ready to sail when Bonnet returned would have seen a similar sight and also began shouting and screaming. On board the *New Adventure* some of the crew, realising what Blackbeard was doing and that their mates were being stranded, also protested.

It is these men and some from the *Revenge* that Konstam suggests made up the seventeen pirates that Johnson claims were stranded on a 'Sandy Island' which may have been Shackleford Bank that lies on the other side of the inlet, far enough away for no-one from Beaufort to see it, and which is also as barren as Johnson describes.[158]

So when Bonnet returns, he finds Blackbeard has betrayed and double-crossed him.

Blackbeard had achieved what he had set out to achieve. He had disbanded his crew and kept only the more capable ones with him; he had discarded a ship that had by now become more of a liability than an asset; and he had rid himself of the other captain, Stede Bonnet, who by this time he no doubt viewed as a pointless addition to the passenger list, and there was no room for passengers on pirate ships. Now it was on to the next stage of the plan.

Blackbeard and his crew board a ship. From *Blackbeard, Buccaneer* by Ralph Delahaye, 1922 (Penn Publishing Co.).

Pirate Rovers, This Lean, Straight Rover Looked the Part of a Competent Soldier. From *Blackbeard, Buccaneer* by Ralph Delahaye, 1922.

Pirate boarding action. From the inner cover of *Blackbeard, Buccaneer* by Ralph Delahaye, 1922.

The pike is a match for the cutlass. From *Releasing a Fearful Weapon* in *Blackbeard, Buccaneer* by Ralph Delahaye, 1922.

Blackbeard fires his pistols under the table, maiming Israel Hands. This piece of art was commissioned for Paine's serialised work on Blackbeard. From *Blackbeard, Buccaneer* by Ralph Delahaye, 1922.

The crews of Blackbeard and Vane's vessels carousing on the coast of Carolina. From Marine Research Society, dated 1837, source Charles Ellms. Originally published in *The Pirates Own Book: Authentic Narratives of the Most Celebrated Sea Robbers* (Dover Publications).

Blackbeard approaching. From 'The Quest For Pirates' Gold' in *Blackbeard, Buccaneer* by Ralph Delahaye, 1922.

Blackbeard: pictured with a rifle while standing on board a ship, by Edward Eggleston (1895).

Blackbeard boards Maynard's ship. By Edward Eggleston, 1904, 'Laws, Punishments, Bond Servants, Slaves, Pirates' in *The New Century History of the United States* (Dr Eggleston's School Histories, American Book Company).

Smoke and flame surround Blackbeard. This was an oil painting on canvas originally commissioned for Paine's serialised work *Blackbeard, Buccaneer* by Ralph Delahaye, 1922.

Blackbeard's head hanging from the bowsprit of the *Jane*.

Blackbeard and Lieutenant Maynard battle it out on the bloody deck of the *Jane*.

Engraving of Blackbeard (Edward Thatch) originally published in the Dutch version of Charles Johnson's *A General History of the Most Notorious Pyrates* (1725).

Blackbeard's last fight. This was originally published in Pyle and Howard's *Jack Ballister's Fortunes* (Century Company, 1894). The oil painting was sold in 1895 under the title *Blackbeard's Last Fight*, and is currently in the Delaware Art Museum's collection.

This engraving of Blackbeard was originally published around 1736 in Daniel Defoe and Charles Johnson's 'Capt. Teach alias Black-Beard' in *A General History of the Lives and Adventures of the Most Famous Highwaymen, Murderers, Street-Robbers, &c. to which is added, a genuine account of the voyages and plunders of the most notorious pyrates. Interspersed with several diverting tales, and pleasant songs. And adorned with the Heads of the most remarkable Villains, curiously engraved on Copper* (some sources give 1726 as the publication date).

Portrait of Alexander Spotswood, oil on canvas by Charles Bridges (1735–45) currently hanging in the Governor's Palace, Colonial Williamsburg, Virginia. The painter made two copies of the work in 1736. One, hanging in the Governor's mansion at Richmond in 1952, was presented by Philip A. Spotswood to the Commonwealth of Virginia in 1874. Another, from which this image is taken, was sold to Colonial Williamsburg Incorporated by I. N. (Louisa Beverley Turner) Jones.

Blackbeard and some of his crew bury treasure. Originally published in 'Buccaneers and Marooners of the Spanish Main' by Howard Pyle in *Harper's Magazine* (August–September 1887); taken from Howard Pyle and Merle De Vore Johnson (ed.), *Howard Pyle's Book of Pirates: Fiction, Fact & Fancy Concerning the Buccaneers & Marooners of the Spanish Main* (1921).

The Old Capitol Building in Williamsburg, Virginia. The flag is incorrect as the red saltire wasn't added to the Union Jack until 1801 after the USA had achieved independence from Britain (National Register of Historic Places in the USA, 66000925).

This photograph, taken by noted photographer and journalist Frances Benjamin Johnston, shows the chamber of the House of Burgesses in the Capitol Building at Williamsburg, Virginia (Library of Congress).

The Courthouse in Williamsburg. Photograph by D.H. Anderson (New York Public Library).

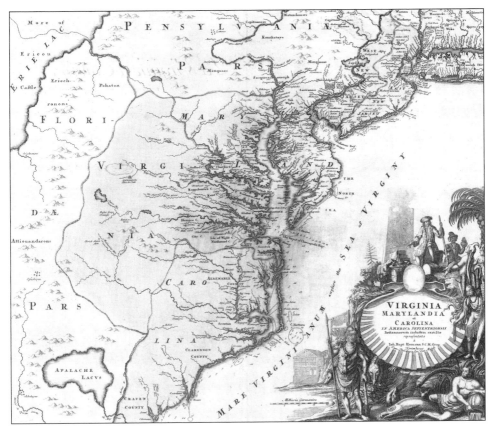

J.B. Homann's map of Virginia circa 1715, covering New York City down the Atlantic coast as far as modern-day Georgia. Homann drew this map in response to Virginia Lieutenant-Governor Alexander Spotswood's plan to settle the interior of Virginia with German immigrants. Though Homann's remarkable representation of Spotswood's plan is extraordinarily up-to-date considering that Fort Christanna was founded in the same year that this map was initially published, the remainder of the map embraces a number of common misconceptions and cartographic inaccuracies common to the region.

The hanging of Stede Bonnet. This engraving was originally published in Johnson's *A General History of Pyrates* (1725).

Colonel Rhett capturing Stede Bonnet. Originally published in 'Colonies and Nation' by Woodrow Wilson in *Harper's Magazine* (1901). Sourced from Howard Pyle and Merle De Vore Johnson (ed.), 'Blueskin, the Pirate', *Howard Pyle's Book of Pirates: Fiction, Fact & Fancy Concerning the Buccaneers & Marooners of the Spanish Main* (1921).

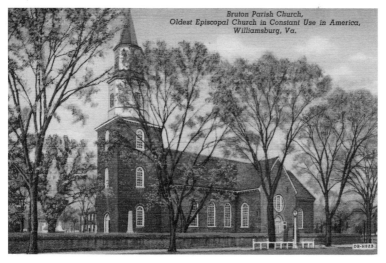

An old postcard image of the Bruton Parish Church.

Chapter 11

Pardon

This Vaine had the impudence to send me word
that he designs to burn my guard ship and visit me very soon ... [159]
Governor Woodes Rogers, 31 October 1718

When Woodes Rogers took up his position as Governor of New Providence (Bahamas today) he was faced with turning a lawless pirate haven into a legal, civilised colony of the British Empire. His appointment had been proposed on 21 November 1717 and the Council of Trade and Plantations approved his Commission a few months afterwards.[160]

Originally founded in 1629, Nassau was an English settlement[161] that was destroyed by the Spanish and then rebuilt as New Providence and the capital renamed Nassau in 1695 to honour the King of England at the time – William III, of the House of Orange-Nassau. As the town became a haven for pirates, most of the activity revolved around the bustling port where merchants and locals mixed with pirates and prostitutes. It was a town filled with taverns that were frequented by cut-throats of all sorts.

New Providence was largely overgrown with woodlands and had some natural resources. The soil was fertile for farming and Rogers knew that industrial growth could take place here. First, though, he had to bring law, order and justice to the island and build fortifications strong enough to repel the Spanish. He considered the local population to be lazy but they were all he had to work with upon his arrival. Disease was rife and the place stank from rotting hides that were lying on the shore in the harbour.[162]

While Spain's influence in the area was diminishing, the threat of war was still an ever-present danger. This part of the Caribbean had old extensive trade routes that were very lucrative. Gold, silver, gems, sugar and cocoa were just some of the goods that filled the holds of merchant ships plying these waters.[163] New Providence was at the heart of these trade routes which had once been the exclusive domain of the Spanish but now were crowded with other European ships as well as the Spanish and, of course, pirates.

On 26 July 1718 Rogers arrived in Nassau on board the *Delicia* commanded by Captain Gale and accompanied by Royal Navy warships, HMS *Rose* and HMS *Milford*. Most of the pirates and inhabitants were cowed and impressed by the small powerful fleet arriving in the harbour. All except one man, who decided to create a special welcome for the new governor.

Notorious pirate Charles Vane, captain of a sloop with twenty guns, had captured a French ship a few days before and brought it into Nassau to be plundered. However, he decided to turn it into a fireship. HMS *Rose* entered the harbour ahead of the other ships and found this burning fireship moving steadily towards them. The crew of the Royal Navy vessel acted quickly, managing to turn their vessel about and heading back out of the harbour, thus avoiding a catastrophe by fire.

Once the danger had passed, the fleet entered the harbour and Vane fled, raising his sails, and hauling up his anchor he sailed away through the eastern passage; a small, narrow channel at the other end of the harbour that led out to the open sea. Firing his guns in defiance, Vane left as quickly as he could and Rogers quickly dispatched vessels to chase after the pirate but they returned with nothing. Vane had at the time around ninety men under his command.[164]

Why is this information so important in the hunt for Blackbeard? Remember that New Providence had been Blackbeard's base of operations. He'd been mentored by the man then considered the king of the pirates – Benjamin Hornigold. That's one reason, but perhaps the most important is that with Rogers' arrival Blackbeard was forced to flee and so he sailed north to get as far away from Rogers as he could and this would bring him ultimately within striking distance of Spotswood.[165]

New Providence had been the pirate kingdom without the kind of civilised law and justice that other colonies and territories enjoyed. The law, if there was any at all, was pirate law. It was only really the arrival of Rogers that offered security and order for the merchants and traders on the island.[166]

Life had been prosperous for the pirates. They'd set up a society of sorts where men could make something of themselves within this pirate community. For example, a pirate captain and his crew would capture a vessel and keep it. One of the crew would display some leadership qualities and rise above the rest and be given a captured prize by a more established captain, such as Hornigold did with Blackbeard. The new captain would fit his ship, pick his crew and set sail. The process would be repeated by the new crew. More vessels would be captured, more captains developed and crews chosen and so it went on. At its height there were around 2,000 pirates operating in the area.[167]

William Moudy was one such pirate. He commanded the *Rising Sun*, a mighty 36-gun ship and had a little fleet comprising a brigantine commanded by Richard Frowd and a sloop with a total combined crew of around 190 men.

His area of operations was around the Bay of Carolina, St Thomas and Antigua. Moudy was known for taking hostages and he would send some of them ashore or onto another vessel to demand a ransom for the release of the remaining hostages and to demand the cargoes of the ships he captured or anchored in the various harbours he attacked. He and his crew had no qualms about abusing their prisoners.[168]

One of the more successful pirates operating in the region was Edward England; an Irishman who some sources claim commanded a 12-gun brigantine with a crew of about ninety, along with another sloop also under his command. Other sources claim he had a crew of 180 and had a ship of twenty-six guns. He was a prolific pirate and had a reputation for beating information out of his victims about where valuable cargo was or where any jewels, money, gold and other treasures might be hidden on board. On one occasion, he threatened to throw a captain overboard, weighted down with a double-headed shot around his neck. Like Hornigold, Blackbeard and Vane, England operated out of New Providence until the new governor, Woodes Rogers arrived, and then he fled to Madagascar where he ended his days penniless.[169]

The task facing Rogers was daunting. London expected him to transform the haven of piracy into a law-abiding prosperous colony. He had to ensure that his reforms were permanent; that there would be no slippage back into the lawless ways of the pirates. The first step was to find out who were the leading and most influential local people – the key merchants, plantation-owners and even those who were trading with the pirates. In short, he needed to know who he could trust of the more prominent local inhabitants. Once he'd confirmed who these people were through interviews and so on, he set up a council that consisted of people who had come with him on the voyage from England and of local merchants and plantation-owners whose dealings with pirates were relatively small. These were Nathaniel Taylor, Richard Thompson, Edward Holmes, Thomas Barnard, Thomas Spencer and Samuel Watkins who were joined on the council by those men who had sailed with Rogers – Robert Beauchamp, William Salter, William Fairfax, William Walker, Wingate Gale and George Hooper. Rogers would later appoint Beauchamp as First Lieutenant and Secretary General making him effectively his deputy. Sadly Salter and Watkins died shortly after they were appointed to the council and they were replaced by Christopher Gale and Thomas Walker. Christopher Gale was a recruit from North Carolina, where he had served for thirteen years as Chief Justice and he assumed the same post on his arrival in Nassau.[170]

Now that he had a new council, Rogers needed to rebuild the defences which were in a poor state. Facing the problem of piracy there was also the threat of war which was never far away:

> If H.M. would please to contribute towards the fortifications necessary
> to be erected in two more places in the harbour of Nassau when I have
> workmen here, the charge would be much less than at any other place in
> the West Indies, and I presume not of less consequence.[171]

Defending the Bahamas was vitally important if it was to become a thriving
prosperous colony. Rogers knew this. Reports of attacks on English shipping
and settlements by the Spanish were coming in. Spanish ships had seized
Thomas Bowling's vessel out of Nassau along with his crew while they were on
a trading voyage. The Spanish took Bowling first to Andros Island to help them
capture English loggers but as this didn't produce results they forced him into
spying for them to gather intelligence on the defences at New Providence. When
the Spanish did finally release Bowling and his crew, they claimed they believed
Bowling and his men were pirates.[172]

Ships arriving in Nassau harbour reported further attacks taking place by
the Spanish. On 19 July 1718, four English sloops were anchored in a lagoon
exploring and plundering some wrecks off the coast of Florida when four
Spanish vessels appeared. The English captains, fearing the approaching vessels
might be pirates, opened fire. In the meantime, the Spanish landed around 130
men on the north side of the lagoon. The fire continued. One Spanish ship
sailed into the mouth of the harbour and began firing its cannon at the English
ships. Neither side gave way and both sides took heavy casualties until an uneasy
truce was negotiated that enabled both sides to work on the wrecks, but the
Spanish broke the truce first by capturing the English and taking them prisoner.
However, during a period of bad weather the English prisoners managed to
escape and reported their experiences to the British authorities.[173] Perhaps more
worrying for Rogers was the arrival of a new Spanish governor in Havana:

> A new Governor was lately arrived at the Havana from Spain, with
> orders to destroy all the English settlements on the Bahama Island: and
> that they had provided for that purpose, one ship of 50 guns and 700
> men, another of 26 guns and 300 men, and three row galleys full of men,
> with instructions in case of surrender, to transport the people and their
> effects to Carolina, Virginia, or some other of the Northern
> Governments, but in case of resistance, to send them to the Havana, for
> Old Spain.[174]

The new governor was interested in taking as many English possessions and
territories as he could. The Spanish took the English sloop *Elizabeth and Mary*
and then on 26 July 1718 they invaded Catt Island where they managed to
capture six women and several children. The men had fled.

We can see that Rogers had a lot to contend with, in addition to putting down piracy. With the rumours of war, the building tension between the Spanish and the English and the re-establishment of law and order and government perhaps Blackbeard felt it was time to leave, that it might be too dangerous to stay, even for him. He likely knew that the seas around the Bahamas would soon be filled with warships from both sides which would make plundering vessels extremely hazardous for a pirate. So he decided to sail north, which for a little while was a lucrative and wise decision.

Governors such as Rogers and Spotswood had limited methods available to them for putting down piracy. One was to send warships to hunt them down but another and certainly more successful was to get the pirates to turn themselves in and begin hunting those pirates who remained at large. Royal Navy warships were scarce and would become even more overstretched as they prepared for war with Spain so the second option was far more preferable – the King's Pardon.

The King – George I – issued a proclamation that effectively pardoned the pirates of their crimes providing they surrendered to the appropriate authorities (the governors) by 5 September 1718. With the words 'every such Pyrate and Pyrates so surrendering him, or themselves, shall have our gracious Pardon', the King had set in motion something that would achieve far more than any pirate-hunter or naval expedition could ever match.[175]

A Royal Pardon meant that in the eyes of the law the pirates were officially forgiven for their actions and they now had the opportunity to wipe the slate clean and start again in a new respectable life. It was hoped that the amount of ex-pirates and pirate-hunters would eventually outnumber the amount of pirates that remained on the wrong side of the law, and so decrease the number of pirates to such a degree that the limited resources available could be better used and directed against those that were left:

> And we do hereby strictly charge and command all our Admirals, Captains and other officers at Sea, and all other Governors and Commanders of any Forts, Castles or other places in our Plantations, and all other Officers Civil and Military, to seize and take such of the Pyrates who shall refuse or neglect to surrender themselves accordingly.[176]

Of course, if some of those pirates who accepted the pardon became pirate-hunters themselves, helping to track down the remaining villains, then so much the better. The plan worked. Many pirates took the pardon and lived by selling the goods they'd plundered while they'd been pirates.[177]

Benjamin Hornigold was one of the pirates who accepted the pardon from Woodes Rogers shortly after the latter's arrival. Because Hornigold was such an influential pirate, many others including Henry Jennings accepted the pardon as well as turning their backs on piracy. While Jennings lived a quiet retirement, Hornigold turned pirate-hunter, and Rogers sent him out to get Charles Vane, the man who had so dramatically escaped from New Providence on the day of the new governor's arrival.

On 1 September 1718, three men from Vane's crew appeared in a boat off the coast of Cuba where they'd arranged to meet their captain. Hearing of this, Rogers realised he had an opportunity to get Charles Vane so he dispatched a vessel, commanded by Captain Whitney, to investigate. He then discovered that Vane had three vessels (two ships and a brigantine) moored at Green Turtle Key near Abacoa. However, with every day passing and Rogers hearing no word he worried that Hornigold might have turned back to piracy which would only add to the new governor's problems. His fears proved to be unfounded, as Hornigold eventually returned with a sloop that had been registered in the Bahamas as a turtle-fisher but had instead been trading with Vane.[178] Vane, however, had eluded him.

What then, does all this have to do with Blackbeard? Did he have any intention of accepting the King's Pardon? We know he couldn't remain in New Providence, so when he sailed north he was likely going to accept the pardon from another governor up the coast of America. However, why he even thought about this is something we will never really know. Some believe it was because he had simply had enough of plundering. Others believe it was because he could see so many pirates turning to the other side of the law that he may have felt that if he didn't, more of the Royal Navy's resources would be directed against him, increasing the chances that a more successful hunt for him would take place and lead to capture. Others believe that he was tired of the life and simply wanted a rest.

Chapter 12

The Beginning of the End

A Royal Pardon could only be issued to a pirate through a colonial governor, and for Blackbeard his choices were extremely limited. Virginia Governor Alexander Spotswood was out of the question because he believed that the pirates were hampering trade along the entire Atlantic coast of America. Giving a pardon to Blackbeard would have been highly improbable. He probably would have had the pirate arrested, tried and executed the moment he set foot in the colony.

In South Carolina, Governor Robert Johnson viewed Blackbeard as Public Enemy Number One since the blockade of Charles Town, so there was no chance of obtaining a pardon from there. Johnson was just as likely to have the pirate arrested and dragged to prison before he had even managed to say the words 'Royal Pardon'.

Down in New Providence it was possible that Rogers might give him a pardon but if the theory that the two men knew each other is correct then Blackbeard could either have played on that knowledge or, if there was animosity there, then he would have no hope of a pardon from Rogers. Then there was the distance. After ridding himself of his flagship and the hundreds of pirates under his command, he was now in the *New Adventure* cruising off the coast of North Carolina, so to get to New Providence before the deadline he would have to head south down into waters where more and more warships were gathering as tensions increased in the run-up to war. There was also the deadline on the pardon – 5 September 1718. If he headed south for the Bahamas he might be able to make it as long as he didn't have to take any detours to avoid Royal Navy warships. If he did he'd never get there in time.

The same was true if he headed for New York. He'd never get there in time, so his only real practical choice was to accept the King's Pardon from Governor Charles Eden of North Carolina, and there are other reasons why he might choose Eden. There has always been mystery and doubt about Eden's complicity with the pirates in many accounts of Blackbeard. Most of these come from Captain Johnson's narrative, on which many others have based their accounts.

The problem is there is no concrete evidence to support the claims of complicity but there is circumstantial evidence. North Carolina was poorer than its neighbours, especially Virginia. It lacked the deep-water access for ports and the natural resources that its wealthier cousin had and it was nowhere near as well-developed, which limited its ability to carry out international trade. Its trade with other North American colonies was also limited to coastal shipping. At the time it was far easier to move goods by sea than it was by land, so the colony lacked the wealth enjoyed by other American colonies and lacked the industrial and agricultural development it needed in order to grow.

The complicity claims are based on Charles Johnson's account, 'Having in the Time cultivated a very good Understanding with Charles Eden.' This understanding is so good that Johnson tells us Blackbeard married Mary Ormond and Eden conducted the ceremony! 'Before he sailed upon his Adventure, he married a young Creature of about sixteen Years of Age, the governor performing the Ceremony.'

However, at the time of writing no marriage certificate had yet surfaced to prove that this marriage ever took place. While many historians point to various examples of Eden's collusion with Blackbeard, most of them cannot really be looked at as concrete, confirmed evidence. Yet, the circumstantial evidence is persuasive.

If Blackbeard was going to accept the offer of amnesty, he had very few alternatives other than Governor Charles Eden, who, for his part, may have been happy to be the one to issue a King's Pardon to a man as infamous as Blackbeard.

If we compare the positions of Governor Eden in North Carolina with Governor Spotswood in Virginia we can draw some interesting conclusions. Virginia had a much larger trading capability and more valuable produce that it could trade with than North Carolina. It had deep-water ports that could accommodate ships from around the world and certainly the large merchant ships from England. Much of North Carolina's trade was coastal and its main export of tobacco was banned from Virginia to ensure it didn't dilute the excellent Virginia tobacco that went across the ocean to England and the rest of Europe. This meant that tobacco from North Carolina had to travel further up and down the coast to trade with other colonies, which meant the coastal vessels carrying tobacco were at sea longer than if they were trading with Virginia, and the longer they were at sea the more vulnerable to attacks by pirates they were. Many of Blackbeard's victims were coastal merchant vessels.

Virginia also had a militia which Spotswood used on occasion to put down insurrection by some of the native tribes on his borders, and he had two warships that were stationed in Virginia to protect its shores and trade routes. On the other hand, North Carolina could only raise a militia to provide a partial defence against attacks from the local native tribes. We have seen in earlier chapters that Spotswood had to intervene in North Carolina to put down an insurrection that the North Carolina militia was unable to do. There were simply not enough men in arms to form a defensive line against land attacks and also defend against and hunt down pirates. Indeed, North Carolina did not have a large enough force to mount offensive operations against well-armed pirates in the way that Virginia did. So when Blackbeard accepted the King's Pardon from Governor Eden the entire colony must have breathed a collective sigh of relief. However, that relief would not last.

While other pirates had taken the King's Pardon as an opportunity to clear all their previous crimes (and escape the gallows) and to start a new life, albeit with the wealth from their piracy, Blackbeard's acceptance was something different.

By the time Blackbeard arrived in North Carolina he'd disposed of his flagship, rid himself of Stede Bonnet and his crew and downsized into the Spanish sloop renamed *New Adventure* and, having accepted the King's Pardon from Governor Eden, settled into a land-based life in Bath Town. His ship remained anchored around the shores of Ocracoke Inlet. He had plenty of treasure because he'd taken it from the flagship and the *Adventure* and transferred it all over to his new vessel, but the question is why was this reduction necessary? He'd been at the height of his power when he'd deliberately grounded his flagship, so what was he up to?

To find the answers we will have to turn to Johnson and other sources as well as speculate to some degree. The first thing we need to look at is his crew. Johnson states: 'Teach goes up to the governor of North Carolina with about twenty of his men.' By implication these men would have been men he could trust; men such as Israel Hands. For him to have pulled off such a large betrayal as he did these men would likely have been involved in some of his plan. Does that make them friends, mates or just men who were devoted to him and would follow him no matter what?

There is another very simple reason why Blackbeard decided to downsize. The cargo/treasure they'd plundered over the course of their voyages must have been considerable, so by drastically cutting the number of men with whom to share it he was ensuring that those remaining with him got a much bigger slice of the pie, as would he. Most pirate ships and pirate crews had their own set of regulations that helped to provide some sort of discipline and ensured that every pirate had an equal share of the loot. The smaller the crew numbers were, the higher the value of each share. Even in the eighteenth century, when many people could not even write their own name, this would have been well understood by everyone; it concerned the one thing that was closest to every pirate's heart – money.

In addition there was also perception. If Blackbeard had presented himself to Eden with more than 300 pirates in tow, the perception would have been as if the pirates were invading which would have spread panic throughout the colony and very likely have caused Eden to send messengers in all directions asking for help. This, of course, would have given away Blackbeard's location and forced him to move on somewhere else. He stood a far greater chance of being received favourably if he only had a small band of followers.

What seems confusing is the number of people Blackbeard had actually selected to take with him. Some historians place the figure at 100, made up of forty white sailors and sixty black men. Others place the size of crew at far smaller; somewhere around thirty, while Captain Johnson states it was forty.

For the sake of clarity we will continue to refer to the sloop that Blackbeard sailed from Topsail Inlet – the Spanish sloop – as the *New Adventure* to avoid confusing it with the vessel of the same name that went aground under the command of Israel Hands. The reality is that Blackbeard renamed this Spanish sloop the *Adventure*. So while Blackbeard and his most trusted men went to see Eden to accept the pardon and then stayed in town, the vessel remained anchored in Ocracoke Inlet. We know from history that, while most pirates accepted this as the end of their pirate lives, for Blackbeard it was to be nothing more than an interlude.

According to Johnson, the first thing that Eden did for Blackbeard that could be construed as collusion was:

> ...To give him a right to the vessel he had taken when he was a-pirating in the great ship called the *Queen Anne's Revenge*, for which purpose a court of vice-admiralty was held at Bath Town. Though Teach had never any commission in his life, and the sloop belonged to the English merchants and was taken in time of peace, she was condemned as a prize taken from the Spaniards by the said Teach. These proceedings show that governors are but men.

In other words, Eden convened a court of vice-admiralty and gave Blackbeard the right to own the sloop now known as the *New Adventure*.

Captain Ellis Brand, commanding HMS *Lyme*, whom we have already looked at, declared that the grounding of *Queen Anne's Revenge* at Topsail Inlet took place on 10 June, and Konstam states it took not more than two weeks to salvage everything from the flagship and the grounded *Adventure* and transfer it all over to the Spanish sloop (*New Adventure*) before Blackbeard made his escape and betrayed his crew. Then there was the voyage to Ocracoke Inlet, some 90 miles north-east by sea which could have been done in a day's sailing around Cape Lookout and then north up through the Outer Banks, and a few weeks where Blackbeard, upon accepting the pardon, would settle into the new life ashore long enough to convince the authorities that he was a changed man, all bringing us to the early part of September 1718 for the end of this interlude.

There are a variety of local stories of how he spent his time during this interlude. If his supposed weakness for women is true then likely he would have frequented bars, taverns and high society such as it was in the colony at the time. He was rich, famous and exciting, and to many of the women who would have captured his attention, the combination of these factors would have been hard to resist.

His supposed marriage to Mary Ormond took place around this time as well. There is a claim that he became interested in Charles Eden's daughter; yet, there is no official record of Eden having a daughter. However, some local legends suggest he had a mansion built for himself, but no such buildings or foundations or remains of such a building have ever been found. Some local stories also state that he took a house just outside of Bath Town on Plum Point. As for Johnson's account of him marrying a girl of 16 and having some of his crew abuse her, that is more than likely Johnson's attempt to spice up the narrative during this interlude in Blackbeard's life. However, as there is no record of such a marriage taking place we can assume that he did take up with a woman who would have been a mistress rather than his wife. Again, local tradition has it that this house where they lived sat on top of a hill above Plum Point and was a good point from which to see Bath Town harbour, as well as being able to see any vessels travelling up the southward approaches to the town via the Old Town Creek. Also, the plantations of Charles Eden and his deputy Tobias Knight on the far side of the creek were easily accessible from Blackbeard's location by rowboat.[179] It is likewise probable that Blackbeard would have spent some of this time mixing with the local high society; introduced to them, no doubt, by his new benefactor, Governor Eden.

While Blackbeard was living the quiet life in Bath Town, back in Virginia his old quartermaster, William Howard arrived in Williamsburg in the company of two negro slaves:

> I gave your Lordships an account that one Capt. Tach a noted pyrate in a ship of 40 guns run ashore in June ... and that he and his crew had surrendered to the Governor of that Province. Since which one Howard, Tach's Quartermaster, came into this Colony, with two negros which he owned to have been piratically taken, the one from a French ship and the other from an English brigantine.[180]

In addition to the pardon, Spotswood had issued a proclamation that all pirates arriving in his colony were to register with the authorities. Once Spotswood heard of Howard's arrival he 'caused them [Howard and the slaves] to be seized pursuant to H.M. Instructions', but Howard did not surrender meekly. Instead he

> commenced a suit against the officer who made the seizure, and his insolence became so intolerable, without applying himself to any lawful

business, that the Justices of the Peace where he resided thought fit to send him on board one of the King's ships as a vagrant seaman.[181]

Blackbeard had betrayed Stede Bonnet who had originally gone to see Governor Eden to obtain a pardon and permission to sail to St Thomas in order to get a privateering commission. Of course, once he returned to Topsail Inlet to tell Blackbeard the coast was clear for getting a pardon from Eden, he found the pirate had betrayed him. Bonnet was left in something of a quandary: to head to St Thomas as a privateer, or to hunt down Blackbeard? History shows that Bonnet returned to piracy in his quest to find Blackbeard and seek his revenge.[182]

Captain Johnson, in his *History*, takes up the story of Bonnet in a separate narrative of the gentleman pirate. He writes that the point at which Bonnet abandoned all hope of becoming a privateer took place while he was preparing to sail to St Thomas when, 'a bumboat, that brought apples and cider to sell to the sloop's men, informed them, that Captain Teach lay at Ocracoke Inlet, with only eighteen or twenty hands'.

With this news, Bonnet immediately set sail for Ocracoke in the hopes of finding Blackbeard but when he arrived there was no sign of his quarry. Indeed, Blackbeard had sailed into Bath Town and Bonnet, who did not know that Blackbeard was only a few miles away, didn't venture any further than the Inlet. Captain Johnson confirms this: 'It happened too late, for he missed him there, and after four days cruise, hearing no farther news of him, they steered their course towards Virginia.'

Whether Bonnet decided to turn to piracy or his crew decided it for him isn't known but turn to piracy they did after being unable to locate Blackbeard. At first their efforts were half-hearted, largely because it seems Bonnet's heart wasn't in it. Captain Johnson describes some of the action:

> Meeting with a pink with a stock of provisions on board, which they happened to be in want of; they took out of her ten or twelve barrels of pork, and about four hundredweight of bread; but because they would not have this set down to the account of piracy, they gave them eight or ten casks of rice and an old cable, in lieu thereof.

We can see that Bonnet is still at sixes and sevens over whether or not he was a bona fide pirate. Such was the state of affairs that Bonnet lost a part of his crew after they'd taken a 60-ton sloop off Cape Henry in July 1718. This sloop carried a large cargo of liquor and molasses, both of which they needed and as Johnson says: 'they bought two hogshead of rum and as many of molasses, which, it seems they had need of, though they had not ready money to purchase them.' Instead, Bonnet sent some men over to the new prize sloop to take command of her and they immediately deserted.

Over the next few days they took four outward-bound ships from Virginia and then later, cruising in the Delaware Bay, they took another vessel out of North Carolina bound for Boston. However, all of this activity was according to Johnson,

> but small game, and seemed as if they designed only to make provision for their sloop after they arrived at St Thomas; for they hitherto had dealt favourably with all those that were so unhappy to fall into their hands.

Suddenly, however, Bonnet changed and decided to become a full-blown pirate. What changed him we shall never know. Perhaps it was his crew threatening mutiny, but whatever it was things changed. Cruising in the Delaware Bay they captured two snows in the mouth of the Delaware River, then the *Francis*, a 50-ton sloop bound for Barbados out of Philadelphia. This time the vessels were plundered and then cast free with no indication of buying or handing the crews anything back. Another 50-ton vessel was captured by the *Revenge* on its way to Barbados and this time Bonnet kept the vessel, sending a skeleton crew across to man it.

A few days later the *Fortune*, a sloop out of Antigua bound for Philadelphia, was captured and completely plundered of her cargo of sugar and mostly rum. Bonnet decided to keep this sloop as well, and as soon as they had secured her cargo and the vessel, the little fleet set sail heading for Cape Fear River where he planned on cleaning and repairing the *Revenge* which was now badly in need of attention. Once there, the two sloops anchored in the river while the *Revenge* was beached inside the river mouth away from prying eyes. Of course what Bonnet didn't know was that by staying in Cape Fear River he was putting himself and his pirate crew in danger of capture. Captain Johnson takes up the story: 'They stayed too long for their safety, for the pirate sloop which they now new named the *Royal James*, proved very leaky, so that they were obliged to remain here almost two months, to refit and repair the vessel.'

During this time they captured a small coastal vessel and used the wood from her hull to replace the damaged and rotten timber on the *Revenge*, now renamed the *Royal James*.

Bonnet had taken the captain and crew of the *Fortune* prisoner and they were now also stranded while the *Royal James* underwent repairs. Later, in his report to the South Carolina authorities Captain Mainwaring, commanding the *Fortune*, stated the pirates had treated him and his crew with some civility and it is partly from him and other witnesses that the facts in the narrative of Stede Bonnet are derived.

So Bonnet remained in the mouth of Cape Fear River, South Carolina, for two months making repairs while not far away, Governor Robert Johnson in

Charles Town had become aware of their presence and was making plans to capture the pirates.

The capture of Bonnet had actually started with a second blockade of Charles Town by Charles Vane. In August 1718 Vane, commanding two vessels, cruised off Charles Town Bar for several days taking as many ships as they could. Still smarting from the blockade by Blackbeard back in June, Governor Johnson was in no mood to just lie down in the face of Vane's blockade. In one day, Vane captured an outbound slave ship and a couple of inbound sloops. The following day he attacked another four vessels and plundered them. Governor Johnson met with the Council of South Carolina and decided to take the fight to the pirates. The colony was in dire financial straits largely because of the disruption of trade caused by piracy, yet they decided to create their own naval squadron to protect them from piracy and to get Vane.

The decision was not a quick one. The politicians argued over the cost and as they did, one of the colony's most prominent citizens offered his help. He was Colonel William Rhett, a British-born rice baron who had first arrived with his wife Sarah in South Carolina in 1698. He was something of a hero as well, having led a small naval force that had stopped a Spanish-Franco raid on Charles Town in 1706.

Rhett offered the use of two of his ships for anti-piracy work. All the Governor had to do was pay for fitting them out, which he readily agreed to and also made Rhett the colony's only official pirate-hunter. Captain Johnson goes into detail about the preparations:

> In a few days two sloops were equipped and manned: the *Henry* with 8 guns and seventy men, commanded by Captain John Masters, and the *Sea Nymph*, with 8 guns and sixty men, commanded by Captain Fayrer Hall, both under the entire direction and command of the aforesaid Colonel Rhett, who, on the 14th September, went on board the *Henry*, and, with the other sloop, sailed from Charles Town to Sullivants Island, to put themselves in order for the cruise.

They were too late to attack Vane, but Rhett knew that Bonnet was still at the mouth of Cape Fear River and he set his little fleet on a course for him.

By 26 September the two South Carolina sloops arrived at Oak Island which lay at the narrow entrance to the river. The whole area was filled with shoals and sand bars and still is today; these change with every winter storm. 'In the evening, the colonel with his small squadron, entered the river, and saw, over a point of land, three sloops at an anchor, which were Major Bonnet and his prizes,' Captain Johnson writes in his narrative of Bonnet.

In the meantime, Bonnet's sentries had discovered the two sloops and as Captain Johnson states the pirates 'manned three canoes, and sent them down to take them, but they quickly found their mistake, and returned to the sloop, with the unwelcome news'.

Both sides now prepared for a dawn attack. Bonnet moved first while it was still dark. As the sun came up the two South Carolina sloops saw the *Royal James* (which had now been put back in the water) moving towards them, gun ports open, guns primed and the gunners ready. However, just as they came within range of musket fire, the pirate ship ran aground, a sitting duck for the two South Carolina sloops. Under way, the *Henry* and the *Sea Nymph* headed straight for the *Royal James* and as they came within pistol-shot range, both sloops ran aground so all three ships were now stuck and could only wait for the tide to come in to float them out of harm's way. The three ships lay on opposite sides of the main channel; the *Royal Fortune* lay on her starboard side, the other two sloops on their port sides. The decks of the two sloops lay exposed to the pirates who were protected by the hull of the *Royal James*, so the South Carolinians would get the worst of the fire, which they did.

A gun battle that lasted for five hours ensued, with both sides peppering each other with pistol and musket fire. Rhett's expedition had lost twelve men dead and eighteen wounded, while there were only nine casualties on the pirate side.[183] Finally, the tide returned and it was the *Henry* that moved first and managed to get into position where it could fire a broadside across the bows of the pirate vessel. The end of the road had arrived for Bonnet and he had no choice but to surrender. He soon found himself in jail awaiting trial and very probably the noose.[184]

Buoyed by this success the hunt for Blackbeard was moved up a notch. The Governor of South Carolina had managed to capture a noted pirate. The Governor of New Providence had managed to successfully turn one of the most well-known pirates, Benjamin Hornigold, into a pirate-hunter. However, in North Carolina perhaps the most notorious pirate of the time was leading the life of Riley with Governor Eden appearing to look the other way when it came to Blackbeard breaking the pardon. It was now down to Spotswood to bag his own pirate. There were a couple on offer: Blackbeard and Charles Vane. The latter had refused a pardon and the former had taken one and then chose to ignore it. Both were fair game but Vane was apparently far away. Blackbeard was nearby.

According to Captain Johnson, Blackbeard was throwing a party while Bonnet was battling Rhett and his men. Indeed, Blackbeard's guest of honour was none other than Charles Vane who had sailed north to the Outer Banks and met up with Blackbeard at Ocracoke Inlet:

> Captain Vane went into an inlet to the northward, where he met with Captain Thatch or Teach, otherwise called Blackbeard, who he saluted

(when he found who he was) with his great guns, loaded with shot (as is the custom among pirates when they meet) which are fired wide, or up into the air. Blackbeard answered the salute in the same manner, and civilities passed for some days, when about the beginning of October, Vane took leave and sailed further to the northward.[185]

There is some doubt if this meeting ever took place, largely because it only appears in Captain Johnson's narrative concerning Vane. If such a meeting between two famous and powerful pirates did take place it would have had serious repercussions throughout the colonies. While Governor Eden in North Carolina seems to have had little influence over Blackbeard, to have a meeting of this magnitude on his doorstep would have been difficult for him to ignore. Vane would have been known and it is possible that Eden had got wind of Vane refusing the pardon offered when Rogers arrived in New Providence. If the two were meeting, he would have to take note and investigate what was transpiring, especially if, as Johnson says, the meeting lasted 'some days'.

Conversely, this meeting could have been the catalyst that gave Governor Spotswood the excuse to act and go after Blackbeard. Here is a man who hated everything that Blackbeard represented and having the beginnings of another pirate haven right on his doorstep, the governor of the colony in which this haven was located unable to do anything about it was just too much. In Virginia, Spotswood was under great political strain and was keenly aware that any attempt to hunt and capture or kill Blackbeard while he was under the protection of another governor in a neighbouring colony could cause his political downfall. He also had a low opinion of Governor Eden and even went as far as to make a claim of '... the insolence of that gang of pyrates and the weakness of that Government to restrain them'.[186]

Spotswood's career was in the balance. One way to salvage it would be to go after a notorious pirate but he would need as much justification as possible to mount an expedition. However, if he failed he could at least salvage something by claiming that, with the gathering of so many pirates in one place, he was both compelled into urgent action before he had completed full preparations and terrified that any lack of action would mean that the pirates, having been expelled from New Providence, could regroup and become stronger off the coast of North Carolina. However, in his papers Spotswood does not mention this meeting between Blackbeard and Vane, so there is some doubt as to whether the meeting took place.

The reason why Spotswood decided to act, according to Johnson, was because of the complaints from traders: '... having at the same time received complaints from divers of the trading people of that Province [North Carolina] of the insolence of that gang of pyrates ...'[187]

Sometime around September 1718 Johnson tells us that Blackbeard broke the conditions of the pardon and returned to piracy. He had sailed towards Bermuda when a chance encounter brought him into the company of two or three English vessels that he plundered in full violation of the restrictions he'd accepted under the King's Pardon.[188]

He then attacked two French vessels sailing together for Martinique. One was laden with sugar and cocoa and the other was apparently empty. His own sloop laden with the cargo from the two English vessels, Blackbeard ordered the crew of the French vessel carrying the goods to transfer to the empty one and then he let them go on their way. The fully-loaded French vessel he kept and now, once again, Blackbeard was in command of a tiny fleet. The two ships headed back for North Carolina, the *New Adventure* leading with the newly-captured French vessel, loaded with sugar and cocoa, in its wake.[189]

Back in North Carolina Blackbeard managed to convince Charles Eden that he had found the vessel adrift, loaded with cargo and without a crew, so he'd claimed it. Such a claim, if true, or believed to be true, was acceptable. Under maritime salvage laws, a vessel found adrift could become the property of the salvager providing no-one came forward with a legal claim to that ship and to protest that it had been taken from them:[190]

> When Teach and his prize arrived, he and four of his crew went to his Excellency and made affidavit that they found the French ship at sea, without a soul on board her; and then a court was called and the ship condemned.

Because an illegal act could not be proved, and Charles Eden could only proceed on the evidence presented before him, or rather the lack of evidence, Blackbeard had to be assumed to be telling the truth. The fact that both Eden and Tobias Knight presided over the court was no coincidence because it was part of their jobs. However, Captain Johnson says 'the governor and the pirates shared the plunder'. It is from this account and others by Johnson and accusations from Spotswood that the charges of complicity by Eden spring. Johnson states, 'the governor had sixty hogshead of sugar for his dividend, and one Mr. Knight, who was his secretary and collector for the province, twenty'. The fact that Eden could claim a portion of the cargo was a fact of maritime and colonial law at the time. The remainder of the cargo was divided between the captain and his crew.

Once the ship had been stripped of its cargo it had to be destroyed, as Johnson states: 'It is possible one or other might come into the river that might be acquainted with her, and so discover the roguery.' Blackbeard then went back to Eden, claiming the ship was leaking and no longer fit for sailing. If it sank in the river it could become a hazard to shipping and removal would be far more difficult and expensive than removing it while it was still afloat. As the colony had no deep-water ports and relied on whatever shipping could navigate its shallow waterways and inlets, the Governor did not want to risk having something blocking a trading lifeline. He issued an order for the vessel to be taken out into the river and burnt.[191] 'She was burnt down to the water's edge, her bottom sunk, and with it their fears of her ever rising in judgement against them.'[192]

Blackbeard had returned to piracy. He was settled at Ocracoke Inlet which was an ideal place to build a pirate base. Perhaps this was Blackbeard's ultimate goal: to build a pirate haven, larger than the one that had been in New Providence before Rogers arrived, one where Blackbeard was king over all the pirates.

Ocracoke had a number of advantages as a pirate base for Blackbeard to have used to build his new pirate empire. There is the close proximity to Bath Town, providing a land base where sloops could be moored. It was ideally placed for attacking the busy and lucrative trade routes running up and down the Atlantic coast. From here, Blackbeard could monitor all the shipping leaving the northern coast of North Carolina, as every vessel would have to pass Ocracoke Island. He could also sail out to intercept shipping from either South Carolina or Virginia. The latter terrified Spotswood. Also, the shallow waters, shoals and tight confines meant that in sloops the pirates could slip in and out unmolested as Royal Navy warships would never be able to navigate through the area.

Exactly where on Ocracoke Island Blackbeard moored his sloop and where he lost his life is debatable. We do know he was moored in shallow water, since this provided him with greater protection from larger vessels. He made a point of anchoring where he knew that Royal Navy warships could not reach him. This is why, once his location had been found, the attacking force used sloops, lightly-armed so they rode high in the water. Local legends put the mooring site at either Springer's Point, Silver Lake or what has become known as Thatch's Hole (or Teach's Hole) on the sound side of the island, shielded from the Atlantic.

Ocracoke Island is around 18 miles long and no more than 2 miles across at its widest point. Covered with sand dunes and low grass and being uninhabited, it was the perfect site for a new pirate base.

It was an ideal spot where Blackbeard and his crew could keep an eye on shipping emerging through the inlets, where he could sail out at almost a moment's notice to plunder ships in the open ocean, and then scurry back into hiding at the first signs of pursuit. The accepting of the pardon was merely a ruse to buy himself more time. He'd decided to ignore it and in Virginia, so had Alexander Spotswood.[193]

Chapter 13

Lies, Damn Lies and Politics

... the several rewards ... for Edward Teach,
commonly known as Captain Teach or Blackbeard,
one hundred pounds, for every other commander
of a pirate ship, sloop or vessel, forty pounds ...[194]
Alexander Spotswood, 24 November 1718

S potswood had problems. As Lieutenant-Governor of the colony of Virginia he was the man in charge and it was going badly.

The colony was originally named in honour of Queen Elizabeth I, the so-called Virgin Queen. It boasted the very first permanent English settlement of all the American colonies that had been established in 1607 – Jamestown.[195] During Spotswood's time in office the colony was a relatively affluent and prosperous place to live, unlike the Carolinas.[196] It had deep-water ports and a thriving transatlantic trade which set it apart from the southern provinces.

Spotswood was determined to ensure the colony remained prosperous and thriving but he faced growing political problems within the Council. Blackbeard was certainly part of these problems – a symbol of the growing anxiety from the plantation-owners over the security of their trade routes. He was facing a serious political crisis that wasn't just to do with security. However, the capture of a villain as notorious as Blackbeard would go a long way to restoring his social and political standing. Of course, if it all went wrong, he would be finished and would simply disappear into political obscurity, never to re-surface.[197]

In late 1718 Spotswood wrote to the Earl of Orkney, the Governor of Virginia, a man who had never set foot in the colony, regarding the unrest in the government. He wished to 'lay open the unreasonable conduct of my adversaries ... what single instance do they give of the many hardships which they say I daily exercise upon the people?' His chief accusers were Commissary James Blair, Philip Ludwell and the Deputy Auditor, Mr Grymes. He goes on to say:

I asked whether Mr Commissary [Blair] whether he would declare himself to be so much your enemy as to vote for paying a solicitor to get your Lordship removed, nevertheless he violently argued, and gave his vote for paying that sum [£300].[198]

However, Spotswood was not a man to allow himself to be bullied. The gauntlet had been thrown down by his accusers and so Spotswood, a military man at heart, was not prepared to turn away from a fight:

Having long struggled with a sett of men here, whose designs for many years have been to engross into their own hands the whole power of the Government and to forme a new plan thereof according to their own caprice, but directly opposite to the interest of their Sovereign, as well as their Mother Country.[199]

In 1716 Spotswood had dissolved the House of Burgesses, determined to show their true colours to the world:

... everyone expected the Burgesses had nothing else to do, but to call for the few bills which remained unfinished at their former Session, and to lay the levy for discharging the publick creditors; but instead of proceeding on any of their bills that lay before them, the first business they went upon was to re-enact a law which H.M. had very lately repealed, that declaring who shall not bear office in this country.[200]

And further:

All petitions brought before them, were immediately referred to the next Assembly, and the Grand Committee converted into a trifling Office of Enquiry into the Capitol furniture; in which they spent five or six days at the expense of £400 to their country to examine into the state of a few old chairs and sconces of less than £50 value. When many of the more sensible members of that House, tired out with these amusements were returned home, as apprehending no business of moment would be brought in, and others believing their presence unnecessary, were gone to take the diversion of a horse race near the town, the Party managers watched that opportunity to bring in an address to the King, with a long roll of Articles; in the first charging me in general with subverting the Constitution of their Government, depriving them of their ancient rights and privileges, and daily exercising hardships on H.M. good subjects, and in the second with divers particulars facts to prove their pretended accusation.[201]

While this political wrangling continued it was evident to Spotswood that the need to capture Blackbeard was growing all the more urgent. Having the pirate in chains would go a long way to stopping some of the mud-slinging. Spotswood was not one to sit around wringing his hands, and the letter he wrote in

December 1718 to the Council of Trade and Plantations set out his defence before a political attack was communicated to England and a vote of no confidence taken. He then goes on to write:

> Without examining the truth of any one of these Articles, the Address containing the general charge was first put to the vote, and carryed by the suffrages of 22 against 14 that opposed it, there being then no less than 15 Members absent, who would have been of the latter opinion. Having thus obtained their Address to pass, the Speaker was immediately commanded to sign three fair copys, which were brought in ready drawn for that purpose; and then they proceeded to consider the Articles, but upon hearing the falsehood of many of them exposed, those who readily voted for the Address upon the faith of their leaders, began to be startled and would not so easily give in to what they found could not be proved, and so put off the debate till next day, when eight of the Articles were entirely struck out as groundless, and the rest which are intended to support their charge so much altered from the first draught, that those who opposed the Address consented to let them pass purely to expose the weakness and malice of my accusers.[202]

He concluded his letter by saying:

> When your Lordships shall be pleased to consider the first of the Burgesses Articles I hope you will be pleased to entertain a more favourable opinion of Virginia than to believe that the persons concerned in that unintelligible composition, are the wisest or most learned of its legislators; but though I ought to quarrel with my accusers' understandings, I may be allowed with justice to expose their dishonesty.[203]

If Spotswood was able to instigate the defeat of Blackbeard it would boost his political career and certainly cement his place in history. It would also convince their Lordships at the Council of Trade and Plantations of his good intent and his ability to control the colony and defend it against any threats, thus ensuring its continued prosperity and security. If the expedition to attack Blackbeard worked, then Spotswood would become safe in his political career and go down in history as the man behind the downfall of one of the most fearsome pirates of the era.

If Blackbeard was either arrested, convicted and hanged for his crimes, or killed during a battle, Spotswood could use this victorious action to dismiss the council members who were a thorn in his side – namely Blair and Ludwell. However, if the expedition to capture or kill the pirate failed and Blackbeard won or got away, Spotswood could use the political unrest as part of his defence, claiming that it failed because his political opponents held him back and prevented him from fully implementing the plan.

Yet, the political wrangling continued:

> Mr Byrd thought fitt soon to withdraw to England, carrying with him all the books of the Revenue (if he ever kept any) and has continued there ever since, ready on all occasions to do me ill offices, instead of returning to clear himself of those frauds which have been discovered in his management during his being Receiver General.[204]

Spotswood's political enemies were quite capable of answering back with their own firepower and wrote to the King:

> We lay before your Majesty several attempts of the Lieutenant Governor towards the subversion to the Constitution of our Government the depriving us of our ancient rights and privileges and many hardships which he dayly exercises upon your Majestys good subjects ... we have desired to appear in behalf of your oppressed subjects of this Colony being deprived of any other means whereby to make known to your Majesty our just grievances by our remote situation, which misfortune we find greatly increased by being governed by a Lieutenant Governor while the Governor in chief resides in Great Britain.[205]

They raised the issue of the Governor's official residence. As we have seen earlier, Spotswood had moved into this grand mansion before it was finished. For him, it was a symbol of the grace, splendour and wealth that Virginia enjoyed over its neighbouring colonies – a symbol of her prosperity:

> That he [Spotswood] hath by a misconstruction of our laws as much as in him lay perverted many of them particularly that for settling ye titles and bounds of lands, which makes it a condition of the patents, that they are to forfeit them if they fail three years of paying their quit rents, which he hath endeavoured to extend to lands granted before that law which have no such condition in their patent or grant. His construction of the law for finishing of the Governor's House, whereby he lavishes away the country's money contrary to the intent of the law.[206]

There were fourteen grievances that accompanied the letter to the King from Spotswood's accusers. Due to the length of time it took for letters to cross the ocean by ship, these accusations would not be seen by London until after the Blackbeard affair was over.

Politics aside, there were other pressing reasons for Spotswood putting together an expedition to go after Blackbeard, and chief among these was the adverse effect the pirate's actions were having on trade. In the early eighteenth century, piracy was so rife that virtually every vessel at one point or another ran the risk of being attacked by pirates and some ships would be attacked several times during the same voyage. Up until 1718 this had been concentrated in the Bahamas and the Caribbean where it didn't really affect Spotswood.

Now it was on his doorstep and that was an entirely different matter. Virginia trade was suffering at the hands of the pirates and that meant that Spotswood's wealth, reputation and political future were at risk. Although he was entitled to a percentage of the trade in Virginia, Spotswood was dedicated to the colony and did not want to lose the power, influence and prestige that it enjoyed on the American continent. The last thing he wanted was for the pirates to 'gather strength in the neighbourhood of so valuable a trade as that of this Colony'.[207]

There was another key factor that made the hunt for Blackbeard urgent – war with Spain was looming. The international political situation was growing worse, and tensions between England and Spain were building which could be seen in the skirmishes between Spanish and English ships. Spotswood knew that the two Royal Navy warships moored on the banks of the James River in Virginia could be called away at any time to be pressed into the war. He also knew that he could lose control of his land-based militia as they could be also subsumed into the war effort:

> I am to acquaint you, that on Tuesday the 16th inst. a great Council was held at St James's, where H.M. signed a Declaration of War against Spain, and ordered that the same should be published the next day by the Heralds at Arms...[208]

However, fortune smiled on Alexander Spotswood when William Howard, Blackbeard's former quartermaster on the *Queen Anne's Revenge* arrived in Williamsburg. The pirates abandoned at Topsail Inlet spread out across the colonies, some heading as far as Pennsylvania and using Virginia as a key route. Many of them were seeking pardons.[209] However, there is no record of Spotswood ever issuing a pardon to a pirate, which meant that pirates ending up in Virginia may not have been as welcome as they might have believed.

So it was the case with William Howard. He was recognised either by someone who had been trading with pirates or by someone who had fallen victim to the pirates and would be quite content to see any of them in jail or, even better, hung.

According to Spotswood, Howard had the sum of £50 and the two slaves we mentioned in earlier chapters. While £50 in today's money isn't much, back in the eighteenth century it amounted to a vast sum. For a sailor to have this amount of money meant that he was likely a pirate and had either stolen the money or sold stolen goods. We can assume that his wealth caught the gaze of the local inhabitants, who notified the authorities. Spotswood had him arrested immediately.[210]

Putting Howard on trial would give Spotswood the opportunity of sending a key message to those pirates who had not yet taken the pardon. Howard was a crucial member of Blackbeard's crew – a quartermaster was always close to the captain, in both confidence and hierarchy. With Howard now under arrest, Spotswood had the chance to gain information about Blackbeard's activities and possible locations. He set to work on building a case.

As in many things with Spotswood this trial was not an easy one, for Howard had managed to obtain legal assistance from one of Virginia's chief lawyers and lodged a complaint against the Justice of the Peace who'd signed his warrant for arrest, and against the captain and lieutenant on the warship on which he was incarcerated. Howard's claim for damages amounted to £500. As far as Spotswood was concerned this was 'extraordinary behaviour' for a pirate. The governor was furious.

Offenders, whether they were pirates or robbers or whatever, were usually considered guilty before they went to trial where they had the opportunity to prove their innocence, and the audacity of such a criminal trying to sue for damages was staggering to Spotswood. Within the government he could find few to uphold his view, which may have been down to the fact that so many key people were part of the campaign against him.[211]

He had to proceed with a quick trial or let the man go free, which would have been a disaster for his political career. Indeed, he would have had to pay the damages from public funds which would have added to his downfall. He encountered a great deal of opposition from within the Council itself, as he expressed in his letter of defence to the Council of Trade and Plantations when he claimed to be alone in the fight to rid the region of piracy:

> ... but found a strong opposition from some of the Council against trying him [Howard] ... Besides the favour shown to Tache's Quarter Master in advising him to sue for his liberty and for his piratical effects; some of the same gang [Blackbeard's abandoned pirate crew] having passed through this countrey in their way to Pensilvania, and contrary to my Proclamation assembling in great numbers with their arms, and endeavouring to debauch some sailors out of the merchant ships to join them, the Officers of the Government could find none to assist in the disarming and suppressing that gang.[212]

The trial of Howard and the ultimate capture or death of Blackbeard were urgent and essential. If Blackbeard managed to build a pirate haven at Ocracoke it would be a catastrophe for Virginia. Trade would drop dramatically, as would their prosperity. The Council was ranged against Spotswood. Something had to be done. If he could bring down Blackbeard it would show that regardless of the pirate's fearsome reputation and strength, he was a man and so could die like a man.

During his trial Howard was questioned about his piratical actions as well as those of Blackbeard. Through this and other snippets of intelligence an accurate picture began to emerge:

> That Tach with divers of his crew kept together in North Carolina went out at pleasure committing robberys on this coast and had lately brought in a ship laden with sugar and cocoa, which they pretended they found as a wreck at sea without men or papers, that they had landed the cargo at a remote inlet in that Province and set the ship on fire to prevent discovery to whom she belonged.[213]

The case against William Howard shows that Spotswood had most of the information he needed to convict the former quartermaster. He would have had depositions from captains and crew of ships plundered by the pirate that would have provided the glue to convict Howard.

Howard was formally accused of being involved in the theft of cargoes from twelve vessels and other acts. Some of these attacks took place before 5 January 1718 and could be wiped off the slate under the conditions of the King's Pardon, but others took place after this date which meant that Howard and Blackbeard were ineligible for the pardon. This meant that the pardon given to Blackbeard by Governor Eden was void. The trial was brief and for Spotswood was politically vital. Howard was found guilty and convicted of piracy. He was sentenced to be hung.

Spotswood now set his sights on Blackbeard.

Chapter 14

Battle Plan

We must plan for freedom, and not only for security,
if for no other reason than that only freedom
can make security secure.
The Open Society and its Enemies, Sir Karl Popper

S potswood was taking an enormous risk. Given the level of political unrest
he was facing, the hunt and capture, or death, of Blackbeard was both
urgent and dangerous; largely because he was overstepping the mark,
something he'd done before and been successful, so why not again?

Blackbeard was in North Carolina and as such was protected by the laws of
the colony and by Governor Eden. Even today, American state police forces
have trouble chasing felons across state lines because they have no jurisdiction
beyond their own state. This was even more pronounced in colonial days where
each of the colonies was virtually an entity unto itself. At the time, each governor
reported directly to the Council of Trade and Plantations in England. Any
armed incursion into one colony by another was seen as an invasion unless the
colony being invaded had asked for assistance. If any attack against Blackbeard
actually worked, then Spotswood would go down in history as the man who
defeated the notorious pirate, but if it failed, that didn't bear thinking about.

In his proclamation authorising the destruction of pirates who threatened
his colony, he refers to boundaries for such an action, writing:

> It is amongst other things enacted, that all and every person or persons,
> who, from and after the fourteenth day of November, in the Year of Our
> Lord One Thousand Seven Hundred and Eighteen, and before the
> fourteenth day of November, which shall be in the Year of Our Lord
> One Thousand Seven Hundred and Nineteen, shall take any pyrate or
> pyrates, on the sea or land, or in case of resistance, shall kill any such
> pyrate or pyrates, between the degrees of thirty four and thirty nine
> Northern latitude ...[214]

The latitudes refer to the coasts of Virginia and North Carolina, and while

Spotswood had every right to specify the coast of his own colony, he had no right to include the coast of a neighbouring colony. There is no record of Spotswood ever having contacted Governor Eden for permission to send an armed expedition into his colony.[215]

To ensure everyone reading the proclamation understood exactly what he was saying, Spotswood spelt it out in even plainer language: '... and within one hundred leagues of ... Virginia, or within the Provinces of Virginia, or North Carolina ...'[216]

Interestingly, this proclamation was issued two days after the battle that took the pirate's life. It's likely that Spotswood would have heard of the outcome through messengers dispatched after the fighting was over and so felt safe enough to issue the proclamation. By doing this he was taking responsibility for the successful operation himself: making the expedition official on the one hand, and telling his critics on the other that he had given permission.

Of course, he could have played it safe and not issued the proclamation at all, or at least issued it but not provided latitude references or mentioned the provinces by name. That way he could have turned to his critics and said he had merely authorised the hunt for the pirate but not for the hunt to take place in the territorial waters of another colony, but Spotswood was not a man to play it safe.

At the time there were just over 100 vessels in service with the Royal Navy and Spotswood was lucky enough to have direct access to two of them, while both South and North Carolina had none they could call on. Despite the scourge of piracy affecting the whole of the Atlantic seaboard, the entire coast from the Caribbean to New England was patrolled by just nine warships; less than 10 per cent of the Royal Navy's entire strength.

Spotswood summoned Captains Brand and Gordon to his residence just outside Williamsburg; the hammering and pounding by the workmen coming from somewhere deep inside the mansion reverberated through the house. Over port they listened as Spotswood laid out the plan for the expedition to get Blackbeard. Remember Brand commanded HMS *Lyme* and Gordon commanded HMS *Pearl*. Since their dispatch to Virginia, neither had seen much action. That was about to change.

Spotswood was operating on the very fringes of his authority. As we have seen, he had authority over military affairs within his colony but he had none over the actions of the Royal Navy warships or their crews. The two captains could easily have listened to his plan, thanked him for the port and said no to his proposal and there would be nothing Spotswood could have done. However, their role was to protect the valuable Virginian trade routes from anyone who threatened them, especially pirates. While they were largely there in a defensive role, both men knew the expedition fitted the requirements of their role in the colony and that it would send a resolute message to other pirates operating in the area. They didn't hesitate; they said yes.

Since Eden didn't seem to be taking a firm stance against the pirate, and according to Spotswood was probably colluding with him, Spotswood sent his spies into the neighbouring colony to gather information. Blackbeard made no secret of where he was living and with the help of Governor Eden he was very likely mixing with high society between his voyages. His considerable wealth, which the King's Pardon had allowed him to retain, would have made his movements very difficult to conceal, and everywhere the pirate captain went, Spotswood's spies would report back to their Governor. Unlike today when information is immediate, it would have taken days for information to get back to Spotswood, either carried by a rider on horseback, a stage coach or a coastal vessel. Nevertheless, the information coming in enabled Spotswood and the two captains to work out Blackbeard's most likely location at any given time. The choices were his residence near Bath Town and Ocracoke Island, where his sloop was moored.

The three men plotting the pirate's downfall decided upon a double-pronged assault. Normally, this classic military manoeuvre involves either attacking a single target from two different directions or attacking two targets simultaneously. The effect of such a move is to divide the enemy's defences and cut off routes of retreat and re-supply in a sustained battle. However, this was not to be a sustained battle; it was to be a fast hard-hitting approach that relied on the element of surprise. The three men chose the strategy of attacking two different targets simultaneously.

On their side, Spotswood and the captains had the resources and manpower advantage. Captain Johnson claims in his narrative that Blackbeard had forty men at his disposal but some reports indicate the number was far fewer than that. Remember when Johnson stated that he went to Eden with around twenty men and there is no mention of the remaining twenty back at the ship? Perhaps that's all the manpower Blackbeard had. Either way, his men would be no match for the well-trained Royal Navy crews, and the military assault had the advantage of surprise, or at least it should, if nothing went wrong.[217]

Yet something nearly did go wrong. Somehow, Tobias Knight in North Carolina learned that something was being planned. He had already been in receipt of several hogsheads of sugar from the pirate, which were increasingly looking like stolen goods. He had been involved in the hearing that awarded Blackbeard salvage rights to the vessel he found apparently abandoned. Knight sent a guarded note to Blackbeard which seemed to warn him of the coming battle when he wrote, 'I would have you make the best of your way up as soon as possible your affairs will let you.' If later the finger of collusion with Blackbeard was being pointed at Charles Eden, perhaps it was being pointed at the wrong man. Knight signed his letter to the pirate saying that he was Blackbeard's 'real and true friend'. If he knew any details of the scheme, he did not put those in the letter; perhaps he was trying to warn his friend something was about to take place while having an eye for his own reputation and any repercussions afterwards, in short, to save his own skin?[218]

The vague note didn't help Blackbeard who, it seems, ignored this warning. Instead of sailing his sloop out into the relative safety of the ocean, he remained where he was, thinking perhaps that he was safe in his hiding-place and protected by the governor and the King's Pardon. This lack of action was a fatal mistake.

However, there may be another reason for his lack of action. When Blackbeard blockaded Charles Town and wanted only a supply of medicine, it pointed to the possibility that his crew may have been ill and that he too, may have been unwell. If he knew he was fatally ill and wanted to go down fighting rather than hiding and wasting away, perhaps his lack of action now at Ocracoke in avoiding a battle would give him the opportunity to die a glorious death in battle rather than die slowly through disease. Win or lose, victory or savage but memorable death, he would win.

Back in Virginia, Spotswood set events in motion, even though he didn't have the full backing from his Council. He was placing a great deal of trust in the abilities of others to carry out the task; an extremely risky thing to do for such an endeavour. If anything had gone wrong, he would be finished, but then these men he was working with were the Royal Navy and they were the best, weren't they?

There would be two attacks. The first was to be a land attack with Captain Brand leading around 200 men across the border between Virginia and North Carolina, near Windsor, heading for Bath Town on the Pamlico River to search for the pirate. Once across the border, his force was to march south, through Plymouth, towards Bath Town, initially avoiding Albermarle where Governor Eden's residence was.

If Spotswood was on shaky legal ground with an attack against a pirate in the coastal waters of another colony, he was certainly on no legal ground whatsoever in sending an armed force across the border into North Carolina. Blackbeard had accepted the King's Pardon, and so was a law-abiding citizen of North Carolina in the official eyes of the law because there was no evidence to prove the contrary. Spotswood knew exactly where the limits of his jurisdiction were, he just chose to ignore them. From the moment the forces crossed the border, stealth and speed in equal measure were essential.[219]

The second attack would be by sea where a small force would sail to Ocracoke Island and attack Blackbeard's sloop *New Adventure* in the hope that the pirate might be aboard her. Provided the sloop did not sail out to sea, Spotswood knew that this was where it would be found. His information told him that he stood a good chance of catching the pirate at one of the two locations. If the alarm was raised and the pirates on the island base headed to Bath to get away from the sea force, they would run right into Captain Brand's army, while if any of the pirates based in Bath headed for the sloop they would run into the force coming in from the sea who would have blocked anyone trying to escape along the river.

As far as the sea assault was concerned, the shallow waters around Ocracoke Island, filled with submerged and partly submerged sand bars, made it almost impossible for large warships to navigate. Before they could get near to Blackbeard's sloops they would have been marooned on any of the sandbanks and shoals lying just under the surface of the water. The only way the sea assault would work would be if they attacked using smaller vessels such as sloops. The Royal Navy had no sloops in the area. Of course, if Spotswood was following the rules to the letter he should have contacted the Admiralty to seek permission for the assault to take place, but he was not a man to let rules stand in the way of results. An answer would take far too long.

Spotswood, Brand and Gordon decided that two sloops would be needed for the sea attack. Spotswood would hire the sloops and the captains would provide the crews from their own ships. Shortly after the meeting Spotswood hired the two vessels and fitted them out from his own finances, which gives us a good indication of the state of his determination and his wealth at the time. Both sloops arrived in Hampton (what was then called Kecoughtan) on 17 November 1718, just four days after the meeting. In his letter to the Council of Trade and Plantations Spotswood wrote:

> Having gained sufficient intelligence of the strength of Tache's crew, and sent for pylots from Carolina, I communicated to the Captains of H.M. ships of war on this station the project I had formed to extirpate this nest of pyrates. It was found impracticable for the men of war to go into the shallow and difficult channels of that country, and the Captains were unwilling to be at the charge of hyring sloops which they had no orders to do, and must therefore have paid out of their own pockets, but as they readily consented to furnish men, I undertook the other part of supplying at my own charge sloops and pilots.[220]

In those days it was not uncommon for governors, Royal Navy crews, privateers or anyone else who captured pirates to claim a percentage of their treasure. Indeed, it would have been one of the motivations for mounting the expedition. As this was common practice, Spotswood offered various sums to the crews that did the fighting as a reward for a successful mission; this would come out of the public finances of Virginia:

... receive out of the public money, in the hands of the Treasurer of this Colony, the several rewards following that is to say, for Edward Teach, commonly called Captain Teach or Blackbeard one hundred pounds; ... for any lieutenant, master or quartermaster, boatswain or carpenter, twenty pounds; every other inferior officer, fifteen pounds and for every private man taken aboard such ship, sloop or vessel, ten pounds...[221]

Spotswood must have decided the amounts before the expedition departed on its historic mission, but he had not yet consulted his Council. There were very few members he could trust and the fewer people who knew about the expedition, the less chance there was for a leak to find its way to Blackbeard, but clearly there was one as Tobias Knight knew that something was in the wind. Every day Spotswood's political standing was growing more tenuous and in the case of the rewards, he'd made the offer before he had permission to do so.

Command of the naval expedition was given to the First Lieutenant of HMS *Pearl*, Lieutenant Robert Maynard. He took command of the *Jane*, the larger of the two sloops and command of the other vessel, the *Ranger*, was given to Midshipman Hyde. In his narrative, Captain Johnson describes Maynard as 'an experienced officer and a gentleman of great bravery and resolution'.

Time was fast approaching for the mission to begin. The crews on both sloops worked quickly, loading an assortment of ammunition, muskets, pistols, cutlasses and naval stores. No cannon were loaded. These men knew that Blackbeard had at least eight big guns on his vessel, giving him a distinct advantage in a battle as he could fire first and at a longer range.

However, by having no heavy guns the two sloops would have been lighter and faster. This was what Maynard and his crews were relying on – speed and manoeuvrability. Without the cannon and the ammunition for them the sloops would sit higher in the water which meant there was less chance of them being grounded on a shoal or sand bar. Then they really would be sitting targets for the pirate's cannons. If Blackbeard had received warning that the Royal Navy was on its way to destroy him and had his crews ready and his guns primed and ready to fire there would be no contest, the entire expedition could turn out to be a disaster. *Jane* and *Ranger* would have been blasted out of the water before either could sail anywhere within range for the crews to fire their muskets.

While Maynard and his men were preparing the two sloops the land forces had already started marching. Once they'd crossed the border between Virginia and North Carolina the force led by Captain Brand was in violation of the law. The crossing of the border was, legally, an armed invasion and the planned capture of pirates and their possessions were technically abduction and armed robbery.

Several influential people from North Carolina aided the land force as they crossed the border. Edward Moseley, the Surveyor General and Colonial Treasurer was one of them. He was against Governor Eden's policies and planned to ride with Brand's force right into Bath Town.

Six days after leaving their base in Virginia, Brand's army was within 3 miles of Bath Town. He sent an advance scout in the form of Colonel Moore, another resident of North Carolina, to establish whether Blackbeard was in the town. He was not.[222]

However, Israel Hands was, along with about twenty-four other pirates from Blackbeard's crew. At this time, Hands was still Blackbeard's first mate and had been captain of the sloop *Adventure* before it was grounded in Topsail Inlet. After Blackbeard had shot him in the knee in an unprovoked outburst the wound prevented him from running. Virtually a cripple, he was unable to escape and all he could do was put up his hands in surrender.[223]

Brand then moved on to Governor Eden's residence while the bulk of his force searched the town for pirates. To Eden's disgust, his house was ransacked by Brand's troops searching for evidence that would link him and his colleague, Tobias Knight, with Blackbeard. Although they located the sixty hogsheads of sugar in Eden's barn and the twenty in Knight's possession, they could not find any definite evidence that could connect either of these officials to the pirate. Perhaps the sea assault would meet with more success.

Chapter 15

Showdown

They were so closely and warmly engaged, the lieutenant
and twelve men against Blackbeard and fourteen, till
the sea was tinctured with blood round the vessel. Blackbeard
received a shot in his body ... yet he stood his ground, and
fought with great fury till he received five-and-twenty wounds
and five of them by shot. At length, as he was cocking another
pistol, having fired several before, he fell down dead.[224]

Captain Charles Johnson

It was 21 November 1718. Night was falling. Far away the land force was still marching towards Bath Town. On the far side of the island, Lieutenant Maynard quietly ordered the anchor to be slowly lowered into the water.

In the darkness, a few men rowed silently away from the *Jane* heading for the shore. They disappeared into the night. They were his eyes and ears.

He knew the morning tide would be favourable for him to launch his attack. He whispered his orders that went from man to man – no noise, no lights, and no fires. If a sound or light alerted the pirates to their presence the mission would be over. Through signals, Maynard ordered the *Ranger* to stop any vessels traversing the inlet and entering the river, ensuring that no word of their presence would reach Blackbeard. But stopping ships also meant he might be able to glean last minute information on where the pirate was lurking and clues on the strength of his defences.

On the far side of the inlet, the sloop *New Adventure* sat moored in its hideaway. The noise of drink-fuelled laughter drifted across the water. In his cabin, Blackbeard was drinking with Samuel Odell, captain of the trading sloop that had brought the letter by Tobias Knight warning Blackbeard of an impending attack. That sloop had been anchored nearby since 17 November. On board the *New Adventure* was a skeleton crew of no more than twenty-five men. The rest of the crew were in Bath Town with Israel Hands.[225]

So the night drifted by. The pirates revelled in their supposed safety, unaware of the danger they were in. No pirate lookouts had been posted by Blackbeard, which meant that come the dawn they would not have been as ready for battle as they should have been. The sailors in the sloops *Jane* and *Ranger* waited for sunrise which seemed to take an eternity to arrive.

Finally, the first light of dawn began to push away the darkness of night and Maynard quickly issued a small cold breakfast to his crews. The tides were higher and the order was quickly passed to move out. Yet, even without cannons weighing them down, Maynard was still unconvinced that he would not become beached on a sand bar just below the surface of the water, despite the fact that he had a local pilot, Master William Butler aboard.[226] In the tides, some of the sand underneath may shift from one day to the next. If he suddenly ran aground, Blackbeard's cannon could blast him to shreds. He sent a small tender, a longboat with four oars, ahead to sound out the perfect route and judge the depths.

Aboard the two sloops a total of more than fifty-seven men waited for the coming battle. Thirty-three men had been chosen from the *Pearl* and the rest were taken from the *Lyme* to crew the two sloops. Each of the two sloops had a pilot familiar with the waters in Pamlico Sound and around Ocracoke Island.

As they waited, many of the Royal Navy crews cleaned their weapons, checked their powder, and said a last prayer. While they had no cannon they were loaded down with the weaponry they would need: cutlasses, daggers, pistols, muskets, grenades, pikes and boarding axes, along with various amounts of ammunition.

> Moderate gales & fair Weather, this day I rec'd from Captain Gordon an Order to Command 60 men out of his Majesties Ships *Pearl* & *Lyme*, on board two small Sloops, in Order to destroy Some pyrates, who resided in N. Carolina, This day Weigh'd and Sail'd hence with ye Sloops under my Command, having on board Proviso of all species with Arms & Ammunition Suitable for ye occasion.[227]

If they won, it would see the end of the most feared and notorious pirate in the region. If they lost, that pirate's fame and reputation would be such that no-one, not even the Royal Navy, would dare come near him. If they lost, nothing could stop him. They had to succeed. The reputation and political life of a colonial governor were resting on their actions, as was the reputation of the Royal Navy in its ability to defeat the scourge of piracy. The future years of trading throughout the colonies also rested on their shoulders, for if Blackbeard was not defeated, the pirates would flock here in droves.

The sloops followed the tender around the island. There was very little wind, the sky was overcast and grey, the water smooth and the crews resorted to using their oars to get them into position to attack. Quietly, the Royal Navy men rowed their two sloops following the little tender ahead of them. The stern of the *New Adventure* slowly came into view as the men rowed and inch by inch, moment by moment, more of it could be seen.

At the south-western tip of the island the *New Adventure* was moored, her bows facing the oncoming force. As the approaching tender came into view the alarm on the pirate sloop was raised as one man rushed below decks to tell Blackbeard. Moments later Blackbeard emerged from his cabin and climbed up to the main deck just as the *Ranger* and *Jane* cleared the shelter of the island. He ordered his master gunner, Philip Morton, to fire on the longboat, sending a shot across the tender's bow. The tender quickly turned away, coming in behind one of the sloops for protection.

There is some confusion as to the order of events immediately following this. Johnson tells us that Maynard hoisted the King's colours, which was standard maritime procedure but it is more likely that Maynard held off raising his colours. Pirates often revealed their identity to their prey at the last possible moment when escape was impossible and it seems plausible that Maynard might have done the same. He needed to get his sloops within 100 yards of the *New Adventure* so they would be within musket range, and giving himself away too early would have meant sure death from Blackbeard's guns. For Maynard to show his hand at this point would have been foolish. So he waited.

Instead of raising his anchor, Blackbeard cut his cable, clearly aware that there was some doubt about who the two sloops were. The pirates then quickly hoisted their sails as the sloop began to drift with the tide running parallel to the shore. Blackbeard could have escaped by sailing north into Pamlico Sound and then out to sea; instead he chose to turn and fight. He ordered the ship to be turned so that her starboard guns would come to bear on the approaching sloops.

On Maynard's port side was the *Ranger*, and the two sloops headed in a line abreast formation towards the pirates. When they were within 500 yards, they were definitely within range of the pirate cannon and completely at Blackbeard's mercy. Once he fired a broadside using grapeshot it would cut the Royal Navy men to pieces. However, Maynard had modified the sloops by ensuring extra ladders had been fitted and hatch covers taken away, allowing the crew to quickly come up on deck and join in on any hand-to-hand fighting. Now, he ordered the bulk of his crew below decks to give them some protection from the broadside that would inevitably come.

As they drew closer Maynard finally raised the King's Colours so Blackbeard knew who he was dealing with.

Captain Johnson tells us that Maynard kept up a barrage of small-arms fire at the pirates. They kept up a running fight, the gap between them getting smaller and smaller. Suddenly, 'Teach's sloop ran aground.' He'd run into a sand bar and beached. Now, unable to move, Blackbeard became the sitting target. Yet, there is some discrepancy about who really beached: whether it was Blackbeard's sloop or Maynard's, or if they both beached. It is more than likely that they both beached at some point during the engagement. We will assume that Blackbeard went aground first and Maynard, seeing the danger of also running aground, barked out orders to the remaining men above decks to throw all the ballast and water casks overboard to lighten the load and lift the vessel higher in the water.

At roughly this point, Captain Johnson's narrative along with other sources includes a heated verbal exchange between Blackbeard and Maynard, which starts with Blackbeard's challenge for the identity of his assailant. There are different versions of this exchange, depending on which source you read. For example, Maynard reported the exchange as follows: 'At our first salutation he [Blackbeard] drank Damnation to me and my Men, who he stil'd Cowardly Puppies, saying, He would neither give nor take Quarter.'

Captain Johnson's version of the exchange, far more verbose, is below:

> Damn you for villains, who are you? And whence came you? The Lieutenant made him Answer, You may see by our Colours we are no Pyrates. Blackbeard bid him send his Boat on board, that he might see who he was; but Mr Maynard replied this; I cannot spare my Boat, but I will come aboard of you as soon as I can, with my Sloop. Upon this, Blackbeard took a Glass of Liquour, and drank to him with these Words: Damnation seize my Soul if I give you Quarters, or take any from you. In Answer to which, Mr Maynard told him that he expected no Quarter from him, nor should he give him any.

Johnson claims that the two vessels were half a gunshot away when the verbal exchange took place, which would be less than 100 yards away, probably closer.

The record of this verbal exchange can be found in Johnson's narrative, from the account of the battle in the *Boston News Letter* which refers to the conversation but not in as much detail, as well as from Maynard's report of the action. Remembering that Johnson's account was written some years after Blackbeard's death, he may have used the report from the *Boston News Letter* and embellished it for his readers; he may also have used Maynard's report if he had access to it. However, Alexander Spotswood also mentioned this in his letter of 22 December 1718 to the Council of Trade and Plantations and the account published in the news letter may not have reached him by then. Indeed, he may have received his information from Maynard:

As soon as he perceived the King's men intended to board him, he took up a bowl of liquor and calling out to the Officers of the other sloops, drank Damnation to anyone that should give or ask quarter ...'[228]

According to Captain Johnson, Blackbeard managed to get his sloop floating again 'as Maynard's sloops were rowing towards him'. Presumably, Blackbeard had done what Maynard did and ordered everything not immediately essential to the battle be thrown overboard. There is also the possibility that the tide had lifted the sloop from the sand bar.

As the two sloops neared each other now side-on, Blackbeard fired a broadside 'with all Manner of small shot'. According to the *Boston News Letter* Blackbeard had ten guns, four on either side, and a lighter swivel gun in the bow with one possibly in the stern. The account continues: 'At that point Blackbeard opened fire. Teach begun and fired some small Guns, loaded with Swan shot, spick Nails, and pieces of old Iron, in upon Maynard, which killed six of his Men and wounded ten.'[229]

Most of the time, a cannon will fire a single ball that might punch a hole in the side of a vessel and kill a few people as it passed through a lower deck, or if the gunner is really lucky, it might bring down a mast. However, from the descriptions and the after-effects, we know that something different was used. Sometimes a gunner would load into the cannon what at the time was called a swan-shot. This was a particularly nasty type of ammunition and was designed for causing maximum death and injury to people rather than damage to the structure of vessels. It consisted mainly of jagged strips of old iron and clusters of nails.

Blasts of these shots from the cannons sprayed slivers of metal across the attacking sloops, spreading the carnage over a wider area than would have been achieved by balls alone. This cascade of sharp strips of metal ripped through the heads and upper bodies of the attackers. The *Boston News Letter* counts six men dead and a further ten wounded, while Captain Johnson's narrative counts the casualties as twenty killed and wounded on Maynard's sloop and nine on the *Ranger*. This number includes Mister Hyde, the commander and the next two men in the chain of command, which meant the *Ranger* now had no-one at her helm and she was drifting away from the fight. One more broadside from the pirates would finish the expedition completely.

Captain Johnson states it was at this point that Maynard sent the rest of the men below decks to join the ones already waiting: 'The lieutenant, finding his own ship had way, and would soon be on board of Teach, he ordered all his men down, for fear of another broadside.' The *Boston News Letter* account states that Maynard 'ordered all the rest of his Men to go down in the Hold: himself, Abraham Demelt of New York and a third at the Helm stayed above deck'.

The broadside had effectively cut Maynard's force by between 30 and 50 per cent. The deck of the *Jane* was littered with bodies and the wounded that were unable to move. Blood flowed over the deck, making it slippery and sticky to walk on.

Despite the losses, this broadside and the after-effects may have been an advantage for Maynard. We've seen that he ordered the rest of his men still intact below decks, leaving only himself and two others above decks with the dead and the wounded. Captain Johnson tells us that this was to prevent further casualties, and perhaps there may have been an element of that but it is also possible that this was part of Maynard's plan to lure Blackbeard onto his vessel and then bring up the rest of the men from below to the fight.

The battle was entering its final phase.

Captain Johnson states that Blackbeard's sloop 'fell broadside to the shore', which could mean that she had run aground. This could have been down to navigational error, or musket fire from Maynard's vessel could have cut the *New Adventure*'s jib sheet. It could even have been the result of the recoil from the firing of the cannon that pushed the sloop onto the sand bar, as some sources claim.

Johnson also implies that it was Maynard who, even after the devastating broadside, continued to row towards Blackbeard's vessel. This is the opposite of what Konstam tells us in his book. He states that Blackbeard steered his vessel towards Maynard's ship, presumably to finish her off. This was his chance to be victorious. Whether he had seen the men that were left standing after the broadside go below deck is debatable. He may have and considered them walking wounded. At that range there would have been smoke from the cannon fire and from the musket fire from his crews. Either way, the ships ended up with their sides touching.

At this point in the battle, Captain Johnson states that Blackbeard's men tossed hand grenades (grenadoes) across onto the *Jane*. Modern grenades contain explosives and strips of metal with the casing designed to split into tiny fragments on explosion, and these older versions were much the same. The naval grenades were usually hollowed-out iron balls, each with a hole bored through the casing with gunpowder inside. A fuse soaked in saltpetre and usually made of cord was pushed through the hole and the fuse was then lit by a match. Others were made of bottles and filled with a combination of pellets, pieces of lead and gunpowder. As in the naval version, the fuse was pushed into the gunpowder and when lit the holder had a few seconds to throw the weapon before it exploded, sending the contents, including shards of glass, flying in all directions. The effect would be devastating enough, but on the deck of a boat filled with people the result would have been horrendous. Had Maynard not ordered the bulk of the crew below, the grenades would have ended the mission then and there because Maynard would have lost so many men that he couldn't have continued.

Blackbeard could clearly see the deck littered with bodies of the dead and wounded with only Maynard, Demelt and Butler left standing. One by one the grenades exploded, creating a thick cloud of black smoke that hung over the deck. Luckily none of the grenades fell through the open hatches into the midst of the waiting men below. If they had it would have been carnage.

At this point we must make an assumption. We know that before the broadside, Maynard had ordered the bulk of his crew below decks to be ready to rush up and attack the pirates when they boarded the *Jane*. This is in virtually every account of Blackbeard. It also must have been done when the *Jane* was far enough away for Blackbeard to see it. We also know that just after the broadside, Maynard ordered those men still fit below decks as well, according to the account in the *Boston News Letter*. We have to assume that Blackbeard didn't see this as the smoke from the cannon fire might have been obscuring his vision, or he saw it and felt it didn't matter because there were so many Royal Navy crew either dead or wounded on the *Jane* that he didn't think the remaining few would pose a problem.

With the smoke from the grenades lying thickly over the deck of the *Jane* (and possibly even the *New Adventure* as the ships were side by side), Johnson tells us that 'Blackbeard seeing there were few or no hands aboard told his men that they were all "knocked on the head, except three or four and therefore," says he, "let's jump on board and cut them to pieces."'

In its account of the action the *Boston News Letter* states that Blackbeard grabbed the *Jane*'s foresheet in order to pull the two ships together. Grappling hooks from the *New Adventure* were thrown over and the lines made fast, pulling the two ships side by side – their beams touching. Calling to his men Blackbeard led fourteen pirates across onto the bow of Maynard's sloop. The close-quarter fighting had begun.[230]

If the popular image of Blackbeard is anywhere near the truth, he would not, on this occasion, have had the chance to equip his hat with those slow-burning fuses. Yet without them he must still have been an imposing figure; one that could have made even the most battle-hardened veteran like Maynard feel a slight twinge of terror. The pirate, with his crew alongside him, bore down on the three resolute but soon to be dead crewmen of the *Jane*.

Suddenly Maynard called to the men below. There were two ladders leading down into the hold and so the well-armed, unharmed crew that had been hiding below rushed on deck to engage the pirates, completely surprising them. They had little choice but to fight.

Both sides fought ferociously using whatever close-quarter weapon they had; from cutlasses, axes, knives, pikes and hatchets to pistols, and whatever else they could find. The men from the holds certainly would have used the time they had to load firearms. However, they would have been able to fire only one shot each before they needed to reload, and more than likely, that one shot would have been used the second they emerged – rendering their pistols useless except for use as clubs. It was a vicious fight to the death and all the while the bodies of those already fallen were still spilling their blood across the decks.

If the details in the accounts are accurate it is likely that no sawdust had been distributed across the deck of the *Jane* to soak up the blood. Instead it was still flowing out of severed limbs and all the other wounds, and those left standing were fighting and slipping on the bloody wood.

Imagine the scene. The main deck of a sloop is typically only about 20 feet long and about 15 feet wide. The deck would have been littered with ropes, open hatches, ladders and other paraphernalia, plus a growing number of bodies. Indeed, the hatch covers had been removed to enable the crew below to swarm up onto the deck and engage the pirates, so it is very likely that some men fell to their death through those open hatchways. Smoke from the grenades and close pistol-firing would still be lingering in the air as the men fought in that small confined space, tripping over bodies and sliding on the blood, fighting viciously, never knowing whether someone was behind them ready to drive a blade through their backs. This was no clean battle and there was only one rule: to win at all costs.

Not all the pirates had jumped across onto the *Jane*. There were still another ten or so on the *New Adventure* who, seeing how the battle was going, could have joined their comrades but for one thing. While the fighting had been taking place on the *Jane*, the *Ranger* had managed to come alongside the *New Adventure* and her men poured onto the decks of the pirate ship, engaging the remaining pirates. 'The sloop *Ranger* came up, and attacked the men that remained in Blackbeard's sloop, with equal bravery,' Johnson wrote. The scales had tipped against the pirates.

Below the deck of the *New Adventure*, one of the crew stood alone. In his hand was a lighted fuse. In front of him was a barrel of gunpowder. Blackbeard had ordered this man, known only as Black Caesar, to set the fuse to the powder and blow up the ship as Johnson tells us:

> Teach had little or no hope of escaping and therefore had posted a resolute fellow, a Negro whom he had brought up, with a lighted match in the powder room with commands to blow up when he should give him orders, which was as soon as the lieutenant and his men could have entered.

The explosion would not only have obliterated the *New Adventure* and everyone on it, but also the attacking sloops and everyone on them. It was a last-ditch suicide attempt that never occurred.

The accounts of how this man was stopped differ. One source claims it was the men boarding the ship from the *Ranger* that stopped the pirate just in time, while Johnson states that when Caesar 'found how it went with Blackbeard, he could hardly be persuaded from the rash action by two prisoners that were then in the hold of the ship'. Another suggestion is that Samuel Odell, the merchantman who was still on the sloop and hiding from the battle he wanted nothing to do with, stopped the pirate. Since he was the only one on board the sloop to be acquitted at the subsequent trial, this seems feasible. Yet, all the sources say that even though Odell was simply caught up in the fighting and was an innocent bystander, he received around seventy wounds and recovered from them all![231]

Back on board the *Jane*, the fighting was intense. The two captains faced each other in a classic scenario. The accounts from the *Boston News Letter* and from Johnson's narrative provide us with details of the final moments. Metal crashed on metal as Maynard and Blackbeard fought with swords. Maynard lunged at Blackbeard and his sword smashed against Blackbeard's cartridge box. The blade broke and Maynard stumbled backwards. He grabbed his pistol and as he was cocking it Blackbeard moved in for the kill. His blade caught Maynard with a blow, but only managed to damage the lieutenant's fingers. Maynard managed to let off a shot from his pistol, which struck Blackbeard but failed to bring him down. Abraham Demelt joined the fight, swinging his sword at the pirate and 'gave him a terrible wound in the neck and throat'.

Blackbeard remained standing, blood pouring from his wound: 'He stood his ground and fought with great fury, till he received five-and-twenty wounds, five of them by shot.'[232]

The *Boston News Letter* tells us a Highlander from among Maynard's men stepped up and

> engaged Teach with his broad sword who gave Teach a cut in the neck. Teach saying well done lad; The Highlander replied, If it be not well done, I'll do it better. With that he gave him a second stroke which cut off his head, laying it flat on his shoulder.

In the thick of a close-quarter battle, with swords sweeping in all directions, men falling at your feet, where any wrong movement or moment's delay spelled disaster and death, is it really likely that a pirate, or anyone, would feel obliged to verbalise congratulations to a man who had just struck him a near fatal blow across the neck? Also, depending where on the neck the cut landed, would that same person even be capable of saying anything? If this Highlander had, in fact, cut off the pirate's head in this manner, then surely his name would in some way be recorded.[233] However, in Johnson's account, he does not mention the Highlander.

Of course, it is very likely these last few seconds of Blackbeard's life were recorded with a degree of embellishment and speculative drama created by the author of the account in the newspaper, in the same way that today's papers embellish, stretch and sometimes ignore the truth.

Once their captain had fallen, the rest of the pirates lost the will to fight and surrendered.

Blackbeard was finally dead. Now it was time to turn to the casualties and here again there are discrepancies as to the actual number of dead and wounded. The *Boston News Letter* in its account states that 'Teach's men being about 20, and three or four blacks were all killed in the Ingagement ...' The same account refers to a letter written by Maynard quoting the loss at thirty-five killed and wounded; a significant number of the men he took with him on the expedition.[234]

Johnson states that nine pirates died, including Blackbeard, and fourteen were taken prisoner. He provides the names of these individuals as well.[235]

Then there is the figure from Spotswood who wrote that

Tach, with nine of his crew were [*sic*] killed, and three white men and six negroes were taken alive but all much wounded. The loss of the King's men is very considerable for the number, their being ten killed in the action, and four and twenty wounded of whom one is since dead of his wounds.[236]

Whatever the real figure, the mission had been a success. The most feared pirate on the high seas at the time was now dead. He'd suffered twenty-five separate wounds according to the sources. However, this cannot be fully verified since the body was subsequently thrown overboard and would have quickly decomposed in the sea, so there is no way of proving otherwise beyond the claims of those involved.[237]

At some point, Blackbeard's head was removed from the body. Johnson states that 'the lieutenant caused Blackbeard's head to be severed from his body, and hung up at the bowsprit end, and then he sailed to Bath Town, to get relief for his wounded men.'

This sounds as if Maynard ordered the head to be removed, although the *Boston News Letter* account states it was the unknown Highlander who gave Blackbeard the final blow that cut off his head. It would be virtually impossible in such close quarters to achieve a single slice across the neck, accurate and powerful enough to sever the head. This means the assailant would have had to swing back his blade, exposing the upper body to attack from either a gunshot or another blade from elsewhere. Most of the sailors were carrying cutlasses and with their short blades the assailant would probably have stood almost shoulder to shoulder with Blackbeard and would need to use more strength than he would have had to achieve anything more than a few hacking movements, exposing himself to further counter-attack.

The scenario is more likely as Johnson described, that the head was removed after the battle. Whoever did it would have had more time and room to make a single cut with enough power to do the job. In those days, the removal of a victim's head was standard practice to prove that the victim was indeed dead. The entire body would not be needed. The head was sufficient for identification, hence the well-known command throughout history of 'bring me his head'. In his proclamation, Spotswood also declared '... upon the conviction, or making due proof of the killing ...'[238]

In addition, the removal of a victim's head displayed an utter contempt for that person's life. It was an execution and nothing more. It took away the dignity and honour of the individual who would not even be afforded a proper burial. By causing Blackbeard's head to be severed Maynard was not only providing proof that the pirate was dead, he was also displaying contempt for the man when he ordered it to be lashed and hung from the bowsprit of the sloop *Jane*.

With the head severed, Blackbeard's body was no longer needed and so without ceremony it was heaved overboard. As it splashed into the water we can only imaging the cheering from the King's men that the scourge of this pirate was over and they had won. Legend has it that the body floated around the sloop up to seven times before it finally sank. This can be discounted as nothing more than gossip and is best left to fiction. It shows perhaps, the fact that the body was not used to being separated from the head and so swam around the *Jane* in some attempt to reconnect, or some might believe it was a last display of defiance and so as a fictional tool is effective in illustrating the character and defiance of Blackbeard.

Shortly after the battle, Maynard set sail for Bath Town, the head of Blackbeard dangling from the *Jane*'s bowsprit; a symbol of the complete victory over piracy. Once back in Bath Town Maynard reported to his commanding officer and remained there long enough for the wounded men to recover before setting sail back to Virginia, the pirate's head still on the *Jane*'s bowsprit for all to see.

Chapter 16

Trials and Tribulations

*If this finds you yet in harbour I would have
you make the best of your way up as soon as
possible your affairs will let you. I have something
more to say to you than at present I can write ...* [239]

Tobias Knight, 17 November 1718

Blackbeard's death was not the end of the story. To follow were the trials and executions of many of his crew, the claims of collusion against Charles Eden and Tobias Knight. There was also the issue of Blackbeard's treasure, if indeed it existed.

Just two days after Blackbeard's death Spotswood issued his proclamation. It was 24 November 1718 and it was here that Spotswood offered the reward for the death or capture of pirates, specifically Blackbeard. The questions of whether Spotswood by now knew of the pirate's demise or whether Maynard knew of the reward on offer are not at all certain. Perhaps it would be a little naive to believe that Maynard did not know of the reward and acted purely because it was his duty as an officer of the Royal Navy, or perhaps not.

It is perfectly possible that he knew there would be a reward waiting for him on his return and so he fought that much harder. Indeed, before his departure the reward may have been offered to encourage him to create that extra desire for success that devotion to duty alone may not have achieved. The actual reward, which was promised to be 'punctually and justly paid', took three years to be paid, longer than the entire time Blackbeard was a pirate.

According to the narrative of Captain Johnson, those who perished alongside their captain were the gunner Philip Morton, the boatswain Garrat Gibbens, the carpenter Owen Roberts, the quartermaster Thomas Miller, and crewmen John Husk, Joseph Curtice, Joseph Brooks and Nath (probably short for Nathaniel) Jackson.

The pirates wounded and subsequently taken prisoner were John Carnes, another Joseph Brooks, James Blake, John Gills, Thomas Gates, James White, Richard Stiles, Black Caesar, Joseph Phillips, James Robbins, John Martin,

Edward Salter, Stephen Daniel, Richard Greensail, Israel Hands and Samuel Odell. They were all put on trial and sadly the trial records do not exist, or they have yet to be found. If they are found at some point in the future they will very likely shed some new light on the life of Blackbeard and hopefully might reveal some new facts.

Most of the information about the trial that follows comes from *North Carolina Colonial Records*, Volume 2 and from Robert E. Lee's book on Blackbeard. However, because there are no original transcripts there must still be an element of speculation here. The pirates were taken to Williamsburg in Virginia where they were to be tried. For three months they rotted in the cells in Williamsburg waiting. All the while Spotswood was building his case against them. Certainly, Alexander Spotswood would have been present and would more than likely have been watching over the entire proceedings, ensuring that the only decision possible was made. Guilty.

Whether legal advisers would have been on hand to ensure that the pirates were provided with a 'fair' trial is debatable. Many other trials for piracy have left it up to the person accused of the crime to defend themselves. In the seventeenth and eighteenth centuries you were guilty until proven innocent and most criminals in those days had to build their own defence for there was nothing like legal aid then.

Some of the accused were black and under the social conditions of the day they were considered as slaves. However, as they were not owned by anyone and had escaped their bonds, the question was whether they should be treated as slaves or as pirates. Since the crime of being an escaped slave held a lesser penalty, it was finally decided to put them on trial for piracy.

Each pirate would have in turn been escorted to the stand. There, alone, he would have been told what he was guilty of and then be given an opportunity to try to prove his innocence. Once the decision had been made that he was indeed guilty, he would have been escorted to the cells and followed by the next pirate in the chain.

If we look back at the King's Pardon, discussed in earlier chapters, we know that pirates who accepted the pardon were officially excused of any previous acts of piracy. The case for the Crown then had to hinge on the acts of piracy that took place after the pirates had accepted the King's Pardon. These acts would include the taking of the French and British vessels and the burning of the French vessel. Blackbeard claimed to Eden that this was a salvage operation and Eden approved the burning of the vessel but the prosecution at the trial claimed this was theft and an act of piracy.

Spotswood could also use this claim to throw doubt on Charles Eden's governorship of North Carolina, since he had approved Blackbeard's pardon and the salvage rights to the vessel that the pirate subsequently burnt. That meant the legal receipt that Blackbeard had given to Eden for the hogsheads of sugar could be turned by the prosecution into an illegal receipt for stolen goods.

Out of those who stood trial, all except Israel Hands and Samuel Odell were sentenced to be hung. Perhaps Spotswood could be content with this. In his authority as a colonial governor, he'd managed to condemn the pirates to death for their crimes. Both Israel Hands and Samuel Odell had been able to convince their accusers of their innocence and so were spared the gallows.

Hands had been in Bath Town at the time of the attack and battle aboard the *Jane*, and while that would not have been sufficient to secure his innocence, the fact that he had been shot by Blackbeard before the acts of piracy his fellows were accused of and, as a result, was no longer capable of carrying out much in the way of activity would have been enough. He also testified against his fellow pirates.

Samuel Odell's defence was robust as well. He must have proved to the court that he was just a trader who happened to be aboard Blackbeard's sloop for an evening of drinking and was still there when the attack took place the following morning. He proved that he was not a pirate and took no part in the fighting except in self-defence. He was simply a man who was in the wrong place at the wrong time. Without the transcripts of the trial we can't be sure how his statements were corroborated but we must assume that witnesses such as the men from the Royal Navy were able to testify, as far as they could tell, that his claims were accurate. Whatever happened in the trial and however he was believed, Samuel Odell was acquitted.

The battle of Ocracoke that ended Blackbeard's life took place on 22 November 1718. Once the battle was over there would have been the task of attending to the wounded and burying the dead. The two battle-scarred sloops, *Jane* and *Ranger* originally sailed to Bath Town for treatment of the wounded, and then sometime later they set sail again and arrived back in Virginia on 1 December 1718. The trial of the pirates is known to have taken place sometime in the middle of March 1719 which gives us the three-month gap before the trial.

Presumably, this gap was the time that Spotswood needed to ensure the case against the pirates was as comprehensive as it could be. From the moment the pirates surrendered they were destined to be executed and, apart from Hands, no amount of delay was going to save them.

From Spotswood's point of view, that gave him three months of questioning the prisoners, to pit each one of them against the other and see what information he could use to build his case. Of the five African American pirate prisoners, four agreed to testify against the rest of the pirates, as did Israel Hands. Their testimony would have been damning indeed. While this was taking place, Spotswood was also trying to build a case against the North Carolina government, to prove there was collusion and conspiracy right at the very top. He was also ensuring that he set up a proper, legal trial with 'fair' people he'd appointed as Vice Admiral Commissioners to sit with him in judgement.[240]

The only evidence against Eden was the pardon awarded to Blackbeard and the sugar found in his barn, which he was entitled to under the salvage rights of the day. The incursion into North Carolina and the battle at Ocracoke also revealed a pirate stash of 25 hogsheads of sugar, 11 barrels weighing between 304 and 330lbs, 145 bags of cocoa, a barrel of indigo and a bale of cotton. These items, along with the sale of the sloop, presumably *New Adventure*, realised a sum of £2,238.[241]

The revenue from these sales went towards the costs of the expedition which included the cost of hiring the sloops, repairing them, the costs of feeding and housing the prisoners for three months, the cost of storing the plunder on the *New Adventure* and keeping it for three months while it was examined. There were also legal costs involved, the costs of the trial and whatever costs were incurred for the mass execution of the pirates – the rope, perhaps?

In his letters to their Lordships at the Council of Trade and Plantations Spotswood maintained that he did not communicate his plan to attack Blackbeard to Governor Eden because he was afraid the plans would be leaked to the pirate. From Tobias Knight's letter to Blackbeard we know that this very nearly did take place but why Blackbeard chose to ignore Knight's letter is something we shall never really know. This letter by Knight to Blackbeard was found among Blackbeard's papers on his sloop.

Despite the political battles that were to take place between the two colonies, the fate of the pirates who had been captured at Bath Town and after the battle at Ocracoke Island was never in doubt. The Vice Admiralty Court ruled that the prisoners were guilty of piracy and so were sentenced to be hung by the neck. Only one man was found innocent and that was Samuel Odell. Israel Hands, as we know, was given a pardon which Captain Johnson claims that:

> just as he was about to be executed a ship arrived at Virginia with a proclamation for prolonging the time of His Majesty's pardon to such of the pirates as should surrender by a limited time therein expressed. Notwithstanding the sentence, Hands pleaded the pardon and was allowed the benefit of it.

This could be Johnson again adding a dramatic twist to the truth, which is more likely that this extension to the pardon had been issued on 23 July 1718 in order for Britain to strengthen its weak naval forces in the colonies and allow any pirates to turn privateer and fight the Spanish. So this extension likely already existed and was given to Hands in reward for him turning state's evidence against his own shipmates. Perhaps this was his way of getting back at Blackbeard for shooting him.

Once the sentence was passed, the execution took place only a few days later, beginning with a procession of the prisoners down the Jamestown road (the same road they had travelled on to their captivity three months before). The prisoners would have been accompanied by members of the militia to guard them and the clergy, along with representatives of the Virginia legislature. No doubt the road would have been lined with crowds of people shouting and jeering at the pirates.

When they reached the place of execution, one by one each man stood on a cart (they would have had no option), his hands bound behind him and a noose tightened around his neck. They were each given the chance to say some last words, the clergy said a quick prayer and then the horse tied to the cart was quickly pulled away leaving the pirate hanging by his neck, dancing in mid-air as the rope bit into his throat until his legs finally went limp. This same procedure happened over and over for each pirate in this mass execution.[242]

The last of Blackbeard's most trusted crew were gone but the saga was not yet over.

Chapter 17

Fate and Collusion

Blackbeard was gone. Those of his crew who had been captured were all dead. All that remained of this intimidating pirate were the many different versions of his stories and the equal number of mysteries surrounding him that persist to this day.

During the short period of his pirate career Blackbeard never became the leader or king of the pirates as was Roberts. At one point, Hornigold held that lofty position among all the other pirates operating out of the pirate haven of New Providence who were plundering vessels throughout the West Indies and along the coast of the American colonies. That stopped when Woodes Rogers arrived as Governor of the Bahamas. He brought with him the King's Pardon.

One of the most well-known pirates who were using this base at the time, alongside Blackbeard before Woodes Rogers arrived to try to rid New Providence of the pirates, was Charles Vane. He started his career at sea as a member of Henry Jennings' crew and in 1716 he was part of a group of sailors who seized the ship on which they were serving and turned to piracy. Vane took command of his own sloop, the *Ranger* and became famous for his cruelty to the crews of vessels he captured. He showed little remorse in torturing them.[243]

After his dramatic escape from New Providence, Charles Vane continued his pirating activities. According to Woodes Rogers, Vane seized two ships leaving Carolina (he does not specify North or South) which were both bound for London. One was the *Neptune* of around 400 tons commanded by Captain King, and the other was the *Emperour* of 200 tons commanded by Captain Arnold Gowers. Both ships carried cargo of rice, pitch, tar and skins. After plundering the *Neptune* Vane sank her and then deprived the second one of all her cargo and provisions. Vane also traded with a merchant who was arrested for dealing in stolen property and awaited transportation to England.[244]

When he refused to attack a warship, Vane was overthrown by the crew of his own vessel and Jack Rackham, another famous pirate replaced him. Known as Calico Jack, he was later to be linked to female pirate Anne Bonny. Vane was later captured when his ship was wrecked in the Bay of Honduras and he was tried for piracy and hung.

Blackbeard's mentor, Benjamin Hornigold accepted the King's Pardon through Woodes Rogers and turned pirate-hunter. Before he'd been a pirate he was a privateer and then resorted to piracy after the War of Spanish Succession was over. He reverted back to being a privateer the moment the King's Pardon became available. With Hornigold effectively at his side, Rogers set about ridding New Providence of pirates and turned it into a law-abiding colony of the Crown. Rogers commissioned Hornigold to capture Charles Vane which he never succeeded in doing but he did capture and bring to justice other pirates, including Nicholas Woodall, John Auger and several others. Most of these men were executed.

Once Rogers settled in he set about giving the pardon to as many pirates that would take it and most of them did. Vane was one of the few who didn't. So with most of the pirates now living off the wealth they'd made as pirates and Hornigold acting as pirate-hunter for Rogers, the wild lawless haven was soon a thing of the past. The period when New Providence was at its height as a pirate haven and the pirates plundered vessels, attacked coastal settlements and blockaded towns throughout the West Indies, up and down the Atlantic coast has been referred to as the 'Golden Age of Piracy'. However, once Rogers arrived and Hornigold, the most influential pirate at the time, turned pirate-hunter that age ended. Indeed, Hornigold was one of the chief architects for the downfall of this golden age. He captured more than thirteen pirates and, according to Rogers, 'Captain Hornigold has given the world to wipe off the infamous name he has hitherto been known by, tho in the very acts of piracy he committed most people spoke well of his generosity.'[245]

Hornigold's end is unclear. Most historians agree that his ship was wrecked and that he drowned in the wreckage, but whether that was through negligence or the effects of drink or was down to a storm or other causes is not known, nor is the date or location of the wreck known.

Israel Hands' fate is also unclear. He'd been the second-in-command for Blackbeard and at one point was put in command of the sloop *Adventure*. He was not involved in the battle that killed Blackbeard but was arrested in Bath Town on charges of piracy. He was released after he had testified against his pirate brothers, which testimony Spotswood used to build a case that incriminated Tobias Knight and Charles Eden as being in collusion with Blackbeard. Most of the information we have of him comes from Captain Johnson. In the Israel Hands affair it is Johnson who details the incident where Blackbeard shoots Hands in the knee, permanently damaging him:

> Blackbeard without any provocation privately draws out a small pair of pistols and cocks them under the table, which, being perceived by the man, he withdrew and went on deck, leaving Hands, the pilot, and the

captain together. When the pistols were ready, he blew out the candle, and crossing his hand, discharged them at his company: Hands, the master, was shot through the knee and lamed for life; the other pistol did no execution. Being asked the meaning of this, he only answered, by damning them, that if he did not now and then kill one of them, they would forget who he was.[246]

Assuming that this story is correct, it then adds weight to the account of Hands ending his days as a beggar, since with such a damaged knee he would have had a great deal of difficulty finding any work, even as a pirate. The name of Israel Hands has since been immortalised in the book *Treasure Island* by Robert Louis Stevenson.

In 1710 Edward Moseley took up the post of Surveyor General of North Carolina and in 1715 he became Colonial Treasurer. His involvement in the Blackbeard case came shortly after the pirate's death when Moseley stormed into Eden's office to look for evidence linking Eden with Blackbeard as more than a casual acquaintance. He failed to find anything and was arrested for his treachery. Through the colonial attorney Governor Eden had Moseley banned from public service and the man did not return until many years later.

Woodes Rogers ended the scourge of piracy on New Providence almost exclusively with local resources and with very little assistance from outside. He publicised a mass execution of pirates to ram home the point that anyone who refused the King's Pardon for piracy and continued plundering vessels for their own profit would be hunted down and hung.[247]

Shortly after Blackbeard's death Spain went to war with England and Rogers was still getting to grips with maintaining order where previously there had been none. He divided his time between organising the colony's defences and ridding it of piracy, something that with war now a reality, it could do without:

> As soon as the fort is finished and all the guns mounted, which I hope will be done before the Christmas holy days are over, I will then do the best I can to make examples of some of them [pirates].[248]

Black Caesar, the man who was captured while attempting to blow up the pirate sloop, was hung with the others accused alongside him. He is referred to by Spotswood, although not by name, in a letter to the Council of Trade and Plantations:

> His [Blackbeard's] orders were to blow up his own vessel if he should happen to be overcome, and a negro was ready to set fire to the powder, had he not been luckily prevented by a planter forced on board the night before and who lay in the hold of the sloop during the action of the pyrates.[249]

Stede Bonnet was betrayed by Blackbeard and turned to piracy after accepting the King's Pardon. He sailed into the estuary of Cape Fear River to careen the very leaky *Royal James*, and to wait out the hurricane season. Here he was attacked by a naval expedition, led by Colonel William Rhett. The pirate was defeated and arrested. Bonnet was hung for piracy, committed after he received his pardon, on 10 December 1718. Ironically, this took place in Charles Town, the port that Blackbeard had blockaded and ransomed, when Bonnet was aboard the pirate's flagship only seven months earlier.[250]

David Herriot, Captain of the *Adventure* when it was seized by Blackbeard, was also captured and charged as a pirate. His defence that he had been forced into the life of piracy fell on deaf ears of the court and he was sentenced to be hung. However, he tried to escape and was killed by soldiers who were hunting him on Sullivan's Island.

What then of Governor Charles Eden and Tobias Knight? It is around them that the charges of collusion with Blackbeard revolve. Spotswood is the one man most influential in propagating these charges, but at the time of writing there is no concrete documentary proof of these allegations. Eden was never found guilty of abusing his political position.

The evidence available is circumstantial. For example, there is the supposed wedding between Blackbeard and Mary Ormond over which Eden presided. Then there is the fact that Blackbeard approached Governor Eden to accept the King's Pardon, which according to Johnson he went on to ignore. There were the hogsheads of sugar that Blackbeard was supposed to have given him as a gift, and then there was the inquiry that Eden presided over concerning giving Blackbeard legal ownership of the sloop *New Adventure*. In addition, there was the inquiry convened by both Eden and Knight that gave Blackbeard the rights to the French vessel, and then the subsequent order to burn the vessel which also came from Eden.

Regarding the wedding, it is only Johnson who relates this event in his narrative where he states that Blackbeard, after sleeping with his new bride, gave her to some of his friends for their pleasure. Johnson also states the pirate had thirteen other wives before he married Ormond: 'And this I have been informed, made Teach's fourteenth wife, whereof about a dozen might be still living.'

We can assume that Blackbeard, like most pirates, probably had a few mistresses in various ports and we have indicated that he very likely had a mistress in Bath Town who lived with him. However, there is no evidence to support Johnson's claims of fourteen wives, just as there is no evidence at the time of writing that suggests this woman's name was Mary Ormond. As for the poor girl's fate, the whole incident comes from Johnson's narrative and so may be suspect. This account could have been invented by Johnson to spice up a pause in Blackbeard's life and to spice up his character. Yet, on this point we leave you with this thought. If the shooting incident is true, then having some of his pirate friends abuse his wife would be perfectly in keeping with Blackbeard's behaviour. We leave you to decide.

Even if this marriage did happen and Eden did preside over the ceremony, it does not point to his collusion with Blackbeard. It merely illustrates the fact that they knew each other.

The question of why Blackbeard approached Eden and none of the other colonial governors to accept the King's Pardon has been discussed earlier. His choices were limited. However, as Johnson tells us he continued his piracy after accepting the pardon, it does not point to Eden being in collusion. In his narrative, Johnson points out that the vessels being plundered in the Ocracoke Inlet by Blackbeard belonged to traders who wanted something to be done:

> The sloops trading up and down this river, being so frequently pillaged by Blackbeard, consulted with the traders and some of the best of the planters, what course to take; they saw plainly it would be in vain to make any application to the Governor of North Carolina to whom it properly belonged to find some redress.

So these traders and planters turned to Spotswood for help. One of Spotswood's claims against Eden was that the North Carolina Governor turned a blind eye to Blackbeard's renewed pirating ways after he'd accepted the pardon, which is supported by the statement above. However, there was no proven evidence at the time that indicated Blackbeard had carried out piracy in North Carolina waters or in any other part of North Carolina jurisdiction.

Unlike some of her wealthy neighbours, North Carolina had neither the financial resources nor the military muscle available to catch Blackbeard in the act of committing piracy and to stop him, once and for all. As far as Eden was concerned there was no evidence that Blackbeard had ignored the pardon and was committing acts of piracy, so he saw no reason to go after a man, who was, in the eyes of North Carolina law, a reformed character.

The charges of collusion were also levelled at Tobias Knight. As the Secretary of the Colony and Chief Justice for North Carolina, Knight was essentially second in the batting order after Eden. Eden claimed that the hogsheads of sugar found in his possession were his legal share of salvaged cargo from Blackbeard. Knight admitted to knowing about these hogsheads and the sixty hogsheads he had in his barn which also came from Blackbeard. Knight admitted to having the hogsheads of sugar in his possession which he claimed were not his but that he was keeping them in store 'at the request of the said Thatche, only till a more Convenient store could be procured by the Governor for the whole'.[251]

The letter from Knight to Blackbeard, found amongst the pirate's papers and warning him of an impending attack, is probably the most solid evidence there is against Knight. However, in his case Knight managed a robust defence that ended with him being acquitted and he died shortly afterwards. Again, Johnson links Eden and Knight with Blackbeard when he discusses the same letter:

> But notwithstanding this caution, Blackbeard had information of the design from his Excellency of the province and his secretary, Mr Knight, wrote him a letter particularly concerning it intimating that he had sent him four of his men, which were all he could meet with, in or about town, and so bid him be upon his guard.

Johnson adds a further link to build the theory of collusion with Blackbeard when he states that after the battle at Ocracoke was over the Royal Navy men 'found several letters and written papers, which discovered the correspondence between Governor Eden, the secretary and collector, and also some traders at New York, and Blackbeard'. Johnson goes on to say that Blackbeard had enough of a regard for his friends that he would have

> destroyed these papers before the action, in order to hinder them from falling into such hands, where the discovery would be of no use, either to the interest or reputation of these fine gentlemen if it had not been his fixed resolution to have blown up together, when he found no possibility of escape.

To make these claims, Johnson must have used a wide variety of sources, from the *Boston News Letter*, Israel Hands' story, other pirates and victims of Blackbeard, and Spotswood's letters to which he may have gained access through the Council of Trade and Plantations.

Yet, in 1726, when the fourth edition of his book came out, Johnson wrote a retraction, changing his mind about Eden's alleged collusion with Blackbeard. He wrote:

> I have been informed since, by very good hands, that Mr. Eden always behaved, as far as he had the power, in a manner suitable to his post, and bore the character of a good governor and an honest man.

He goes on to say that he was 'at a loss to know what acts of Piracy he had committed after this surrender to the Proclamation'. He is referring here to Blackbeard. Johnson continues in his retraction that the French ship was 'lawfully condemned' then, with regard to the complaints of the planters against Blackbeard, he states:

If he had committed any depredations amongst the planters, as they seemed to complain of, they were not upon the high sea, but either in the river, or onshore, and could not come within the jurisdiction of the Admiralty, nor under any laws of Piracy.

Finally, Johnson turns to Eden's character and states that there 'did not appear from any Writings or Letters found in Blackbeard's Sloop, or from any other Evidence whatsoever, that the said Governor was concerned at all in any malpractice'.

This retraction then makes the entire expedition to get Blackbeard completely illegal and the reasons behind it, that the planters and traders complained of Blackbeard's actions, spurious. Spotswood went after the pirate on the grounds of his acts of piracy but as we can see there is no evidence to support these claims under Admiralty law. Spotswood was in the wrong.[252]

Just two days after the death of Blackbeard, Spotswood issued the proclamation that offered a reward for anyone who could bring the pirates to justice. It was not until 1722 when the political wrangling that had been the hallmark of Spotswood's time in office came to an end when he and his council reached an agreement of detente. Spotswood was replaced that same year and retired into his estate in Virginia, which measured about 80,000 acres. It became known as Spotsylvania, and here he owned a number of iron furnaces. On a brief return to London he married, before returning to the colonies, where he died in 1740 survived by his widow and four children.

When Spotswood issued his order that all pirates, pardoned or otherwise, who entered into Virginia had to register with the authorities, William Howard, Blackbeard's former quartermaster was one of the first to fall victim to this proclamation. Abandoned by Blackbeard at Topsail Inlet he was arrested on the spot, placed in chains and left to languish in the hold of a ship while his trial was prepared. Spotswood ignored the fact that Howard had not committed any acts of piracy since his break with Blackbeard, claiming that Howard's time to accept the King's Pardon had expired. However, the man escaped the gallows in the same way that Israel Hands had. While awaiting his execution a new proclamation arrived that extended the date of the pardon for acts of piracy to 23 July 1718, and since he had been marooned by Blackbeard he'd not committed any acts of piracy, he accepted the pardon and was freed. No further acts of piracy could be attributed to him. After this lucky reprieve nothing more was ever heard of William Howard again.

Chapter 18

Legacy

*... one of his [Blackbeard's] men asked him in case anything
should happen to him in the engagement with the sloops,
whether his wife knew where he had buried his money?
He answered 'That nobody but himself and the Devil
knew where it was, and the longest liver should take all.'*[253]

Captain Charles Johnson

This, then, is Blackbeard's story. The hunt to find the truth has shown us the facts of his life but left a mystery about the man himself. In just over two years he managed to carve out a career in piracy that has endured throughout the centuries after his spectacular death. Perhaps it is the manner of his dying that fascinates us. Unlike so many other pirates captured and tried for piracy, he did not end his days thrashing and dangling from the end of a rope. He did not die in mysterious circumstances like his mentor, Benjamin Hornigold. He did not die of disease, like so many other sailors of the time. Instead, he died fighting and not just by a pistol shot or by a single cut of the sword but by many cuts and many shots. He died in a vicious, no-holds-barred ruthless fight for survival which he lost.

His actions as a pirate are common knowledge, as is the way he died but his early life and his origins are surrounded in mystery. He was known by a number of names: Edward Teach, Thatch, Tach, Tache and so on. Indeed, it is highly likely that Edward Teach was not his name at all. No-one really knows who his parents were and until there is definite proof of what his surname really was, any trace of his parentage is impossible.

Captain Johnson tells us he had fourteen wives or, more likely, mistresses in various places but who these women were and whether he fathered any children by these women remains unknown. In a letter referred to earlier in the book, Governor Johnson of South Carolina wrote that he believed Blackbeard had a wife and children in London. However, like the other mysteries surrounding him, who they were and what happened to them is not known. Indeed, on occasion letters from people claiming to be descendants of some of Blackbeard's men and of the pirate captain himself are received at the North Carolina Maritime Museum, recognised as being one of the leading authorities on Blackbeard. However much people claim they are Blackbeard's descendants, until we have concrete proof of his real surname these claims cannot be verified.

The mystery of Blackbeard is how has he endured over all the other pirates of his day? He was not the most prolific pirate during the 'Golden Age of Piracy'. Charles Vane, for example, and Bartholomew Roberts plundered far more ships than Blackbeard. Indeed, he was not known as the king of the pirates; that was a title that fell to Bartholomew Roberts. Blackbeard didn't command vast numbers of pirates as others did. Yet, these names do not trip off the tongue as Blackbeard's does. Nor are they as well-known, or infamous if you will. Most people, certainly in the UK and North America, have heard of the pirate known as Blackbeard. Indeed, he is probably the only pirate ever heard of by people who have no interest in piracy.

There are other mysteries surrounding Blackbeard. The location of his skull is one of them. After the head had been hung up at Hampton Harbour it disappeared. One legend has it that the skull was used as a drinking chalice, though who would use this gruesome cup does not bear thinking about. Other legends lay claim to its location but it would be very difficult to determine if any of these claims were correct. As we don't have any DNA of Blackbeard and don't even know his real name, trying to discover if a particular skull that someone claims is his would be close to impossible.

Legend also states that Blackbeard buried some of his treasure, and people have been searching for it for years. The location of this treasure, like the location of his skull, is another of the many mysteries in the Blackbeard affair. No treasure has ever been found but since he could not have spent all of it during the last few months he was in North Carolina before his death then, if it does exist, it must be somewhere.

In Captain Johnson's narrative we are told that one of Blackbeard's crew asked him one night if anyone, such as his wife, knew the location of his treasure. Blackbeard answered the man by saying that 'nobody but himself and the Devil knew where it was, and the longest liver should take all'. Ironically, the pirate captain died the following day.

While we know a lot about Spotswood and some of the other players involved in the Blackbeard saga, we know little of the man himself. Yet he is remembered in many different ways. For example, every year Hampton in Virginia holds a Blackbeard Festival. The recently-discovered wreck that appears to be his flagship, the *Queen Anne's Revenge* that went aground near Beaufort, is being carefully excavated and studied. Stories about local people seeing the headless ghost of Blackbeard abound, and almost any cafe, restaurant or park that claims to have the most tenuous connection to the pirate blows that connection out of all proportion in order to attract tourists.

For centuries his story has filled the pages of books, comics, magazines and now recently, computer games. Films, television productions, a theme park and a painting have all immortalised him. Of all the pirates operating in the Caribbean and coastal waters of the American Colonies during the 'Golden Age of Piracy', none are more famous, or infamous, than Edward Teach, alias Blackbeard.

Through his actions we can see that Blackbeard was a man on a mission. If his goal was for his life in piracy to be remembered throughout history, and his actions point to this being the case, then he certainly achieved it.

We've laid out the facts of Blackbeard's story but there are still many questions that remain unanswered. Who was he and where did he come from? We leave that for you to decide.

Further Reading &
Information

BBC Drama, *Blackbeard* (Dangerous Films)

Cordingly, David, *Under the Black Flag: The Romance and Reality of Life Among the Pirates* (Harvest Edition, New York: Random House, 1996)

CSPCS – Calendar State Papers Colonial Series (For ease of reference, these can be found at British History Online)

Gosse, Philip, *The History of Piracy* (New York: Longmans, Green & Co., 2007)

Havighurst, Walter, *Alexander Spotswood: Portrait of a Governor* (New York: Hold, Reinhart and Winston Inc., 1967)

Johnson, Captain Charles, *A General History of the Robberies and Murders of the Most Notorious Pirates* (London: Conway Maritime Press, 2002 (First published in 1724))

Konstam, Angus, *Blackbeard – America's Most Notorious Pirate* (Hoboken, New Jersey: John Wiley & Sons Inc., 2006)

Lee, Robert E., *Blackbeard the Pirate – A Reappraisal of His Life and Times* (Winston-Salem, North Carolina: John F. Blair, 1974)

Parry, Dan, *Blackbeard – The Real Pirate of the Caribbean* (London: National Maritime Museum Publishing, 2006)

Pickering, David, *Pirates* (London: Collins Gem, 2006)

Spotswood, Alexander, *The Official Letters of Alexander Spotswood, Lieutenant-Governor of the Colony of Virginia, 1710–1722: Now First Printed from the Manuscript in the ... of the Virginia Historical* Society, Volumes 1 & 2 (Virginia Historical Society, 2010)

Appendix I

Spotswood's Version of the Truth

The following is the complete letter written by Governor Alexander Spotswood to the Council of Trade and Plantations, dated 22 December 1718. Its significance to this work is that it illustrates in detail Spotswood's precarious political position and the accusations that had been levelled against him by his opponents. It touches on the issue of William Howard, Blackbeard's quartermaster on the *Queen Anne's Revenge*, on the attack at Ocracoke Island and on the issue of what to do with the plunder seized from the captured pirates and what was left on board the *New Adventure*. It is currently found in *Colonial and State Papers, America and the West Indies*, Volume 30:

> Having long struggled with a set of men here, whose designs for many years have been to engross into their own hands the whole power of the Government and to form a new plan thereof according to their own caprice, but directly opposite to the interest of their Sovereign, as well as of their Mother Country; It is no wonder that I now share with the rest of my predecessors, the effects of their resentment: it being too well known for these thirty years past, that no Governor has longer escaped being vilified and aspersed here, and misrepresented at home, than he began to discover the intrigues and thwart the politicks of this formidable party, etc. Thus a Governors asserting the undoubted prerogative of the Crown in the nomination of Judges, is in the language of these men, a subversion of the Constitution; and his endeavours to obtain a just payment of the Kings Rents a depriving the people of their ancient rights and privileges, and by such false glosses the ignorant are imposed on to believe, and the knavish encouraged to hope for mighty liberties and advantages by adhering to this Party, and choosing such Representatives as are agreeable to them. But notwithstanding these and many other artifices to foment dissatisfactions among the people, the Country in general is so sensible of its present happiness, that with all the industry

of the Party, not one grievance came to the Assembly which mett here on the 11th of last month; and indeed if ever any people had reason to be easy under a flourishing trade and moderate taxes, an exuberant Treasury, and a profound Peace, it is certain those of Virginia ought to be so.

Under these happy circumstances this last Session of Assembly mett, and as the peaceable state of the country gave me no occasion to demand anything in behalf of the Government, everyone expected the Burgesses had nothing else to do, but to call for the few bills which remained unfinished at their former Session, and to lay the levy for discharging the publick creditors: but instead of proceeding on any of their bills that lay before them, the first business they went upon was to re-enact a law which H.M. had very lately repealed viz. that declaring who shall not bear office in this Country. This bill brought in by Mr. Grymes the Deputy Auditor, soon passed the Burgesses without removing the very objection for which it was formerly repealed; and being sent to the Council found as easy a passage there, though not without the opposition of some of that Board and particularly Colonel. Jenings, who having been at your Lordships Board, when the repeal was under deliberation, argued for leaving out those parts agt. which your Lordships took exception; but all objections were in vain, the avowed design of this bill being to exclude from offices, all persons recommended from England.

The reasonableness of this set of Counsellors will further appear by the enclosed Minutes of Council, wherein they advise me to pass this bill, notwithstanding the many just exceptions; I represented it liable to. After passing this bill and one other which I shall mention hereafter, the Burgesses seem'd inclined to no other business. All petitions brought before them, were immediately referred to the next Assembly, and their Grand Committee converted into a trifling Office of Enquiry into the Capitol furniture; in which they spent five or six days at the expense of £400 to their country to examine into the state of a few old chairs and sconces of less than £50 value. When many of the more sensible members of that House, tired out with these amusements were return'd home, as apprehending no business of moment would be brought in, and others believing their presence unnecessary, were gone to take the diversion of a horse race near the town, the Party managers watched that opportunity to bring in an Address to the King, with a long roll of Articles; in the first charging me in general with subverting the Constitution of their Government, depriving them of their ancient rights and privileges, and daily exercising hardships on H.M. good subjects: and in the second with divers particulars facts to prove their pretended accusation.

Without examining the truth of any one of these Articles, the Address containing the general charge was first put to the vote, and carried by the suffrages of 22 against 14 that opposed it, there being then no less than 15 Members absent, who would have been of the latter opinion. Having thus obtained their Address to pass, the Speaker was immediately commanded to sign three fair copies, which. were brought in ready drawn for that purpose; and then they proceeded to consider the Articles, but upon hearing the falsehood of many of them exposed, those who readily voted for the Address upon the faith of their leaders, began to be startled and would not so easily give in to what they found could not be proved, and so put off the debate till next day, when eight of the Articles were entirely struck out as groundless, and the rest which are intended to support their charge so much altered from the first draught, that those who opposed the Address consented to let them pass purely to expose the weakness and malice of my accusers. I herewith transmit to your Lordships a copy of the Address and Articles as they passed the House, whereby your Lordships may judge whether the latter, if they were really true, are sufficient to convict me of subverting the Constitution of the Government, or oppressing the King's subjects. I have also added the whole Articles given in that your Lordships may see the malice of these men in charging me with crimes which they themselves could not justify to be true. Time will not allow me at present to enter upon a full answer to this charge neither would it be proper to send one by this uncertain conveyance: but I shall in a very short time send over a Gentleman well acquainted with the affairs of this Country etc., who will be able to give your Lordships a true light into those things which my adversaries have industriously misrepresented, or which their Agent Mr. Byrd may craftily insinuate to my prejudice: and besides I have not the least doubt of your allowing me a reasonable time to be heard etc. In the mean time refers to enclosures as a brief answer.

When your Lordps. shall be pleased to consider the first of the Burgesses Articles I hope you will be pleased to entertain a more favourable opinion of Virginia than to believe that the persons concerned in that unintelligible composition, are the wisest or most learned of its legislators: but though I ought not to quarrell with my accusers' understandings, I may be allow'd with justice to expose their dishonesty, which in this particular is very notorious etc. I am accused of putting a misconstruction on the law for settling the titles and bounds of lands, and of endeavouring to extend that clause thereof making three years non-payment of quittrents a forfeiture of the land granted after the passing that law, to other lands which were granted long before. Now, my

Lords, I do affirm, that this charge is utterly false. I never had a thought of extending that law etc. and no occasion. The Law cited was passed in 1710, and in less than three years thereafter viz. in 1713 another Act of Assembly was made declaring what shall be accounted a sufficient seating etc., wherein there is a clause declaring in express words, That all lands for which the quittrents shall be three years in arrear, shall revert to the Crown. This I acknowledge to have construed according to the sense it will naturally bear, according to the intention of those that made it, and the interpretation the whole country put on it till of late, that a party of the Council thought fit by their own absolute will and pleasure to declare it to have no meaning at all etc. I challenge them to produce one single instance of any man's paying more quittrents than he is bound to, by the condition of his patent, or that I have diseased any one of his freehold for non-payment by colour of this Act: a power being still lodged in the Governor to regrant the land forfeited to the same proprietor from whom it reverts.

As the chief design of this law was to obtain, justice to the King without the least intention to injure the subject, so I have on divers occasions declared that if the Burgesses would by a new law, make a reasonable provision for the just payment of the quitt rents, I would consent to the repeal of this, and I even offered to consent, that it might be declared by law that whoever should enter the true quantity of his lands on the Receiver Generals books, should incur no forfeiture for the non-payment of his quittrents until a reasonable time after the same should be demanded by the Kings Officers: But the party who have always opposed the Kings interest, foreseeing that this would necessarily tend to the obtaining a true rent roll of the Colony, would by no means hearken to this proposal. From all which your Lordps. will judge, whether my endeavouring to obtain a just payment of the Kings rents, according to the express words of a law in force, or this party of men aiming to defraud their Sovereign of the acknowledgment due by the very condition of their own patents, be most like an attempt to subvert the Constitution? And whether a people have just cause to complain of the hardship of a law, who refuse all overtures for amending it?

My accusers designed to represent me as a person so ignorant as not to understand the common sense of their laws, or such a tyrant as to wrest them to purposes quite foreign to the true intent thereof etc. They knew very well that the law made in 1713 is that which I have always contended for etc. As soon as they found the people alarm'd at this law, and preparing to give up a true account of their lands to prevent the forfeiture thereof, they spread a report about the country that the Kings Attorney General in England had declared his opinion that this law extended only to lands granted after the passing thereof, and that no man had occasion to fear the forfeiture of any lands patented before: they declared this to be their own opinion too on all occasions, and to make it the more publick took an opportunity to argue it on the General Court Bench, without having any case in judgment before them which required their opinion in that point: and to show the people how little they valued the effect of that law, divers of the same party let their lands run in arrears, as an example to others to act the same part. I can scarce believe that the Kings Attorney General gave any such opinion, unless it was on the law with which I am now charged, for all the lawyers here are clear that the Act in 1713 doth extend to all lands whatsoever, as indeed it was the intention of the makers that it should. The other three Articles will appear to be very frivolous, when I come to set forth the truth of the matters etc. I shall only now give a brief character of the persons chiefly concerned in framing the present accusation against me etc. The two late Officers of the Revenue are particularly offended at my enquiry into their mismanagements.

Your Lordships may be pleased to remember that in Aug. 1714 I received a particular charge from your. Board to transmit an account of the several branches of the Kings Revenues, the application, and manner of auditing thereof; I no sooner began this inquiry, than I found many abuses in the collection and the utmost confusion in the accomplishments of these Revenues, which I thought highly necessary to reform: but as both the Officers strenuously opposed any such regulation, so Mr. Byrd thought fit soon to withdraw to England, carrying with him all the books of the Revenue (if he ever kept any) and has continued there ever since, ready on all occasions to do me ill offices, instead of returning to clear himself of those frauds which have been discovered in his management during his being Receiver General. This Gentleman (as is publicly talked here) has advised his accomplices that they had no other way to carry their point, than by getting the Assembly to petition H.M. to remove me. And Councillor Ludwell his chief correspondent here undertook that task. As both these gentlemen were closely united in their opposition to my endeavours for reforming the abuses in the Revenue, so the latter (who is a man of implacable malice and resentment) can never forgive my suspending him from the office of Auditor: He it is, who with the assistance of his brother in law Mr. Commissary Blair, the constant instrument of faction against all former Governors, has set himself up for the Head of that Party etc.

Amongst the two and twenty Burgesses who voted the present

accusation against me, there are Mr. Grymes the Deputy Auditor son in law to Mr. Ludwell, a man of the same principles with him in relation to Government, and pursuing the very same schemes in the management of the Kings Revenue. Mr. Corbin married to one of the same family etc., and turned out of the place of Naval Officer, for no less an offence than forging the late Queen's letter, for clearing a ship in his district etc., and consequently a person disobliged etc. Mr. Blair brother to the Commissary and both partners in trade with Mr. Ludwell; a member chosen (by much industry) for the almost deserted corporation of James City, merely for his remarkable scurrility and insolence. Three more of the same party displaced from being Justices of the Peace, and one from the office of an Agent under the Tobacco law for evil practices in their offices by the advice of these very Counsellors who now use them as their tools; and divers others disobliged for being refused the employment they had a mind to, as indeed it is very common for some here to look upon anything that's refused them to be so much taken away from them, and the less they are qualified for the offices they aim at, so much the greater is their resentment for being denied. These are my only accusers, for as to several others drawn in to vote on the same side, they have already owned their error in being so easily imposed on, by the crafty insinuations of these Party managers, and it will not appear strange if among two and fifty men (of which the Burgesses House is composed) there should be found some of weak understandings, as well as others liable to corruption and neither proof against the arts of an industrious party when they have so great a point to carry. But however this Party of men may triumph in their gaining a small number of the Burgesses to join with them in an unrighteous accusation, their joy is like to be but short lived, the people in general beginning already to condemn their proceedings, and as the principal gentlemen of the country are resolved to given publick testimonies of their satisfaction with my administration, and their dislike of the late Assemblies behaviour I doubt not in a short time to send your Lordships Addresses from most parts of the Colony vindicating me from what I am charged with; as I now send copies of what I have already received on this occasion.

In my letter of the 14th of August last, I gave your Lordships an account that one Capt. Tach a noted pyrate in a ship of 40 guns run ashore in June, at the mouth of Ocracoke Inlet in North Carolina where that ship and two of the four sloops he had under his command were lost, and that he and his crew had surrendered to the Governor of that Province. Since which one Howard, Tach's Quartermaster, came into this Colony, with two negroes which he own'd to have been piratically taken, the one from a French ship and the other from an English brigantine. I caused them to be seized pursuant to H.M. Instructions, upon which, encouraged by the countenance he found here, he commenced a suit against the officer who made the seizure, and his insolence became so intolerable, without applying himself to any lawful business, that the Justices of the Peace where he resided thought fit to send him on board one of the Kings ships as a vagrant seaman. Hereupon he caused not only the Justice who signed the warrant but the Captain and Lieutenant of the man of war to be arrested each in an action of £500 damages. And one of the chief lawyers here undertook his cause.

This extraordinary behaviour of a pyrate well known to have been very active in plundering divers vessels on this coast but the year before, occasioned a more strict enquiry into his course of life after his departure from hence, and at last it came to be discovered that though he and the rest of Tache's crew, pretended to surrender and to claim the benefit of H.M. Proclamation, they had nevertheless been guilty of divers piracys after the fifth of January for which they were not entitled to H.M. pardon. I therefore thought fit to have him brought to a tryal, but found a strong opposition from some of the Council agt. trying him by virtue of the Commission under the great Seal pursuant to the Act of the 11th and 12th of King Wm. though I produced the King's Instruction directing that manner of tryal; but having at length overcome their scruples, I had this person tryed and convicted of taking and destroying no less than twelve ships and vessels after the 5th of January and long after notice of H.M. Proclamation.

About the time of this tryal I received advice from North Carolina, that Major Bonnet who was one of Tach's associates and surrendered with him, was gone out again in a sloop, and betaking himself to fresh piracys had been taken by some vessels fitted out for that purpose by the Government of South Carolina. That Tach with divers of his crew kept together in North Carolina went out at pleasure committing robberies on this coast and had lately brought in a ship laden with sugar and cocoa, which they pretended they found as a wreck at sea without either men or papers, that they had landed the cargo at a remote inlet in that Province and set the ship on fire to prevent discovery to whom she belonged: and having at the same time received complaints from divers of the trading people of that Province of the insolence of that gang of pyrates, and the weakness of that Governmt. To restrain them, I judged it high time to destroy that crew of villains, and not to suffer them to gather strength in the neighbourhood of so valuable a trade as that of this Colony.

Having gained sufficient intelligence of the strength of Tache's crew, and sent for pilots from Carolina, I communicated to the Captains of H.M. ships of war on this station the project I had formed to extirpate this nest of pyrates. It was found impracticable for the men of war to go into the shallow and difficult channels of that country, and the Captains were unwilling to be at the charge of hiring sloops which they had no orders to do, and must therefore have paid out of their own pocketts, but as they readily consented to furnish men, I undertook the other part of supplying at my own charge sloops and pilots. Accordingly I hired two sloops and put pilots on board, and the Captains of H.M. ships having put 55 men on board under the command of the first Lieutenant of the *Pearle* and an officer from the *Lyme*, they came up with Tach at Ocracoke Inlet on the 22nd of last month, he was on board a sloop which carried 8 guns and very well fitted for fight. As soon as he perceived the King's men intended to board him, he took up a bowl of liquor and calling out to the Officers of the other sloops, drank Damnation to anyone that should give or ask quarter, and then discharged his great guns loaded with partridge shot, which killed and wounded twenty of the King's men who lay exposed to his fire without any barricade or other shelter; he resolutely entered the first sloop which boarded him, nor did any one of his men yield while they were in a condition to fight. His orders were to blow up his own vessel if he should happen to be overcome, and a negro was ready to set fire to the powder, had he not been luckily prevented by a planter forced on board the night before and who lay in the hold of the sloop during the action of the pyrates. Tach with nine of his crew was killed, and three white men and six negroes were taken alive but all much wounded.

The loss of the King's men is very considerable for the number, there being ten killed in the action, and four and twenty wounded of whom one is since dead of his wounds. I do myself the honour of giving your Lordships the particulars of this action because, it has, I hope, prevented a design of the most pernicious consequence to the trade of these Plantations, which was that of the pyrates fortifying an Island at Ocracoke Inlet and making that a general rendezvous of such robbers. While the preparations for this service were carrying on, I proposed to our late Assembly and prevailed with them to pass an Act giving rewards for apprehending and destroying of pyrates, by which there is to be paid particularly for Tach £100, and half the rewards promised by H.M. Proclamation, for every one of his, or any other crew of pyrates taken on this coast, to be paid out of the publick money now in the hands of the country's Treasurer: but I did not communicate to the Assembly nor Council, the project then forming agt. Tach's crew for fear of his having intelligence, there being in this country and more especially among the present faction, an unaccountable inclination to favour pyrates, of which I beg leave to mention some instances.

Besides the favour shown to Tache's Quarter Master in advising him to sue for his liberty and for his pyratical effects; some of the same gang having passed through this country in their way to Pennsylvania, and contrary to my Proclamation assembling in great numbers with their arms, and endeavouring to debauch some sailors out of the merchant ships to join them, the Officers of the Government could find none to assist in the disarming and suppressing that gang.

On the tryal of some pyrates lately brought hither, arguments have been used to justify their villainies, and to acquitt them, upon the bare allegation of their being forced into that wicked Association without any proof, or so much as a probability of their acting by constraint. I received some days ago the honour of your Lordships of the — of August and H.M. Commission for pardoning pyrates, which came very seasonably to save Howard the Quartermaster then under sentence of death, but by H.M. extending his mercy for all piracys committed before the 18th of August, is now set at liberty. I must on this occasion entreat your Lordships directions as well concerning the effects of this man as of others which appear to have been piratically taken.

By H.M. Instructions I am commanded to seize and secure the effects of all pyrates brought in here; until H.M. pleasure be signified therein: and by H.M. late Commission, I observe that all forfeitures are remitted to such as surrender within the time therein mentioned: what I am therefore in doubt of is, whether by the remitting all forfeitures, H.M. intends only to restore the pyrates to the estates they had before the committing their pyracies, or to grant them a property also in the effects which they have piratically taken. There is besides the two negro boys, about £50 in money and other things taken from the aforenamed Howard, and now in the hands of the Officer who seized it on H.M. behalf, of which an inventory is lodged in the Secretary's Office here. I therefore pray your Lordships advice and commands how these effects are to be disposed, where the person in whose possession they were found is pardoned. I also expect from North Carolina a considerable quantity of sugar and cocoa, which were in the possession of Tach and his crew, and appear to have been the lading of that ship which they lately brought in there under pretence of a wreck, but in reality was taken piratically near Bermuda from the subjects of the French King, and the men put on board a ship of the same nation taken at the same time, as some of Taches crew now in custody allege. If these men were saved alive it is probable they may lay claim to the lading of their ship: but if they are not, there is some consideration due to the Officers and men who rescued the same out of the hands of the pyrates etc. Observing by the publick prints as well as the letters from divers of the merchants that the French settlement on Mississippi, begins to make a considerable noise in the world, I cannot forbear taking notice of one particular circumstance thereof, for which I cannot find any foundation.

It is advised by a letter from South Carolina inserted in the Political State for the month of August last, that the French had formed a design in conjunction with some of their neighbouring Indians to cut off the Cherokees, and the writer of that letter is so particular as to mention the precise time, when, and the number of men by whom, it was to be put in execution. The traders employed by the late Indian company who have been among the Cherokees all the last summer arrived here a few days ago with about 70 horse load of skins, and brought in with them four of the Great men of that Nation, declare that they heard of no such discourse there; though they left the Cherokee country long after the time mentioned for this supposed attack from the French: besides that the Cherokees being a numerous Nation consisting of upwards of 4000 fighting men, and seated in the fastnesses of the great mountains are not so easily to be destroyed by the small numbers which the Carolina intelligence says are marching against them.

So that it is not improbable, but that the French hopes from their new settlement may be as ill grounded, as the Carolina fears of their Indian neighbours. But whatever may be the progress of this new Colony, it is certainly the British interest to obstruct its growth, not only by interrupting the communication between that, and Canada, but by extending our commerce among the Indians, and particularly by cultivating a good correspondence with these Cherokees who are now very friendly to the English, and especially to those of this country employed among them by the gentlemen of the late Indian Company and who have furnished them with arms and ammunition in greater proportion than the people of Carolina are capable of supplying.

By the account I have had from our Indian traders these Cherokees are little farther distant from Virginia than they are from Charlestown: They are an increasing people, and the rather to be courted because of the barrier they may afford us agt. this new settlement of the French: whereas those Indian Nations that inhabit among or near the British settlements are of small account, by reason of their daily decrease, such are the Cattawbaws who from a powerful nation, are of late become much lessened, by a remarkable dispensation of Providence in rendering their women for the most part barren; as if Heaven design'd by the diminution of these Indian neighbours, to make room for our growing settlements. The scarcity and dearth of iron, which the merchants of England have for some time complained of, and the people here have sensibly felt, may I hope be happily remedied by the late discoverys of mines in this Colony: one of which has been found at the head of Rappahannock River, by some German miners which I employed in that service, which is reputed richer than any in Europe, and lies within less than ten miles of water carriage. Several gentlemen here are concerned with me, and ready to set up an iron works if it may be allowed: and I am not without hopes of discovering other mines of a nobler metal, as soon as the country comes to be seated nearer the Great Mountains (over which I discovered the passage) and which may serve to check the vain boasts of the Spaniards, as if the Treasures of the Universe are solely committed to them. I shall conclude this letter with informing your Lordships of the death of Mr. Berkeley one of the Council here, in whose stead I humbly recommend Mr. Cole Digges, a gentleman of good parts, and of an estate which may be reckoned amongst the first in this country, he is descended of an honourable Family in England, and his father served for divers years with great reputation in the office of a Councillor and Deputy Auditor here. This gentleman lives near the seat of Government, and is on that account preferable to others whose remoteness makes them unwillingly attend on the business of the Council.

Signed,
A. Spotswood

Appendix II

Unhappiness in the Colonies:
Various Letters

Letter from South Carolina Governor Robert Johnson to the Council of Trade and Plantations dated 18 June 1718. He sends an impassioned plea for naval protection from the pirates operating off the coast of his colony:

> The unspeakable calamity this poor Province suffers from pyrates obliges me to inform your Lordships of it in order that his Majesty may know it and be induced to afford us the assistance of a frigate or two to cruse hereabouts upon them for we are continually alarmed and our ships taken to the utter ruin of our trade; twice since my coming here in 9 months time they have lain off of our barr taking and plundering all ships that either goe out or come in to this port, about 14 days ago 4 sail of them appeared in sight of the Town tooke our pilot boat and after wards 8 or 9 sail with several of the best inhabitants of this place on board and then sent me word if I did not immediately send them a chest of medicines they would put every prisoner to death which for their sakes being complied with after plundering them of all they had were sent ashore almost naked.
>
> This company is commanded by one Teach alias Blackbeard has a ship of 40 guns under him and 3 sloops tenders besides and are in all above 400 men. I don't perceive H.M. gracious proclamation of pardon works any good effect upon them, some few indeed surrender and take a certificate of there so doing and then several of them return to the sport again; notwithstanding there has for this 3 months last past been a man of war Capt. Perce Comr. at Providence several sloops have fitted out a pyrating from thence during her being there and I am credibly informed there are above 20 sail now in these seas so yet. Unless ships are sent to cruse upon them, all the trade of these American parts will be stopped, for hardly a ship goes to sea but falls into their hands.
>
> As to the war with the Indians I have since my coming made peace

with. several nations particularly the great nation of the Creeks who live to the southward near St. Augustine, but Treaties with them are very precarious, so long as the French from Movele and Spaniards from St. Augustine live and have built forts amongst them and doe continually by presents and furnishing them with arms and ammunition and buying the slaves and plunder encourage them to war upon us, this is certainly fact and I can have no redress although have several times demanded it. Servants slaves robbers and debtors frequently escape from hence there and when demanded can have no return from the Governor but that he will send to the King his Master to know his pleasure therein and so are always Kept and protected; a sloop arrived here from Providence about six days ago but I can't learn Capt. Rogers Governor of those Islands is yet arrived there, 'tis to be hoped he has frigates with him and a good force of land men otherways he will run some risk of being attacked by pyrates for it being there nest and rendezvous they will be unwilling to have the place settled, I am advised there are 6 or 700 now there, etc.

Signed,
Robert Johnson[254]

The following letter is from a Mr Godin dated 17 December 1717, outlining Blackbeard's activities off the South Carolina coast among other matters:

Our Assembly by a late Act has increased the duty of goods imported here etc. There is likewise a late Act that 18 months after the ratification thereof lays an additional duty upon negroes of £40 etc. Negroes will now fetch a better price than ever etc. The Act for carrying on the Indian trade by the publick is continued for 5 years which in the opinion of many is not thought to be for the advantage of the country. We are very much afraid we shall by that means loose in a few years all our Indians who will goe over to the French interest and become greater enemies than ever, the Act is in itself a monopoly and the country has no further to doe in it then to oblige such as should goe amongst the Indians to trade to give security for their good behaviour among the Indians and the Indians themselves are already averse to this manner of carrying on the trade amongst them and deem it as a hardship imposed upon them.

There have already been some vessels in the Bay of Mexico Pensacola and Moville with our Indian trading goods and have sold them to the French and Spaniards and are return'd hither with considerable quantities of skins and more will be going, though' there is now since passed a Law to prevent them, here are in port some Bristol man who now talks of fitting out directly from Bristol to these places which will prove of very evil consequence to this country and by which means we may lose all our Indians and this chiefly by reason that the country has engrossed the whole trade thro' a mercenary and ignorant temper which reigns in most of our people. 'Tis highly reasonable this should be remedied by disannulling the Act at home as they have done that of the Virginia Company for carrying on that trade by a Company Virginia, our Assembly has at length posted the Act for cancelling their bills of credite, this next March is to be paid in a tax of £47,000 of which £24,000 is to sink the same of bills and the remaining £27,000 to pay of sundry orders and debts contracted by the Publick. In March 1718 is to be paid in another tax of £30,000 to sink the same value in bills, so that by March come 12 months will be cancelled £54,000 bills, unless they'll think fit to break again thro' their Act and forfeit their publick faith, etc.

The next letter is dated 13 June 1718 and this is about the blockade of Charles Town and other matters:

South Carolina, 13th June, 1718. Capt. Mede sailed over our barr 18th May in company with Capt. Hudson and Capt. Clarck in the *Crowley*, the latter put back for his passengers and boats that he lost going over the barr and the 22nd as he was just proceeding from the barr was unfortunately taken by two pirates, one a large French ship mounted with 40 guns and the other a sloop mounted with 12 guns with two other sloops for their tenders having in all about 300 men all English the ship is commanded by one Theach and the sloop by one Richards who have been upon this account in those and other vessels about two years and is the same sloop and company that was off of our barr the last summer and took two vessels inward bound they now took besides Capt. Clarck, Capt. Craigh in a small ship belonging to this place as he went over the barr bound for London and the *William* Capt. Hewes from Weymouth.

Whilst these ships were in their possession they sent one of Clark's passengers with Richards and another person master of one of their tenders to towne with a message to send them a chest of medicines which if was refused by the Government they would immediately put to death all the persons that were in their possession and burn their ships etc. and threatened to come over the barr for to burn the ships that lay before the Towne and to beat it about our ears, as the Town is at present in a very indifferent condition of making much resistance if them or any other enemy should attempt it and that we were very desirous to get them off our coast by fair means which we could not do otherwise for want of such helps as other Governments are supply'd with from the Crown, the chest of medicines was sent etc. Soon after they dismissed our people and their ships having first taken from the two vessels that were homeward bound what little money they had on board and all their provisions and from the two others the same and destroyed most of their cargoes etc. all for pure mischief sake and to keep their hands in. They made no farther stay (thanks to God) but are gone to the Northward etc. Those people are so accustomed to this easy way of living that nothing can reclaim and most of those that took up with the Proclamation are now return'd to the same employment which has rather proved an encouragement than anything else, there now being three for one there was before the Proclamation was put out.

They are now come to such a head that there is no trading in these parts, it being almost impossible to avoid them and nothing but a considerable force can reduce them which at first might have been done at an easy charge, had the Government but rightly appraised what sort of people they generally are and how most of them that first turn'd pirates have formerly lived being such as had always sailed in these parts in privateers and lived in the Bay of Campechia they had not we believe thought that a pardon would have suppressed them that being of so near akin to their present way of living.

The Spaniards and French are very industrious in improving their settlements in these parts and will stick at no charges to bring the Indians entirely under their Government, the latter are like to become very powerful at their settlements of Mobile in a very short time. By the care our Government takes of its Plantations one would imagine that they are of no further concern to the Government than they are an opportunity of advancing and gratifying a Courtier or a considerable party man. The neglect of this upon a sudden war with any of neighbours it's greatly feared may prove of the utmost ill consequence to the rest it being the only barrier we have. We wish it may be thought of before it proves too late, it cannot be expected that it can ever become a place well settled under a Proprietary Government and able to defend itself or of any security to our other Plantations etc.[255]

The following letter, dated 21 October 1718, was written by the Governor and Council of South Carolina to the Council of Trade and Plantations outlining the attack by William Rhett that culminated in the capture of Stede Bonnet:

Lately two pirate vessels, commanded by one Vane, lay of the barr of this harbour, as they have often done, and took a ship from Guiney with negroes, and two sloops bound in, and the next day attacked four ships outward bound, but what success, he had with them wee could not be informed, however their insults, and receiving advice that we might expect the same usage from another, who was careening, and refilling in Cape Fear River, obliged the Governor. (though very unable both for want of men and money) to fit out a force to go and attack them, and accordingly two sloops, one commanded by Capt. Masters and the other by Capt. Hall, with about, 130 men were got ready with. All the dispatch we could. and Colonel William Rhett commanded the whole, who sailed southerly first, in search of Vane, but not being able to meet with, or gain intelligence of him, he steered for Cape Fear River, in which he found a sloop of 8 guns and 50 men, commanded by a Major. Stede Bonnet, and two prizes, sloops belonging to New England.

On seeing our vessels enter the River, they endeavoured to get out, and in the chase, all the three sloops run aground on some shoals, But that commanded by Capt. Masters, in which Colonel Rhett was, lay within musket shot of the pirate, and the water falling away (it being ebb) she keel'd towards him, which exposed our men very much to their fire, for near six hours, during which time they were engaged very warmly, until the water rising sett our sloops afloat, about an hour before the pyrate, when Colonel Rhett making the signal, and they prepared to board him, which the pirate seeing, sent a white flag, and after some short time, surrendered, on Colonel Rhett's promising he would intercede for mercy.

We had killed on board Colonel. Rhett eight men and fourteen wounded, of which four are since dead, and on board Capt. Hall, two killed and six wounded. The said pirates are now prisoners here, and we are preparing for their tryal. This undertaking, besides that it has been a considerable expense to us, will (wee apprehend) very much irritate the pirates who infest this coast in great numbers. We become therefore humble suitors to your Lordships, that you will be pleased to lay before H.M. the great danger our trade and Colony are in from them, they having at some times blocked up our harbour for eight or ten days together, and taken all that have come in or gone out, and plundered them, where they have not thought the vessels fit for their purpose. In procuring a vessel it will be of the greatest service to the trade not only of this Colony, but of all these parts etc.

Signed,
Robert Johnson, A. Scene, Nicholas Trot, Though. Broughton, Char. Hart, Far. Younger[256]

Appendix III

Spotswood Timeline

• **1676** – Alexander Spotswood is born in the English colony of Tangier, Morocco, to Robert and Catherine Spotswood.

• **October 1683** – Catherine Spotswood and her son Alexander move from Tangier to England.

• **1693** – Spotswood joins the British military, beginning his career as an ensign in the Earl of Bath's infantry regiment in Flanders.

• **August 13, 1704** – Spotswood is wounded at the Battle of Blenheim during the War of Spanish Succession.

• **July 11, 1708** – the French take Spotswood prisoner during the Battle of Oudenarde in the War of Spanish Succession. John Churchill, Duke of Marlborough, negotiates Spotswood's release.

• **February 18, 1710** – Queen Anne signs Spotswood's commission as Lieutenant-Governor of Virginia.

• **June 21, 1710** – the new Lieutenant-Governor, Alexander Spotswood, lands in Jamestown, Virginia.

• **June 23, 1710** – Spotswood publishes the Royal Commission outlining his power and authority as Governor of Virginia and assumes his post as Lieutenant-Governor.

• **1710** – Spotswood proposes the construction of a new Bruton Parish Church in Williamsburg.

• **1710–1716** – Spotswood helps to rebuild the College of William and Mary, which was damaged in a fire in 1705.

• **1710–1722** – Spotswood pursues the completion of the Governor's Palace in Williamsburg.

• **1711–1712** – Spotswood sends the Virginia militia to the North Carolina border in response to that colony's request for help in quelling Indian uprisings.

• **November 1713** – Spotswood introduces the Tobacco Inspection Act, which requires tobacco to be inspected before entering the European market. The Act incorporates a patronage scheme, creating forty tobacco inspectorships worth £250 a year. Spotswood will award twenty-nine of these inspectorships to sitting burgesses.

• **December 1714** – Spotswood endorses the Indian Trade Act, which gives the Virginia Indian Company a twenty-year monopoly on American Indian trade and charges the company with maintaining Fort Christanna, a settlement in southern Virginia for smaller Indian tribes.

• **1715** – Spotswood helps construct a powder magazine in Williamsburg.

• **September 7, 1715** – Spotswood dissolves the House of Burgesses after a five-week session, calling them 'a Set of Representatives, whom Heaven has not generally endowed with the Ordinary Qualifications requisite to Legislators'.

• **1716** – Spotswood takes up residence in the Governor's Palace in Williamsburg. Promotes expansion into the Blue Ridge Mountains when his 'Knights of the Golden Horseshoe' expedition crosses into the Shenandoah Valley. He and a party of about fifty gentlemen embark on the expedition; German and Scots-Irish families from Pennsylvania soon follow.

• **1717** – in response to pressure from influential Virginia politicians, the Privy Council disallows the Tobacco Inspection Act and the Indian Trade Act, both sponsored by Spotswood.

• **November 22, 1718** – the pirate Edward Teach, known as Blackbeard, is killed in a fight with a party of soldiers and sailors, led by Robert Maynard and commissioned by Spotswood.

• **April 29, 1720** – Spotswood and the Governor's Council end a ten-year period of tense relations by resolving 'to act for the future as cordial friends in the administration of the government'.

• **December 1720** – the Governor's Council awards Spotswood 86,000 acres in the newly-created Spotsylvania County.

• **1721** – James Blair leaves on a third trip to England to lobby for the removal of an executive, this time Lieutenant-Governor Alexander Spotswood. While abroad Blair arranges for the publication of a five-volume collection of his sermons.

• **April 3, 1722** – Hugh Drysdale is appointed Lieutenant-Governor of Virginia after the King's ministers decide to replace Spotswood.

• **September 27, 1722** – Hugh Drysdale takes the oaths of office as Lieutenant-Governor of Virginia in Williamsburg, and with his wife Hester takes up residence in the Governor's Palace.

• **1724** – Spotswood sails to England to secure title to his Virginia lands and to settle taxation issues. He marries Anne Butler Brayne while in England. They will have two sons and two daughters.

• **February 1729** – Spotswood returns to Virginia with his wife Anne and his sister-in-law Dorothea Brayne.

• **1730** – Spotswood is appointed deputy postmaster-general of North America for a ten-year term. During his tenure, he extends postal service south to Williamsburg and appoints Benjamin Franklin postmaster of Philadelphia.

• **1739** – the British decide to use colonial troops in their military campaign against Spanish provinces in the Americas. Alexander Spotswood is appointed brigadier general and quartermaster-general of troops in America.

• **June 7, 1740** – on a trip to Annapolis, Maryland, to raise troops and consult with colonial governors in preparation for an attack on the Spanish in Cartagena, Colombia, Spotswood dies after a brief illness. His burial site is unknown.

Notes

[1] Captain Charles Johnson, *A General History of the Robberies and Murders of the Most Notorious Pyrates* (London, Conway Maritime Press, 1998), p. vii. This was originally published in 1724 as *A General History of Pyrates*.

[2] David Cordingly, 'Introduction' to Johnson's *A General History*, p. x.

[3] Ibid., p. ix.

[4] David Pickering, *Pirates* (London, Collins Gem, 2006).

[5] Most of these letters can be found in 'America and The West Indies', Volume 30, *Calendar State Papers, Colonial Series* (*CSPCS*) (Kew, The National Archives).

[6] Angus Konstam, *Blackbeard: America's Most Notorious Pirate* (New York, John Wiley & Sons, 2006), p. 215.

[7] Captain Charles Johnson explains that Maynard not only led the sea assault but was also directly involved, perhaps even dealing some of the multiple wounds that the pirate suffered.

[8] Konstam, *Blackbeard*, p. 237.

[9] Ibid.

[10] Johnson, *A General History*, p. 47.

[11] New Providence Island had previously been a hive of pirate activity but this changed when the new Governor, Captain Woodes Rogers arrived. His commission was approved in Council and is filed at 'America and the West Indies', *Calendar State Papers, Colonial Series*, Volume 30, Section 305.

[12] See David Cordingly's introduction in Johnson, *A General History*, p. xiii.

[13] Johnson, *A General History*, pp. 50–1 referring to the most famous wife of Blackbeard, one Mary Ormond.

[14] Ibid., p. 46.

[15] See *CSPCS*, Volume 29, Section 635.

[16] The spelling of Edouard Titche comes from the claims of Captain Pierre Dosset, the captain of *La Concorde* before it was stolen by Blackbeard and renamed *Queen Anne's Revenge*, and routed through Charles Mesnier, Intendant of Martinique.

[17] Alexander Spotswood, Lieutenant-Governor of Virginia, letter to the Council of Trade and Plantations, *CSPCS*, Volume 30, Section 800.

[18] According to the North Carolina Maritime Museum, the reference on this chart depicts a likely version of the name of Blackbeard.

[19] Robert E. Lee, *Blackbeard the Pirate – A Reappraisal of His Life and Times* (North Carolina, John F. Blair, 1974), p. 102.

[20] The letter from Tobias Knight was found on Blackbeard's ship after the pirate captain was killed in the Battle of Ocracoke.

[21] Lee, *Blackbeard the Pirate*, p. 4, citing *Encyclopaedia Britannica*, 1973, XXI, 741, 'Teach, Edward' along with several other documents to say that Blackbeard was a Bristol man.

[22] Konstam, *Blackbeard*, p. 12.

[23] The history of Bristol comes from *Bristol-Link online* and from the *Wordsworth Encyclopaedia*.

[24] Konstam, *Blackbeard*, p. 13.

[25] Graham A. Thomas, *Pirate Hunter, the Life of Captain Woodes Rogers* (Barnsley, Pen and Sword, 2008), p. 13.

[26] Konstam, *Blackbeard*, p. 14, suggesting this could be the reason why Blackbeard left New Providence.

[27] See Johnson, *A General History*, p. 50.

[28] Lee, *Blackbeard the Pirate*, p. 198.

[29] See Johnson, *A General History*, p. 199.

[30] Konstam, *Blackbeard*, p. 157.

[31] A BBC production *Blackbeard*, produced by Dangerous Films, picks up on this marriage and dreadful treatment, perhaps for little more than a good bit of television drama.

[32] Most of this information comes from one source, A.B.C. Whipple's *Pirate Rascals of the Spanish Main* (New York, Doubleday & Co., 1957).

[33] Hugh F. Rankin, *The Pirates of Colonial North Carolina* (North Carolina, N.C. State Department of Archives and History, 1963).

[34] Johnson, *A General History*, p. 60.

[35] This description forms part of a deposition written by Henry Bostock, dated 19 December 1717, *CSPCS,* Volume 30, Section 298, Part III.

[36] From Johnson, *A General History*, p. 60.

[37] Konstam, *Blackbeard*, p. 239.

[38] Randal Shrock, Professor of History, Earlham College, *Biography of Alexander Spotswood*, published on www.encyclopediavirginia.org entitled *Spotswood, Alexander, 1676–1740*.

[39] Konstam, *Blackbeard*, p. 214.

[40] See www.encyclopediavirginia.org for details on this story of Spotswood being wounded.

[41] Alexander Spotswood, letter to the Council of Trade and Plantations, *Official Letters of Alexander Spotswood*, dated 18 August (Williamsburg, Virginia Historical Society, 1710), Volume 1.

[42] Ibid.

[43] Spotswood, *Official Letters*, Volume 2, dated 25 July 1713, to the Council of Trade and Plantations.

[44] Spotswood, *Official Letters*, Volume 2, dated 28 July 1713, to the Council of Trade and Plantations.

[45] Spotswood, *Official Letters*, Volume 2, dated 28 July 1713, to the Lords Proprietors of Carolina.

[46] Ibid.

[47] Spotswood, *Official Letters*, Volume 2, dated 31 July 1713, to the Lords Proprietors of Carolina.

[48] Spotswood, *Official Letters*, Volume 2, dated 29 December 1713, to the Lords Commissioners of Trade.

[49] Ibid.

[50] See the biography of Spotswood on www.encyclopediavirginia.org entitled *Spotswood, Alexander, 1676–1740*.

[51] Spotswood, *Official Letters*, Volume 2, dated 27 January 1714, to the Bishop of London.

[52] Ibid.

[53] Spotswood, *Official Letters*, Volume 2, dated 24 October 1715, to Mr Secretary Stanhope.

[54] See the biography of Spotswood on www.encyclopediavirginia.org entitled *Spotswood, Alexander, 1676–1740*.

[55] Spotswood, *Official Letters*, Volume 2, dated 27 February 1717, to the Lords of Trade.

[56] See the biography of Spotswood on www.encyclopediavirginia.org entitled *Spotswood, Alexander, 1676–1740*.

[57] Much of the information on Dick Turpin has come from the www.stand-and-deliver.org.uk website.

[58] BBC *Online History* web pages, account of Queen Anne.

[59] Ibid.

[60] Philip Gosse, *The History of Piracy* (New York, Longmans, Green & Co., 2007), p. 114.

[61] Ibid., p. 193.

[62] Some pirate crews had very detailed codes, like the crew serving Captain Bartholomew Roberts which had no less than eleven articles of agreement.

[63] Captain Kidd resorted to this deception, claiming in his statement for his defence against the charges of piracy to have raised 'French Colours with a design to decoy', *CSPCS*, Volume 17, Section 680, Part XXV.

[64] Johnson, *A General History*, p. 47.

[65] Konstam, *Blackbeard*, p. 62.

[66] Captain Charles Johnson informs us that Blackbeard and Hornigold served together.

[67] Lee, *Blackbeard the Pirate*, p. 11 where Lee states that Hornigold was considered 'the dean of the school of pirates' infesting the West Indies.

[68] *Wordsworth Encyclopaedia*, reference Privateer.

[69] If March 1717 is accurate as Johnson states and according to *CSPCS*, Volume 29, Section 635, it provides some indication that Hornigold and Blackbeard had sailed together for some time.

[70] Captain Mathew Musson, letter to the Council of Trade and Plantations, *CSPCS*, Volume 29, Section 635, *British History Online*.

[71] Johnson implies that Blackbeard took the *Revenge* after the *Queen Anne's Revenge*; however, most other sources suggest the vessels were taken in the opposite order. See the *Boston News Letter*, Issue 708, concerning Teach being in command of the *Revenge* a full month prior to the capture of the *Queen Anne's Revenge*.

[72] See Lee, *Blackbeard the Pirate*, p. 102.

[73] *Boston News Letter*, Issue 708, report filed in Philadelphia on 24 October 1717.

[74] Johnson, *A General History*, p. 47.

[75] *Boston News Letter*, Issue 708, 24 October 1717, Philadelphia.

[76] Konstam, *Blackbeard*, p. 69.

[77] Ibid.

[78] Lee, *Blackbeard the Pirate*, p. 31.

[79] Konstam, *Blackbeard*, p. 84.

[80] Wikipedia (reference *Queen Anne's Revenge*) and North Carolina Maritime Museum.

[81] Konstam, *Blackbeard*, p. 80.

[82] Until its abolition some years later, the slave trade was considered an acceptable form of business at the time.

[83] The Royal African Company was created by the British monarch and a consortium of London-based merchants. The company also dealt in gold, some of which was sold to the English Mint and used to press the coin that would later become the guinea.

[84] Much of the future prosperity of the eastern Americas and the Caribbean Islands had been built upon the undervalued and hard work of thousands of slaves and the often brutal treatment they received at the hands of their wealthy owners.

[85] Salt was widely used as a method of preserving food, and as such was a valuable commodity. Some cultures used it as a form of currency, providing the origin of the term that someone may not be worth his salt.

[86] Scurvy was brought on by the lack of citrus fruits in the diet of a sailor and one of the initial signs was the decaying of teeth.

[87] Konstam, *Blackbeard*, p. 82.

[88] At the time, Britain and France were using different calendars and did not agree until almost half a century later.

[89] In his letter regarding the capture of *La Concorde*, Charles Mesnier described

the event in as much detail as he could from the report by Captain Pierre Dosset. The reference for this is Aix-en-Provence Centre des Archives d'Outre-Mer, AN Col C8A 22 (1717) f447.

[90] Lee, *Blackbeard the Pirate*, p. 14. Lee cites the captain's name as D'Ocier rather than Dosset, as Konstam does.

[91] See Konstam, *Blackbeard*, p. 83.

[92] Spotswood, *CSPCS*, Volume 30, Section 800, letter to the Council of Trade and Plantations where he states Blackbeard had some blacks in his crew who were likely freed slaves or men he had chosen because of their overall fitness.

[93] In his letter regarding the capture of *La Concorde*, Charles Mesnier mentions the figure of 455 negroes.

[94] Konstam, *Blackbeard*, p. 84.

[95] The excavation of the site believed to be the wreck of Blackbeard's flagship is ongoing and much information and advice on this has been received from David Moore of the North Carolina Maritime Museum.

[96] For all the reasons stated for the discrepancies in the number of cannons, we have decided to go with forty since this is what many reports claim.

[97] The method of placing cannons facing to either side was well-established. Despite the military advantage of placing some guns forward and aft in a battle against ships that could only fire broadsides, it would take navies a further century to wise up to the concept. A classic example of broadside firing being a restriction to effectiveness can be seen in the battle that took the life of Admiral Nelson, but which the smaller British force ultimately won.

[98] Konstam, *Blackbeard*, p. 81.

[99] See Lee, *Blackbeard the Pirate*, pp. 14–5. While Konstam suggests that Hornigold was removed by his crew as pirate, Lee states that Hornigold decided to retire from piracy and that it was he who gave Blackbeard command of *La Concorde*.

[100] Taken from the report of Lieutenant Ernaut of *La Concorde*.

[101] Konstam, *Blackbeard*, p. 87.

[102] Ibid., p. 85.

[103] *In Search Of Blackbeard: Historical and Archaeological Research at Shipwreck Site 0003BUI* by Richard W. Lawrence and Mark Wilde-Ramsing, 1 February 2001.

[104] The *Betty* features in the Articles issued against William Howard, Blackbeard's quartermaster for *Pyracy and Robbery* found in Lee's *Blackbeard the Pirate*, pp. 94–105.

[105] Konstam, *Blackbeard*, p. 69.

[106] *Boston News Letter*, Issue 708, dated 4–11 November 1717 from a report filed in Philadelphia on 24 October 1717.

[107] Ibid.

[108] Ibid.

[109] *Boston News Letter*, Issue 708, dated 4–11 November 1717 from a report filed in New York on 28 October 1717.

[110] Ibid.

[111] Ibid.

[112] Lee, *Blackbeard the Pirate*, pp. 94–105.

[113] *Boston News Letter*, Issue 716, dated 30 December 1717–6 January 1718 from a report filed in Philadelphia on 10 December 1717.

[114] A brigantine is a vessel that has two masts. At least one of these, usually the foremast, is square-rigged. However, during the early eighteenth century, brigantine referred to the type of rigging rather than the type of vessel.

[115] *Boston News Letter*, Issue 725, dated 3–10 March 1718 from a report filed in New York on 24 February 1718.

[116] *CSPCS*, Volume 30, Section 298, Part III, deposition from Henry Bostock.

[117] *CSPCS*, Volume 30, Section 298, Part II, deposition of Thomas Knight.

[118] Some believe that Captain Kentish was an alias used by Teach, but there is no clear understanding one way or the other.

[119] *CSPCS*, Volume 30, Section 298, Part I, deposition of Richard Joy.

[120] *CSPCS*, Volume 30, Section 298, Part III, from a deposition by Henry Bostock.

[121] *CSPCS*, Volume 30, Section 298, letter from Governor Hamilton, dated 6 January 1718.

[122] Konstam, *Blackbeard*, pp. 125–6.

[123] HMS *Scarborough* is mentioned in a letter by Governor Hamilton to the Council of Trade and Plantations, *CSPCS*, Volume 30, Section 298 where it states that the warship 'did last year destroy a pirate ship'.

[124] Konstam, *Blackbeard*, p. 90.

[125] By the end of 1717 only a few territories remained in Spanish hands, one of which was the island of Hispaniola, now Haiti, and much of its ownership was transferred to France. However, in 1606 the King of Spain ordered the entire populace to move close to Santo Domingo in the south to avoid the pirates, which resulted in pirates setting up bases in the north and west of the island unhindered by the local population or the authorities.

[126] Konstam, *Blackbeard*, p. 126, citing report filed by Captain Hume commanding HMS *Scarborough*.

[127] Johnson, *A General History*, pp. 47–62.

[128] *Boston News Letter*, Issue 739, June 9–16 1719.

[129] Ibid.

[130] *CSPCS*, Volume 30, Section 556, letter of Governor Robert Johnson to the Council of Trade and Plantations.

[131] The town's original name was actually spelled Charles Towne, in keeping

with the English custom at the time of adding an 'e' to many words that have since dispensed with it.

[132] David Herriot does provide us with a clue when he writes that this vessel was a Spanish sloop captured off Havana. He describes it as having been found empty.

[133] *CSPCS*, Volume 30, Section 556, letter from Governor Robert Johnson to the Council of Trade and Plantations.

[134] Ibid.

[135] Ibid.

[136] Konstam, *Blackbeard*, p. 136.

[137] Lee, *Blackbeard the Pirate*, p. 39.

[138] *CSPCS*, Volume 30, Section 660, letter extracts 19 August 1718.

[139] Johnson, *A General History*, p. 48.

[140] See Konstam, *Blackbeard*, p. 144.

[141] Ibid., p. 143.

[142] *CSPCS*, Volume 30, Section 660; this quote and much of the information for this chapter has been taken from a variety of letters written by South Carolina residents around 19 August 1718.

[143] Konstam, *Blackbeard*, p. 143.

[144] Interestingly, Lee supports this theory but Konstam does not. Johnson makes no mention of it.

[145] Johnson tells us the booty was worth £1,500, which would be worth around a quarter of a million pounds today.

[146] *CSPCS*, Volume 30, Section 556, letter from Governor Johnson to the Council for Trade and Plantations, dated 18 June 1718.

[147] *CSPCS*, Volume 30, Section 660.

[148] Johnson, *A General History*, p. 49.

[149] Konstam, *Blackbeard*, p. 150.

[150] Taken from a letter from Captain Ellis Brand of HMS *Lyme* to the Admiralty, dated 12 July 1718.

[151] Lee, *Blackbeard the Pirate*, p. 51. Both Lee and Konstam mention this important event, though Konstam goes into greater detail.

[152] Konstam, *Blackbeard*, p. 183.

[153] It is unlikely that anyone without special equipment could have plundered the vessels after they had sunk, so it is reasonable to assume that there was ample time for these items to be removed.

[154] Benjamin Cowse, *The Tryals of Major Stede Bonnet and Other Pirates* (London, Benjamin Cowse, 1719, held at The National Archives, Kew, *CSPC 1710*, Volume 31), Herriot's deposition.

[155] We mentioned this previously as the extra sloop involved in the blockade of Charles Town.

[156] Konstam, *Blackbeard*, pp. 184–5.

[157] Ibid., pp. 184–5.

[158] Ibid., pp. 186–7.

[159] *CSPCS*, Volume 30, Section 737, letter from Governor Woodes Rogers to the Council for Trade and Plantations, dated 31 October 1718.

[160] See *CSPCS*, Volume 30, Section 305.

[161] *Wordsworth Encyclopaedia*, reference Nassau.

[162] *CSPCS*, Volume 30, Section 737, letter from Governor Woodes Rogers to the Council for Trade and Plantations, dated 31 October 1718.

[163] The period covered by the 'Golden Age of Piracy' has been hotly debated and for the purposes of this book we will go with between 1713 (the end of the War of Spanish Succession) to around 1720. This period encompasses the whole of Blackbeard's known activities of piracy.

[164] *CSPCS*, Volume 30, Section 737, letter from Governor Woodes Rogers to the Council for Trade and Plantations, dated 31 October 1718.

[165] This other governor is, of course, Alexander Spotswood. From the arrival of Woodes Rogers in Nassau onwards, the net was tightening around Blackbeard and other pirates like him.

[166] *CSPCS*, Volume 30, Section 737, letter from Governor Woodes Rogers to the Council for Trade and Plantations, dated 31 October 1718.

[167] We saw this sequence with the working relationship between Hornigold and Blackbeard.

[168] *CSPCS*, Volume 30, Section 797, Part I; information concerning *Rising Sun* is from a deposition of John Brown, Commander of the *John*. The information about the tender was taken from the deposition of Robert Leathers, Commander of the *Upton Pink* and filed at *CSPCS*, Volume 30, Section 797, Part V. The calculation on the crew was made by simply adding together the crew estimates from both depositions. *CSPCS*, Volume 30, Section 797, letter from Governor Hamilton to the Council of Trade and Plantations, dated 19 December 1718, refers to the sloop in the flotilla.

[169] *CSPCS*, Volume 30, Section 797, Part IV, deposition of Jonathan Bull, Commander of the *Christiana*; and *CSPCS*, Volume 30, Section 797, Part VI, deposition of Robert Leonard, Commander of the *Eagle*. The reference to the larger crew and firepower figures comes from the deposition by John Bois, a carpenter on board the frigate *Wade*, filed at *CSPCS*, Volume 30, Section 797, Part II. The reference to Edward England's death comes from *Pirates* by David Pickering, published by Collins.

[170] *CSPCS*, Volume 30, Section 737, letter from Governor Woodes Rogers to the Council for Trade and Plantations, dated 31 October 1718.

[171] Ibid.

[172] *CSPCS*, Volume 30, Section 737, Part III, deposition by Thomas Bowlin and

four others, dated 8 September 1718.

[173] *CSPCS*, Volume 30, Section 737, Part IV, deposition by William Dewick of Kingston, Jamaica, dated 15 September 1718.

[174] *CSPCS*, Volume 30, Section 737, Part VII, deposition by Richard Taylor, Captain of the sloop *Elizabeth and Mary* and three others, dated 4 August 1718.

[175] This quote comes from the Royal Pardon issued by King George I on 5 September 1717.

[176] Ibid.

[177] *CSPCS*, Volume 30, Section 800, letter from Alexander Spotswood to the Council of Trade and Plantations stating that: 'I am therefore in doubt as, whether by the remitting all forteitures, H.M. intends only to restore the pyrates to the estates they had before the committing their pyracies, or to grant them a property also in the effects which they have piratically taken.'

[178] *CSPCS*, Volume 30, Section 737, letter from Governor Woodes Rogers to the Council for Trade and Plantations, dated 31 October 1718.

[179] Konstam, *Blackbeard*, p. 199.

[180] *CSPCS*, Volume 30, Section 800, letter from Alexander Spotswood to the Council of Trade and Plantations, dated 22 December 1718.

[181] Ibid.

[182] Ibid.

[183] Konstam, *Blackbeard*, p. 195.

[184] *CSPCS*, Volume 30, Section 730, letter from Governor Robert Johnson to the Council of Trade and Plantations, dated 21 October 1718, referring to attack on and capture of Stede Bonnet.

[185] Johnson, *A General History*, pp. 106–7.

[186] *CSPCS*, Volume 30, Section 800, letter from Alexander Spotswood to the Council of Trade and Plantations, dated 22 December 1718.

[187] Ibid.

[188] It would be more accurate at this point to refer to these vessels as British, since Great Britain as a combined Kingdom and nationality had by now existed for a decade.

[189] Information on these activities was provided by Captain Charles Johnson in his narrative and by Alexander Spotswood in letters to the Council of Trade and Plantations. In the case of the narrative, we have discounted various parts already, so may wonder about the accuracy of this. In the case of the letters, Spotswood was by this time building a case against Blackbeard, both for any possible trial and to justify his actions if he were to hunt and attack the pirate in the territorial waters of another colony. Their accuracy could be open to speculation, but since they are the only documents available and there is nothing to contradict the accuracy, we have very little reason to dispute the contents.

[190] The more astute readers might wonder at why Blackbeard then allowed the

crew to continue on its way. Surely they would report the incident the moment they reached a port, thus nullifying Blackbeard's claim to the vessel and effectively destroying the protection he was enjoying under the King's Pardon. So far, no evidence has surfaced that the crews ever arrived on land to lodge a report, so Blackbeard was legally safe in his claim and Eden was legally safe in believing it.

[191] Johnson, *A General History*, p. 51.

[192] Ibid.

[193] In his book, Captain Charles Johnson alludes to the idea that Blackbeard did not make much of a pause in his ways of piracy and continued, even during this quiet time, to bother shipping, albeit restricting himself mostly to a very local area. Alexander Spotswood also makes a brief mention of this continued activity in his letter filed at *CSPCS*, Volume 30, Section 800.

[194] Johnson, *A General History*, pp. 53–4.

[195] *Wordsworth Encyclopaedia*, reference Virginia.

[196] At the time, the areas of the eastern coast of North America that eventually became the thirteen original states, each represented by a stripe on the current US flag, were not referred to as states. They were colonies and the current borders between each only represent a passing resemblance to the original lines. Virginia was much larger than it is now and there were several ongoing border disputes with North Carolina.

[197] We saw a similar political victory during one of the general elections when Margaret Thatcher was re-elected as Prime Minister, shortly after the military victory over Argentina during the Falklands War. Had this military victory not been in favour of Britain, it is very doubtful that the subsequent election would have been in favour of the then current Prime Minister.

[198] *CSPCS*, Volume 30, Section 799, letter from Lieutenant-Governor Spotswood to Governor Earl of Orkney, Governor of Virginia.

[199] *CSPCS*, Volume 30, Section 800, letter from Alexander Spotswood to the Council of Trade and Plantations, dated 22 December 1718.

[200] *CSPCS*, Volume 30, Section 800, letter from Alexander Spotswood to the Council of Trade and Plantations, dated 22 December 1718.

[201] Ibid.

[202] Ibid.

[203] Ibid.

[204] Ibid.

[205] *CSPCS*, Volume 30, Section 800, Part II (a), address of the House of Burgesses of Virginia to HM the King, dated 20 November 1718.

[206] Ibid.

[207] *CSPCS*, Volume 30, Section 800, letter from Alexander Spotswood to the Council of Trade and Plantations, dated 22 December 1718.

208 *CSPCS*, Volume 30, Section 803, circular letter from Mr Secretary Craggs to Governors of Plantations.

209 We know from a letter written by Spotswood that several of the pirates were passing through Virginia on their way further inland and were assembling in larger numbers than were permitted in his Proclamation. For this reason, and to deprive those pirates of an opportunity to re-form under their leader, the hunt for Blackbeard was becoming more urgent. The letter is filed at *CSPCS*, Volume 30, Section 800.

210 *CSPCS*, Volume 30, Section 800, letter from Alexander Spotswood to the Council of Trade and Plantations, dated 22 December 1718. The sum of £50 referred to is more than many people at the time could earn in a whole year, so for someone to be carrying that in loose change meant he was either a well-to-do gentleman or a criminal.

211 If we look at the figures, Howard lost two slaves of undisclosed value and £50 when he was arrested. He was then advised to sue for damages for the seizing of those effects and depriving him of his liberty to a sum of ten times the monetary figure. This would be not dissimilar to someone accused of theft stealing your car, crashing it, ending up in hospital and then suing you for loss of future earnings. It is no wonder Spotswood appeared riled by the whole situation.

212 *CSPCS*, Volume 30, Section 800, letter from Alexander Spotswood to the Council of Trade and Plantations, dated 22 December 1718.

213 Ibid.

214 Johnson, *A General History*, pp. 53–4, from the Proclamation written by Alexander Spotswood regarding the hunt for and capture of pirates.

215 There would not be any record of such a request since Spotswood would never have gone down that route. He was convinced, as we knew from subsequent legal proceeding, that Eden was allied with Blackbeard, and so any request for permission to send an armed party across the border would, Spotswood was no doubt convinced, have alerted Blackbeard and the hunt would have had to start all over again.

216 Johnson, *A General History*, pp. 53–4.

217 Johnson, *A General History*, p. 50.

218 Lee, *Blackbeard the Pirate*, p. 146.

219 In the days of the early colonies, each was treated as a separate governing body, independently answerable to the Council of Trade and Plantations. They were almost like separate countries, and as such, to send armed troops across a border from one to another was tantamount to an invasion.

220 *CSPCS*, Volume 30, Section 800, letter from Alexander Spotswood to the Council of Trade and Plantations, dated 22 December 1718.

221 Johnson, *A General History*, pp. 53–4.

[222] Much of the information on the land expedition to Bath Town can be found in the Public Records Office, under the Admiralty papers 1/1472.

[223] In several sources, including the BBC drama produced by Dangerous Films, the injury sustained by Israel Hands is caused by Blackbeard shooting his knee to enable him to escape the battle the captain knew would happen soon. The narrative by Captain Charles Johnson alludes to this also but informs us that the incident was created purely as an example to the rest of the crew of Blackbeard's authority and that if he did not wound people occasionally, they might forget who he was. As if.

[224] Johnson, *A General History*, p. 57.

[225] Konstam, *Blackbeard*, p. 245 provides information regarding the trading sloop but does not refer to Samuel Odell. That reference comes from Lee, *Blackbeard the Pirate*, p. 137.

[226] Konstam, *Blackbeard*, p. 246.

[227] Konstam, *Blackbeard*, p. 243, citing Maynard's report held at the National Maritime Museum at the time of writing.

[228] *CSPCS*, Volume 30, Section 800, letter from Alexander Spotswood to the Council of Trade and Plantations, dated 22 December 1718.

[229] Konstam, *Blackbeard*, p. 252, citing the *Boston News Letter*, February 16–23 1719.

[230] Johnson, *A General History*, p. 56.

[231] Johnson is the key source for this but both Lee and Konstam say it is quite probable that Odell was one of the two men Johnson tells us stopped Black Caesar from blowing up the ship.

[232] Johnson, *A General History*, p. 57.

[233] The account of the verbal exchange and the removing of the pirate's head in this way is given in the *Boston News Letter*.

[234] The figure of pirate casualties here is taken from the *Boston News Letter* report on the battle. The figure for the King's men comes from a letter written by Lieutenant Maynard to his sister.

[235] Johnson, *A General History*, p. 62.

[236] *CSPCS*, Volume 30, Section 800, letter from Alexander Spotswood to the Council of Trade and Plantations, dated 22 December 1718.

[237] Johnson, *A General History*, p. 57, referring to the number of wounds that apparently brought Blackbeard down; also found in the *Boston News Letter*.

[238] Johnson, *A General History*, p. 54.

[239] Taken from a letter written by Tobias Knight to Blackbeard on 17 November 1718 and later used against him. In our opinion, these words imply a definite warning to leave port, but without actually going into details of when and why.

[240] Konstam, *Blackbeard*, p. 269.

[241] Ibid., p. 272.

242 Ibid., p. 271.

243 Konstam, *Blackbeard*, p. 110 for further insight into the character of Charles Vane.

244 *CSPCS*, Volume 30, Section 737, letter from Governor Woodes Rogers to the Council of Trade and Plantations.

245 *CSPCS*, Volume 30, Section 807, letter from Woodes Rogers to Secretary Craggs regarding Benjamin Hornigold.

246 Johnson, *A General History*, p. 59.

247 *CSPCS*, Volume 30, Section 807, letter from Woodes Rogers to Secretary Craggs regarding Benjamin Hornigold.

248 Ibid.

249 *CSPCS*, Volume 30, Section 800, letter from Alexander Spotswood to the Council of Trade and Plantations, dated 22 December 1718.

250 A description of Stede Bonnet's capture is made by Governor Robert Johnson, Governor of South Carolina, in *CSPCS*, Volume 30, Section 730 and Section 787. This is also mentioned by Alexander Spotswood in his letter to the Council of Trade and Plantations filed at *CSPCS*, Volume 30, Section 800.

251 Lee, *Blackbeard the Pirate*, pp. 148–51.

252 Lee, *Blackbeard the Pirate*, p. 142.

253 Johnson, *A General History*, p. 61.

254 'America and West Indies: June 1718', *CSPCS*, Volume 30, 1717–1718, Sections 264–287.

255 'America and West Indies: August 1718', *CSPCS*, Volume 30, 1717–1718, Sections 327–343.

256 'America and West Indies: October 1718', *CSPCS*, Volume 30, 1717–1718, Sections 359–381, also found on www.british-history.ac.uk accessed 10 November 2011.

Index